Media Convergence

The public br... past decade h... 'communicati... 'mediated' and ... the face of the wor... instant messaging.

The development of digital media presen... ...que opportunity to reconsider what communication is, and what individuals, groups, and societies might hope to accomplish through new as well as old media. At a time when digital media still provoke both utopian and dystopian views of their likely consequences, Klaus Bruhn Jensen places these 'new' media in a comparative perspective together with 'old' mass media and face-to-face communication, restating the two classic questions of media studies: what do media do to people, and what do people do with media?

Media Convergence makes a distinction between three general types of media: the human body enabling communication in the flesh; the technically reproduced means of mass communication; and the digital technologies facilitating interaction one-to-one, one-to-many, as well as many-to-many.

Part 1 undertakes a critique of communication, retracing the very notion of communication in the history of ideas.

Part 2 revisits key moments of media history, highlighting the characteristic features of new, digital media.

Part 3 outlines a research agenda emphasizing the relationship between communication and action – digital media enable new forms of social action from the local to the global level.

Features include:

- Case studies, for example, of mobile phones in everyday life, the Muhammad cartoons controversy as an instance of networked communication, and climate change as a global challenge for human communication and political action;
- Diagrams, figures, and tables summarizing key concepts beyond standard 'models of communication';
- Systematic cross-references. Major terms are highlighted and cross-referenced throughout, with key concepts defined in margin notes.

Klaus Bruhn Jensen is Professor at the University of Copenhagen, Denmark. Recent publications include *A Handbook of Media and Communication Research* (2002) and *International Encyclopedia of Communication* (12 vols, 2008), for which he served as Area Editor of Communication Theory and Philosophy. His current research interests include internet studies, mobile media, and communication theory.

Media Convergence

The three degrees of
network, mass, and
interpersonal communication

Klaus Bruhn Jensen

Routledge
Taylor & Francis Group

LONDON AND NEW YORK

First published 2010
by Routledge
2 Park Square, Milton Park, Abingdon, Oxon, OX14 4RN

Simultaneously published in the USA and Canada
by Routledge
270 Madison Ave, New York, NY 10016

Routledge is an imprint of the Taylor & Francis Group, an informa business

© 2010 Klaus Bruhn Jensen

Typeset in Janson by
Keystroke, Tettenhall, Wolverhampton
Printed and bound in Great Britain by
CPI Antony Rowe, Chippenham, Wiltshire

British Library Cataloguing in Publication Data
A catalogue record for this book is available from the British Library

Library of Congress Cataloging in Publication Data
Jensen, Klaus Bruhn.
    Media convergence : the three degrees of network, mass, and
    interpersonal communication / Klaus Bruhn Jensen.
        p. cm.
    Includes bibliographical references and index.
    1. Communication--Technological innovations. 2. Digital media.
    3. Communication models. I. Title.
    P96.T42J46 2010
    302.23—dc22   2009032242

ISBN10: 0–415–48203–8 (hbk)
ISBN10: 0–415–48204–6 (pbk)
ISBN10: 0–203–85548–5 (ebk)

ISBN13: 978–0–415–48203–5 (hbk)
ISBN13: 978–0–415–48204–2 (pbk)
ISBN13: 978–0–203–85548–5 (ebk)

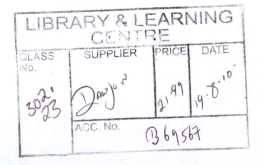

Contents

Illustrations

Figures

Case study boxes

Preface

This book grows out of my involvement in research projects and collaborations concerning the internet, mobile phones, and other digital media over the last decade. It is an attempt to understand new media in the light of old media, and to make sense of the common practice of communication at a time of technological transition and social change.

In preparing the volume, I have been privileged to receive both local and global inspiration and guidance. Since 2002, I have directed – and have learnt from – the research group on Digital Communication and Aesthetics at the Department of Media, Cognition, and Communication, University of Copenhagen, Denmark. During the same years, actually since 2000, the Association of Internet Researchers has been a second collegial home – a community of peers, facilitated by Steve Jones, Nancy Baym, Matt Allen, and Charles Ess as presidents. For a shorter, though no less inspiring and intense period, I served as Area Editor of Communication Theory and Philosophy for the *International Encyclopedia of Communication* (IEC) that came out in twelve volumes from Blackwell in 2008, and which, appropriately, is now being updated in its online version. I enjoyed a most pleasant and professional collaboration with its chief editor, Wolf Donsbach, and my advisory editor, Bob Craig; I also was challenged to write this book on some of the many loose ends that seem never to fit in encyclopedias.

In writing and revising the text, I have received many constructively critical comments on conference papers and other presentations, not least in the context of the International Communication Association, the biannual Nordic conferences on media and communication research, and, again, the Association of Internet Researchers. For detailed and helpful input on draft chapters, I am especially grateful to Mats Bergman, Rasmus Helles, Peter Larsen, Russ Neuman, and John Durham Peters.

Portions of the present text, inevitably, draw on and develop some of my previous publications; as far as possible, these are referenced in the text. In addition, it is appropriate to acknowledge some earlier versions of certain sections. The case studies of climate change and of search engines, in Chapters 1 and 5, respectively, build on work that was presented, in a first version, as an invited presentation entitled, "Search engines as communication and meta-communication: A theoretical perspective," to a workshop on 'Gatekeepers in a digital Asian-European media landscape: The rising structural power of internet search engines,' Singapore, February 28–March 1, 2008; and, in a second version, as a paper entitled, "Searching audiences – Search engines, meta-communication, and new media audiences," to the twenty-sixth World Congress of the International Association for Media and Communication Research (IAMCR), Stockholm, Sweden, July 20–25, 2008. The case study of mobile phones in Chapter 6 was first presented as a lecture entitled, "What's mobile in mobile communication? – Reconsidering senders, messages, and receivers," at a conference on 'Media and mobility,' University of Copenhagen, September 7, 2007. A few sections of Chapter 7 have been adapted from an article entitled "New media, old methods – Internet methodologies and the online/offline divide" (K. B. Jensen, in press); other sections of Chapter 7 rely, in part, on my own contributions in Jensen (2002e). Finally, the treatments of Jürgen Habermas and Richard Rorty in Chapter 8 re-develop Chapter 11 in Jensen (1995).

Klaus Bruhn Jensen
Copenhagen, July 2009

Note

Key concepts and terms are indicated by a marginal note when they are first mentioned in the text.

The symbol > in notes (and the symbol < beside note numbers in the text) indicates a cross reference to another section of the text.

Each of the eight chapters includes a case study that examines a key problem area of media and communication. While case studies are most frequently understood as concrete empirical analyses of some delimited domain (Gomm *et al.*, 2000; Yin, 2003), in this book 'case studies' include theoretical investigations of how particular domains of study should be delimited and defined in the first place.

A critique of communication

Introduction

1

Communication – the very idea

Introduction

Communication – the very idea

New media have historically given rise to utopian as well as dystopian perspectives on the role of communication in society – from Plato's concern that writing would promote forgetfulness rather than memory and wisdom, via recurring debates about print and broadcast media as instruments of either enlightenment and education or entertainment and escapism, to recent accounts of the internet and other digital media as resources for enhanced public participation in politics, economy, and culture. The very idea of communication has been informed over time by the available media, and by the hopes and fears associated with them. As demonstrated by John Durham Peters (1999) in his agenda-setting history of the idea, communication was only recognized as a general category of human activity following the rise of electronic communication media from the last half of the nineteenth century, beginning with the telegraph.[1] These developments encouraged scholars and other commentators to think of diverse practices of social interaction – in the flesh, via wires, and over the air – in terms of their family resemblances. In Peters' (1999: 6) felicitous formulation, "mass communication came first." With digitalization, the idea of communication is, once again, in question. For more than a decade, research has been struggling to understand what comes after mass communication.

In this book, I take the most recent generation of 'new,' digital media forms, typified by the networked personal computer and the mobile telephone, as an opportunity to revisit the idea of communication, and to develop a framework for studying communicative practices across media of three different degrees:[2] the human body enabling communication face-to-face; the technically reproduced means of analog mass communication; and the digital technologies facilitating networked interaction one-to-one, one-to-many, as well as many-to-many. My approach seeks to avoid, on the one hand, the increasingly untenable divides of mass versus interpersonal communication, and of online versus offline interaction. Occasionally implying a dichotomy of technologically mediated versus 'non-mediated' face-to-face communication, the field of communication research has tended to produce separate bodies of mass and interpersonal communication studies (Rogers, 1999). The dichotomy reappeared with a vengeance in 'new media' studies of the 1990s, when cyberspaces and virtual realities came to be conceived of as worlds apart (for a critical discussion, see Slater, 2002). On the other hand, the book aims to counter a second widespread notion in research,

1 history of the idea of communication

2 media of three degrees

policy, and public debate, namely, that previously distinct technologies are all being merged seamlessly into shared platforms and similar formats in a sweeping process of media convergence, and that the sum of new media might even be displacing face-to-face contact. Old media rarely die, and humans remain the reference point and prototype for technologically mediated communication.

My aim is to synthesize and systematize a number of contributions to scholarship, inside and outside the media field, and to outline an agenda for further research, including some of the inherently normative implications of both the practice and the study of communication. Communication configures society. Communication also prefigures society, addressing what is, what is not (yet), what could be, and what ought to be done. Communication supports great leaps of the individual imagination and grand collective projects. Communication articulates alternatives and choices. Human communication constitutes a brief window of opportunity between chance and necessity.

The end of communication

We seem to be endlessly communicating, and to generally trust the positive potentials of communication. As long as people are talking, so the saying goes, they are not fighting. While the recent motto of 'information wants to be free'[3] in relation to file-sharing and peer production (R. Clarke, 2001) remains debated on legal as well as ideological grounds, a motto of 'communication wants to go on'[4] has appeared uncontroversial for decades. In the political domain, Michael Schudson (1997: 307), for one, has critiqued a resulting "romance of conversation" that tends to confuse ordinary sociable conversation with problem-solving conversation, which is of a formal, rule-governed, and public nature. It is counterproductive, to the point of undermining political democracy itself, to think of public debate among citizens as just another conversation among either intimates or strangers. Democracies also need experts to examine and present complex issues, so that citizens may make informed decisions in their own best interest (Schudson, 2006). At least as far as democracy is concerned, the response to the familiar rhetorical question, 'Can't we just talk about it?', must be: No.

This book refocuses attention on the end of communication – its translation into locally as well as globally coordinated actions. Communication serves to manage extreme cognitive and cultural complexities for endless practical purposes. Communication, accordingly, comes with a deadline, imposed on communicators by their natural as well as their social circumstances. The end of communication is to end:[5] ideally, having been enlightened and empowered through communication, individuals, groups, and institutions as well as entire societies and cultures go on to act.

Certainly, communication often has inherent value. Communicative practices range from the mundane to the extraordinary – from getting by

3 'information wants to be free'

4 'communication wants to go on'

5 the end of communication is to end

and going on in the private and public contexts of our everyday lives by asking questions and telling jokes, to transcending ourselves in elaborate aesthetic make-believe and organizing ourselves for political revolution. An end-of-communication perspective implies neither a narrowly instrumental approach to human communication as only a means to an end, nor a general faith in the capacity of communicators to agree in the end. We resume communication, and we repeat ourselves. Communication ends, however, whether by explicit procedures or as a contingent outcome of the process, sometimes behind communicators' backs.

Communication constitutes both a natural and a cultural resource. It has provided the human species with a distinctive evolutionary advantage as well as a precondition for civilized interaction within and between cultures, even if this potential often is not actualized. According to evolutionary biology, human consciousness is defined, in part, by its unique capacity for simulation, including models of itself in externalized and exchangeable forms (Dawkins, 1989: 59). The positive potentials of communication can be understood in terms of the doubt and delay that it introduces into human activities, enabling reflection and negotiation – in the short or long term, through fiction, science, and other forms of experimentation – before individuals, institutions, and societies do things that may have irreversible consequences. Communication is the human capacity to consider how things might be different.[6]

6 communication – the human capacity to consider how things might be different

Communication involves contestation, mostly of trivial things, sometimes of momentous matters. The discipline of philosophy has referred to "essentially contested concepts" (Gallie, 1956), for example, 'freedom' or 'art,' whose implications remain intensely debated, even if most people agree about their core meaning. As noted by Clarke (1979), an additional distinction should be made between what is contested as a matter of fact, and what is contestable – most concepts, like most attitudes and actions, can be contested.[7] This was illustrated in the so-called breaching experiments of the ethnomethodological research tradition (Garfinkel, 1967) – for instance, behaving like a guest in one's own home – which brought out the arbitrary, yet extremely practical routines of everyday social interaction. We may question anything, anytime, but then again, we mostly do not, because it would not be practical. Like the very idea of science (Woolgar, 1988), or of conceptual schemes (Davidson, 1973–74), the very idea of communication is contestable, but it is mostly not contested in either research or ordinary conversation. It is, not least, when new media are introduced that the concept of communication comes to be contested.

7 contested and contestable concepts

Both spoken language and other signs enable us to communicate about that which is not present in immediate space, time, or experience. "In the writings of Aristotle we find explicitly stated for the first time the conception of a sign as an observed event or state of affairs that is evidence for its interpreter for what is at least temporarily absent" (D. S. Clarke, 1990: 11). In one of the first attempts at a grand theory of communication, Jurgen Ruesch and Gregory Bateson (1987/1951: 209) noted the human capacity to identify the signals emitted by other organisms *as signals* – signals of *something else* and signals *for somebody*. Speech sounds and gestures provide access to various possible worlds that can be shared with others in communication. Present signs allow for absent realities. Writing, print, electronic, and digital media, each in specific ways, have radically extended the capacity of humans to imagine, represent, and communicate about possible as well as actual worlds, also in each other's absence. Present media allow for absent realities, absent communicators, or both.[8]

The stakes of communication are especially high when it addresses alternatives and choices, and when it involves a critical mass of people, challenging received worldviews, vested interests, and heartfelt identities. For most of human history, of course, both the availability of information and the accessibility of the means of communication have been limited by technological as well as institutional circumstances. The availability[9] of information – what is known by *anyone at all* in a particular historical and cultural context – has depended on material tools and mental frames of reference for describing the world as found and transforming it for human purposes: telescopes and microscopes, natural as well as formal languages of description and inquiry. The combination of material and mental resources for articulating information in more or less stable forms constitutes media in Marshall McLuhan's (1964) broad sense: extensions of human beings into their natural environments and social settings, but also into imagined worlds – past, present, and future. The accessibility[10] of information in communication – what *someone in particular* comes to know, compared with others – has been a function of the invention and diffusion of information and communication technologies, and of the cultivation of literacy, numeracy, and other communicative competences among different groups in society. The social organization of the means of information and communication, finally, conditions performativity[11] – how people are able to do things with words (Austin, 1962) and, by extension, to do particular things with particular media (Katz, 1959). Digital media – from political websites, to e-banking and online gaming, to the microcoordination of everyday life through mobile media – have directed renewed attention to the performative aspect of communication. Also historically, however, the link between communication and action has been key to the survival and quality of life of individuals, communities, societies, cultures, and, indeed, the human species. We communicate for our lives.

8 present and absent realities, media, and communicators

9 availability

10 accessibility

11 performativity

Case study: speaking of the weather

Human communication explores a margin of indetermination in the material universe. Beyond trial-and-error, as preserved in individual memory and in the gene pool of the species, the scope for human intervention into nature is established through communication and documented in more or less durable media. The record of lessons learnt in the past, provides an invaluable resource for future actions. As noted by the American author, Mark Twain (who was quoting his colleague, Charles Dudley Warner (http://en.wikipedia.org/wiki/Charles_Dudley_Warner, accessed July 15, 2009)), everybody talks about the weather, but nobody does anything about it. While people continue to converse casually about the weather, by the early twenty-first century global warming had become a central topic of public debate and international politics. Maybe humans already did something to the weather that should be talked about some more. Climate change[12] – how to understand it, what to do about it – situates communication in a longer perspective of human history and natural evolution.

12 climate change

To be clear about the illustration, I am not arguing for a specific coupling of environmental issues with new information and communication technologies, nor am I advocating, in the present context, a particular position on the ends and means of environmental policy. My first point is simply that, unlike just a generation ago, it now makes sense to communicate, and to disagree vehemently, about the natural environment as a public issue that calls for collective action:

> down to about 1960, it was generally assumed that for all practical purposes and decisions climate could be considered constant. . . . In any case, many people now know that there have been significant shifts of climate during the twentieth century: at first, a more or less global warming to about 1950, then some cooling. More recently, a notable increase in the incidence of extremes of various kinds in almost all parts of the world has hit agriculture and created difficulties for planning in many fields.
>
> (Lamb, 1995: 2)

My second point is that communication about, and action upon, such knowledge, depends on publicly available and accessible media. One main position, of environmental activism, has been widely associated in international media with Al Gore, the former US vice president, who starred in a documentary on global warming, *An Inconvenient Truth* (Davis Guggenheim, 2006). An opposite position, questioning both the evidence of global warming and the proposed solutions, has been represented by the book *The Skeptical Environmentalist* and its author, the political scientist Bjørn Lomborg (2001), appearing in the media to ask people to *Cool It*, the title of a second book (Lomborg, 2007). The awarding of the Nobel Peace Prize in 2007 to Al Gore, jointly with the United Nations Intergovernmental Panel on Climate Change, did not resolve the matter, but constituted yet another turn in the communication trying to make sense of nature and the place of humans in it.

An assessment of appropriate actions in response to climate change depends, first of all, on the availability of meteorological and geological information and, to a degree, written records from historical time. Some such records have been preserved for the so-called Little Ice Age[13] – a period of unusually cold weather around the middle of the last millennium – which has been examined in several disciplines and fields across the great divide still

13 the Little Ice Age

separating natural and human sciences (Snow, 1964). A classic contribution by the French historian, Emmanuel Le Roy Ladurie (1972/1967), charted "the history of the climate since the year 1000" as a backdrop to the conditions of life among ordinary people during the period, relying, among other things, on sources about the dates of wine harvests. Another study, combining meteorology and art history, showed how, over the centuries, the Little Ice Age affected the color and style of nature paintings (Neuberger, 1970).

The dating of the Little Ice Age is subject to disagreement, but its earliest beginning is normally set around 1300, its end around 1850. The disagreements bear witness to conflicting interpretations of the mediated evidence, and to different theoretical approaches to the relationship between climate change and human civilization, nature and culture. While environmental determinism in a strong sense, like technological determinism, is untenable, the natural environment, as found and modified by humans, helps to explain certain longterm historical developments and social changes:

> Consider, for instance, the food crises that engulfed Europe during the Little Ice Age – the great hunger of 1315 to 1319, which killed tens of thousands; the food dearths of 1741; and 1816, "the year without a summer" – to mention only a few. These crises in themselves did not threaten the continued existence of Western civilization, but they surely played an important role in the formation of modern Europe. . . .Some of these crises resulted from climatic shifts, others from human ineptitude or disastrous economic or political policy; many, like the Irish potato famine of the 1840s, from a combination of all three – and a million people perished in that catastrophe. Its political consequences are still with us.
>
> (Fagan, 2000: xv)

Most famously, a catastrophic wheat harvest in France in 1788, and the resulting shortage of grain and bread, were among the factors contributing to the revolution of 1789.

During the hard times of several centuries, the implications of the weather gave rise to the expression of all manner of practical and metaphysical reflections. A very small portion of these reflections was put into writing by "country clergymen and gentleman scientists with time on their hands," one of whom, in 1316, found that the mass of rain "seemed as though it was THE FLOOD" (Fagan, 2000: xiii, 38). In addition to verbal accounts, the empirical evidence includes, as noted, the records of wine harvests and changing prices of grain, as well as analyses of tree rings and ice cores. Each new type of evidence has required specific measurement techniques, scales, and notations. While providing the basis of qualified scientific (dis-)agreement, feeding into policy deliberations, the findings remain estimates, "acquired by statistical regression analyses from modern instrument records or by proxies from historical records and other sources, [that] are vital to establishing just how warm the late twentieth century has been in comparison with earlier times" (Fagan, 2000: 54).

To sum up, formal instruments have gradually replaced informal observations in the attempt to predict and plan for shifting weather conditions. Such information was, evidently, unknown – unavailable – to both scientists and lay observers at the time of the Little Ice Age. Today, the evidence is widely available, but accessible primarily to small scientific communities with specialized informational and communicative competences. That will remain the case, also for the current period, when it is generally recognized that, since the mid-nineteenth century, human activity came to affect the natural environment in fundamental ways and with longterm consequences. For all practical purposes, public knowledge of and debate about climate change is possible only when the relevant information is rearticulated in ordinary language, texts, and images – to geographically distributed and culturally differentiated publics – through mass media. Climate change ups the ante of communication to the global level of the species. And yet, each person must act locally on information that has been mediated in multiple steps and registers of communication. Media and communication studies examine how people go about conducting and concluding their communications to resolve their differences, so that they might solve environmental and other practical problems in common.

Communication in theory and practice

Theories and double hermeneutics

In an important intervention a decade ago, Robert T. Craig (1999) called for more reflection on the relative merits of different positions in communication theory. Identifying seven main research traditions (rhetorical, semiotic, phenomenological, cybernetic, sociopsychological, sociocultural, and critical), he compared and contrasted their distinctive features in a meta-theoretical perspective that might serve to facilitate dialogue between them.[14] While initially staying within the field of communication, Craig (1999: 155), in a note, considered its interrelations with other fields:

14 theory and
meta-theory

> Might communication studies even claim to be *the* fundamental discipline that explains all other disciplines, since disciplines themselves are social constructs that, like all social constructs, are constituted symbolically through communication? Yes, of course, but only as a joke!. . .The irony that makes the joke funny is that every discipline occupies the precise center of the universe in its own perspective. Communication is no exception, but communication as a metaperspective – a perspective on perspectives – may help us to appreciate the irony of our situation.

I suggest that communication is key to appreciating both the irony and the seriousness of our situation, and that communication studies could reasonably be expected to specify both the potentials and the limitations of communication as a common practice – in other fields of research, and in society at large. Elsewhere in his article, Craig (1999) hinted at two respects in which communication might, after all, be special, even if communication studies as a field is not. First, he proposed to redefine (communication) theory, not as an unended quest for *the* grand theory, but as a meta-perspective "in which to discuss the relative merits of alternative practical theories." Communication deliberates on the relative merits of different conceptions of the business at hand, whether theory development, climate change, or social change. Second, Craig noted the close link between communication theory and practice: "In a practical discipline of communication, theory is designed to provide conceptual resources for reflecting on communication problems" (p. 130). Whereas, in other scientific and social domains, communication may not be the problem at the center of attention, it is frequently considered part of the solution.

Being a communicative practice in its own right,[15] research describes and reflects on a delimited object of study. In this regard, all academic fields engage in hermeneutics, interpreting the world from particular positions of insight. Compared with natural and physical sciences, the social sciences and the humanities study historical and cultural realities that have always already been interpreted by the individuals and institutions inhabiting them. Importantly, researchers may modify these realities when *their* interpretations are communicated back into the rest of society. Karl Marx's works, as interpreted and applied in the Soviet Union and elsewhere, shaped the course of twentieth-century history in decisive ways; Sigmund Freud's writings introduced 'the unconscious' into psychology, advertising, and common parlance. Media and communication research is among the fields which, thus, engage in what Giddens (1979) summed up as double hermeneutics,[16] interpreting, not least, people's own interpretations of how and why they communicate. In the words of the anthropologist, Clifford Geertz (1983: 58), studies of human communication and culture seek to determine "what the devil they think they are up to."

Media are unique constituents of the communicative process of double hermeneutics in two different ways. First, media of description, analysis, and interaction enable and constrain the kinds of interpretation that various fields of inquiry can undertake. Historically, the available media have conditioned and framed the ways in which both researchers and the general public have understood their common past, present, and future. Second, the diffusion of media to a growing number of people has served to democratize, however imperfectly, the means of knowing about, interpreting, and acting on reality, facilitating communication by more people about more things that they would like to be up to. It is the interdependence between communication and action that made mass media a renewed focus of social conflict as well as academic interest during the twentieth century. In the end, communication has consequences for human agency and social practice.

15 research as communicative practice

16 double hermeneutics

Practice and pragmatism

The dialogic and inclusive spirit of Robert T. Craig's (1999) article helps to explain why it received two major professional awards in the year following its publication: the Golden Anniversary Monograph Award of the National Communication Association, 2000; and the Best Article Award of the International Communication Association, 2000. The meta-model also informs recent textbooks of primary-source readings (e.g., Craig and Muller, 2007). As a matter of fact, however, the seven traditions did not respond to Craig's invitation in any kind of sustained dialogue. "Although widely cited," Craig (2007: 125) noted in a later article, "my 1999 article has not been critically discussed in the primary scholarly literature." In coming chapters, I argue, first, that there is much to be gained by not only discussing and comparing, but also converging some key positions in the field. In order to assess whether, and in what sense, media convergence may be taking place, it is useful to engage in theoretical and methodological convergence.

A second argument has to do with the status of whatever synthesis might be the outcome of convergence in research. As recognized by Craig (2007: 141), "there can be no absolutely neutral metamodel." Also within scientific fields, each tradition occupies the precise center of the universe in its own perspective. Prompted by one of the few explicit responses to his original article (Russill, 2005), Craig (2007: 141) amended his metamodel, describing his own vision of theories in terms of tools addressing practical problems of communication as an eighth tradition and "a largely pragmatist project . . . although it also includes and welcomes dialogue with other incommensurable approaches." Throughout this book, I elaborate on pragmatism both as an inclusive meta-theoretical and epistemological framework, and as an ecumenical approach to the theory–practice divide. Whereas epistemologies, like theories, are contested, philosophical pragmatism[17]< merits specific attention as an undercurrent in the history of ideas whose explanatory value for media and communication research has only recently begun to be tapped in a common effort. James W. Carey's (1989b/1975) influential cultural approach to communication as a social ritual[18]< had invoked pragmatism as an alternative to what he described as a narrow main-stream studying transmissions and effects. By the beginning of the present century, a pragmatist conception of communication had become an identifiable position, going on a tradition (Bergman, 2008; Perry, 2001; Simonson, 2008).

Pragmatism presents a third way[19]< down what its originator, Charles Sanders Peirce, described as the road of inquiry (Skagestad, 1981). Balancing between subjectivist and objectivist, interpretive and causal, hermeneutic and materialist, micro and macro approaches to human culture and communication, pragmatism can be understood as an inter-disciplinary style of reasoning (Hacking, 1992) that seeks to bridge also the classic divides between arts and sciences (Snow, 1964). Pragmatism is premised on a communicative conception of how knowledge is produced:

17 > philosophical pragmatism, Chapter 2, pp. 28–35

18 > the ritual model of communication, Chapter 3, p. 50

19 > pragmatism as a third way, Chapter 8, pp. 163–165

its court of appeal is interpretive communities, not individual measurements. Pragmatism entails an end-of-communication perspective on knowledge, asking what practical difference research questions, analytical categories, and empirical findings may make at the end of inquiry. Pragmatism assumes that knowledge is forever fallible – even though scientists and laypersons alike must act on their imperfect knowledge day by day, even moment to moment. It is the potential as well as the actual uses of different technologies and institutions of communication in this ubiquitous process that I address in three steps – retracing the idea of communication in the history of ideas and into the field of new, digital media studies; reexamining the lines of division between embodied and technologically mediated communication; and developing a research agenda that focuses on the distinctive, yet delimited role of communication in social interaction.

Outline of the volume

Part I – a critique of communication

Research that describes itself as 'critical' normally signals a rejection of certain predominant forms of communication in society and, by implication, of certain other approaches to research that might serve to reaffirm the legitimacy both of the communications and of the society. Grounded in classic Marxism and Frankfurt School critical theory, two main variants within the media field include the traditions of political economy (Murdock and Golding, 1977; Schiller, 1969) and cultural studies (S. Hall, 1980; Williams, 1975/1958). In this volume, I engage in critique in a different, if related sense that goes back to that pivotal figure in modern philosophy, Immanuel Kant.[20] In three book-length critiques from the late eighteenth century, Kant sought to establish the foundations upon which the individual human being might recognize the true, the good, and the beautiful. Kant's critiques addressed the conditions of possibility of knowledge as such – any form of knowledge. In a pragmatist optic, these conditions are worked out not by individuals, but by communities of knowers – which makes communication key. Communication articulates differences and distinctions: representations of reality and beliefs that people will be willing to act on as individuals and as collectives. Communication in public is a unique case of human inquiry, involving any and all citizens of a democracy. Communication, thus, accomplishes the mediation of human agency and social structure.[21]< A critique of communication, as begun in this chapter and elaborated in Chapters 2 and 3, examines the conditions under which individuals, groups, and institutions consider how things might be different – which leads to communication about and criticism of things as they find them.

In *Chapter 2*, I take my cue from Aristotle. Whereas Plato had advanced a conception of reality as a unified and transcendental realm of ideas, Aristotle suggested the existence of a diversified and distributed

20 critique and/vs. criticism

21 > agency and structure, Chapter 6, p. 105

reality with diverse empirical manifestations. The Aristotelian perspective facilitates the exploration of how various material, institutional, and discursive factors, in combination, condition communication. Tools and technologies hold communicative potentials, only some of which are

22 > potential and actualization, Chapter 2, pp. 22–25

actualized via the social institutions of a given historical setting.[22]< The history of ideas during the modern period, since Kant, can be told as a sequence of turns toward the concrete vehicles and processes of communication by which humans come to know about and engage with reality. Contrasting Kant and Peirce, I note a shift of emphasis from cognitive toward communicative conceptions of knowledge. Considering another pivotal figure, Ludwig Wittgenstein, I recount the two turns that he signaled for twentieth-century philosophy, first, toward the structure of language and, second, toward the uses of language in so-called language games – socially situated communication. Along with the 'eternal' questions of philosophy, these several turns are part of the inheritance of communication theory and media studies, even if the fertile borderlands of philosophy and communication have not normally been cultivated in research on either side.

Chapter 3 takes stock of media and communication research, extending the critique of communication to its contemporary field of study. My critique entails criticism, less of particular traditions (seven or more or different ones than those identified by Craig (1999)) than of their entrenchment at a time when profound changes in the contemporary media environment should prompt the field to think again, theoretically and methodologically. Emerging over the last half-century in response to the growing global centrality of information and communication technologies in politics, economy, and culture, the field has taken shape internationally as two largely separate social-scientific and humanistic mainstreams, with some additional inspirations from the natural

23 social-scientific, humanistic, and natural-scientific communication research

24 information, communication, action

sciences.[23] With reference to three key concepts – information, communication, and action[24] – which both unite and divide the field, I explore the substantial common ground of these mainstreams, restating them in the vocabulary of pragmatism: differences that make a difference, ideas that are real in their consequences, and transitions from beliefs to actions. Being a specific window of opportunity between chance and necessity, communication has both upper and lower thresholds, depending on the

25 > programmability, Chapter 3, p. 57

distinctive programmability[25]< of the available media. Despite the pervasiveness of communication and the ubiquity of media, not all forms of difference amount to communication; not all meaningful objects qualify as media.

Part II – media of three degrees

The middle part of the book outlines a framework for making sense of the currently emerging media environment. First, I propose a shift of

26 communication and/vs. media

focus from media toward communication[26] – a research agenda emphasizing the recombination and reconfiguration of one-to-one, one-to-many, and many-to-many communication. Media convergence can be understood as a historically open-ended migration of communicative practices across diverse material technologies and social institutions. Second, I include humans among the platforms hosting communication.[27] While primary in a historical as well as an evolutionary sense, face-to-face communication does not necessarily represent the standard or ideal against which all other forms of communication should be measured. As noted by John Durham Peters (1999: 8f., 21, 264), "the dream of communication" as authentic "contact between interiorities" may not even come true in the flesh: "Neither is physical presence assurance that 'communication' will occur . . . dialogue may simply be two people taking turns broadcasting at each other." We have always been virtual in each other's company (K. B. Jensen, 2000). A central task for current media research is to think again about the interrelations between embodied and technologically mediated communication, while avoiding past hyperbole concerning artificial intelligence – coming soon to a computer near you – and moderating present speculations about an imminent cyborg future. Part II is a contribution to such theory development, presenting a three-part definition of media as material, discursive, as well as institutional phenomena.

Chapter 4 addresses the material conditions of communication.[28] Revisiting the tradition of medium theory, as most famously associated with Marshall McLuhan (1964), I review the distinctive ways in which writing, print, electronic, and digital media have extended the human capacity to communicate. I note, in particular, that networked or multistep communication has been the rule, rather than the exception, also before the advent of digital media; I examine the present configuration of one-to-one, one-to-many, and many-to-many communication in terms of a three-step flow.[29]< Compared with medium theory, which highlights the inherent biases of different technologies in fostering new forms of consciousness and culture, I reemphasize the notion of affordances: the potential of various materials to be programmed as media; their emergence in specific social and cultural forms; and their momentum (structural impact) over time. Material technologies condition communication, but only in the first instance.[30] New media of the third degree will themselves grow old, giving way to what promises to become a fourth degree of media[31] increasingly embedding communicative capacities in natural objects and artifacts, including the human body and the physical infrastructures of society. Placing 'new,' digital media in historical perspective, embedded media constitute the next challenge to the very idea of communication – and to the idea of media as entities with interfaces.

Chapter 5 elaborates on the relationship between media as material means of transmission – telephone lines or bit streams – and media as discursive forms of expression – speech or moving images.[32] Being general registers of human expression and experience, the modalities of communication – speech, music, writing, drawing, modeling, and so on – constitute a central intermediate level of analysis between media as material resources and as meaningful discourses. To capture some of the

27 humans as media

28 the material conditions of communication

29 > three-step flow, Chapter 4, pp. 71–74

30 determination in the first instance

31 media of the fourth degree

32 the discursive conditions of communication

linguistic and pictorial complexity of digital media, I return to the humanistic concept of intertextuality: the understanding of discourse as textual networks rather than stand-alone texts. To address the corresponding communicative complexity, I refer to the social-scientific concept of meta-communication: communication about communication that helps communication along, and which has taken on a different order of importance with digital media, for better or worse. In digital media, meta-communication about who says what to whom, in which medium and context, is recorded and recycled in ways that raise major political and ethical issues. While meta-communication, like communication, necessarily ends, both have an afterlife that presents a number of choices for individuals, institutions, and societies to deliberate upon and enact.

Chapter 6 describes media as a distinctive kind of institution – institutions-to-think-with[33] – that enable societies to reflect on and negotiate their common existence. Communication solidifies as culture; it lends meaning to human actions and social structures over time. To lay out the place of media of the second and third degree in modern societies, I return to Jürgen Habermas' model of the public sphere.[34] Like other civic and human rights, the right to communicate,[35] as represented by the public sphere, was hard won, and has required constant reaffirmation and redevelopment. Digital media have facilitated not just new forms of communication, but also new types of political, economic, and cultural action that are pushing at the boundaries of the classic public-sphere model, as exemplified by personal blogs and peer-production communities. At the same time, digital media have reopened debates about the flip side of the right to communicate – the right *not* to send or receive information. The alternative copyright principle that has been advanced by the Creative Commons movement – some rights reserved – suggests the more general point that individuals, groups, as well as institutions will seek to reserve certain rights of communication for themselves. The balancing of these rights presents the key political, ethical, and practical issues currently facing communication as a field of practice.

Part III – the double hermeneutics of media and communication research

Media and communication research can neither predict the future of media, nor prescribe ideal practices of communication. In addition to documenting, interpreting, and explaining media as they currently exist, however, the field feeds into deliberation and debate – double hermeneutics – on how they might be different. If media are institutions-to-think-with, research is a second-order institution-to-think-with. Media studies are the product of a historical period in which new technologies and institutions created a structural demand for more knowledge about communication in society. With each generation of new media, the question is what the field has to say, to whom, and with what effects.

33 institutions-to-think-with

34 > the public sphere, Chapter 6, pp. 111–114

35 the right to communicate

In *Chapter 7*, I first address the methodological state of the field, suggesting that new media lend themselves to old methods.[36] This is in spite of the fact that digital technologies represent important additions to the general toolbox of research and a necessary component of studies of networked communication – means as well as objects of analysis. New media also return the field to old struggles over the existence of one or more scientific methods. I emphasize the complementarity of different methods and methodologies. On the one hand, communication study depends on multiple kinds of evidence and analysis – qualitative and quantitative, naturalistic and experimental, historical and contemporary. On the other hand, the field requires several different kinds of inference and generalization. Beyond deduction and induction, I note a third type of inference – abduction[37]< – which has a specific role to play in theory development. More than an abstract ideal, the openness to a diversity of research approaches represents a practical strategy – we want to know more about communication through all the methodologies we can think up in common. In sum, I advocate both a realist and a pragmatist theory of science:[38] material, institutional, and discursive aspects of communication are all real. They must be tapped through an appropriate range of methods and methodologies that are to be unified, not in the first instance – at the level of elementary categories and procedures of research – but in the final instance, in response to shared issues and problems of communication.[39]

Chapter 8, finally, explores some of the practical, political, and ethical implications of media and communication studies. Researchers are frequently called upon to assess and amend communicative practices; the calls come from political interest groups, from policy makers, and from journalists on behalf of the general public. The common ground of theorists, practitioners, and citizens is so-called normative communication theories: more or less elaborate defenses of good media institutions and good communicative practices that may serve the good society and the good life of its members. Philosophical pragmatism has taken a special interest in communication as a mediator between theory and practice. With reference to two influential developments of pragmatism – by Jürgen Habermas and Richard Rorty – I discuss some of its unrealized potentials for communication theory and communication practice. Pragmatism presents an agenda for further research as well as public debate on how media of the first, second, and third degrees might be different, and how network, mass, as well as interpersonal communication might end differently.

36 new media, old methods

37 > abduction, Chapter 7, pp. 137–142

38 realist theory of science

39 unification in the final instance

Erro, ergo sum

2

Communication and pragmatism
in the history of ideas

Erro, ergo sum

Communication and pragmatism in the history of ideas

Communicating with the classics

Communication theory is heir to classic questions and proposed answers throughout human history. If Western philosophy has traditionally asked how human knowledge about various aspects of reality may be possible in the first place, communication studies examine the media and messages by which people exchange, reflect on, and enact their different perspectives on reality. In the fourth century BCE, Aristotle had identified three constituents of a basic model of communication:

> Spoken words are the symbols of mental experience and written words are the symbols of spoken words. Just as all men have not the same writing, so all men have not the same speech sounds, but the mental experiences, which these directly symbolize, are the same for all, as also are those things of which our experiences are the images.
> (Aristotle, 2007b: n.p.)

Things in the world, mental impressions of them, and people's oral or written expressions about the things as well as the impressions – those are minimal elements of most theories of both knowledge and communication. It is the status and interrelations of the elements that have continued to trouble philosophy and the range of natural, human, and social sciences. And, it is only in comparatively recent times, from the last half of the nineteenth century, that human knowledge of reality has come to be widely and specifically associated with the idea of communicating with others about it, or the failure to do so (Peters, 1999). The foundational statement of modern philosophy had been René Descartes' *cogito, ergo sum* (*je pense, donc je suis*, in *Discourse on the Method*, 1637) – I think, therefore I am. I depart from an alternative premise, *erro, ergo sum* – I err, therefore I am, always already in relation to something else, the natural environment as well as those other humans that I necessarily depend on in communication for survival and, at best, a good life.

This chapter traces a few key perspectives on cognition, communication, and action in the history of ideas. The tradition of philosophical pragmatism,[1] in particular, provides the constituents for a contemporary theory of communication that foregrounds the interdependence of human knowledge, communicative practice, and social action. At the height of the Enlightenment, Immanuel Kant's *Critique of Pure Reason* (1781/1787) posed three questions from the perspective of the individual human being: "What can I know?", "What ought I to do?", and "What may I hope?" (Kant, 1998/1787: n.p.). Pragmatism went on to restate Kant's questions in collective and communicative terms: What can *we* know? What ought to be the ends and means of social coexistence? And, how can communication serve to articulate our hopes and fears in negotiable forms? Departing from Aristotle, and briefly characterizing Kant's theory of knowledge, the chapter focuses on the work of Charles Sanders Peirce, the originator of American pragmatism. While most frequently associated in media and communication research with semiotics, Peirce contributed additional conceptual and methodological insights that are only beginning to be recognized and integrated into communication theory and theory of science.

I should emphasize that the aim of this chapter is neither a detailed account of the thinkers in question in their historical contexts, nor a reinterpretation of their writings as prototypes of communication theory; the purpose of the book is systematic rather than historical.[2] Performing a double hermeneutics[3]< (Giddens, 1979) of selected historical positions for present purposes, I undertake what Richard Rorty (1991b: 94) referred to as recontextualizations:[4] "As one moves along the spectrum from habit to inquiry – from instinctive revision of intentions through routine calculation toward revolutionary science or politics," one's notions or beliefs are placed in a "new context [which] can be a new explanatory theory, a new comparison class, a new descriptive vocabulary, a new private or political purpose, the latest book one has read, the last person one has talked to." This process, inevitably, treads a fine line between old and new contexts – between, on the one hand, historical and biographical settings, as described and disagreed about in massive literatures on major thinkers, and, on the other hand, current problem situations and analytical issues. In each case, I seek to provide sufficient contextualization of matters that may be considered controversial, even while giving priority to recontextualization. In this regard, I observe the distinction between priestly and prophetic interpretations[5] of philosophers (Liszka, 1998). Whereas a priestly reading tries to stay as close as possible to the letter and spirit of a work, and to an established interpretive community of scholars, a prophetic reading allows for inferences about the relevance of the work in an unforeseen context.

Just as readings of past thinkers run the risk of exaggerating their present relevance, the readings may overdo the differences, sometimes in a self-assertive, agonistic fashion. Assessing Aristotle's contribution to a typology of the categories of human consciousness, and comparing it to his own, Kant found Aristotle's approach sorely wanting:

> It was a design worthy of an acute thinker like Aristotle, to search for these fundamental conceptions. Destitute, however, of any

2 systematic and/vs. historical analysis

3 > double hermeneutics, Chapter 1, p. 11

4 recontextualization

5 priestly or prophetic interpretation

guiding principle, he picked them up just as they occurred to him, and at first hunted out ten, which he called categories (predicaments). Afterwards he believed that he had discovered five others, which were added under the name of post predicaments. But his catalogue still remained defective.

(Kant, 1998/1787: n.p.)

Kant himself was undoubtedly the main influence on Peirce, who commented that he knew the *Critique of Pure Reason* almost by heart (Peirce, 1931–58: 1.560). Nevertheless, in a summary assessment, Peirce noted that "Kant (whom I more than admire) is nothing but a confused pragmatist" (Peirce, 1931–58: 5.525).

In communicating with the classics, I try to observe, as far as possible, what has been called a principle of charity[6] (Wilson, 1958/59: 532). The point is to apply the strongest possible interpretation to other people's statements and arguments on the assumption that they are, most likely, rational and relevant (see Davidson, 1973–74). This principle might be considered an ethical norm that serves to recognize the rights of others in communication.[7]< I take it, instead, as a pragmatic principle that can help to ensure the quality of communication, equally in one's own self-interest. As long as our communication is ongoing, it is in my interest to gain the strongest possible understanding of what you are saying, including any attempts at misleading me – which could be quite rational and relevant. As noted by the sociologist, Erving Goffman (1983), in one of his last works, communication requires both cognitive patience on my part and the granting of social sanity to others. In the case of communication with historical sources, it is in my interest to benefit from the unforeseen, even unforeseeable relevance of the classics' statements and arguments.

6 principle of charity

7 > the ideal
communication
situation,
Chapter 8, p. 151

Re-actualizing Aristotle

Plato had suggested, in the *Republic* and other dialogues attributed to Socrates, that the world as we commonly perceive it, is only a secondary realm of shadows and that, beyond it, there exists a primary reality of ideal forms. Aristotle, in contrast, allowed for a diversified and distributed kind of reality – several different manifestations of the same thing can be considered equally real, depending on perspective and context. What we commonly think of as the 'content' of communication is a case in point. The content occupies a meeting ground between a sender and a receiver, and between reality as possible and manifest. Any discourse of either fact or fiction represents but a small portion of reality, and the discursive representation will only be received and reproduced to some degree by its audience – who may, next, accept or reject (some of) its implications, and act upon them or not, whether in the short or the long term. In each stage of a process of communication, a transformation occurs of what could be, into what is – in some discursive, cognitive, or behavioral manifestation. Such transitions and transformations are cap-tured by Aristotle's principles of potential and actualization.[8]

Along with his first drafts for diverse specialized sciences, Aristotle's realist position helped to make his philosophical framework readily applicable to empirical forms of inquiry. Its canonical status during the Middle Ages and the Renaissance was challenged, however, from the seventeenth century. As part of the breakthrough of modern experimental sciences, Aristotle's *Physics* came to be understood more as soft natural philosophy than as hard natural science. The principles informing that book – matter, form, potential, actualization, and so on – arguably could not provide the building blocks for a comprehensive descriptive system of nature. The principles, however, are better understood as general tools for thought (*Hilfsmittel*) (Wieland, 1962: 230) – premises and procedures for exploring the possible existence of particular systems of nature (and culture) and the appropriate ways of studying them. According to Wolfgang Wieland's (1962) reinter-pretation of Aristotle, the main point of the principles is not their descriptive, but their reflective uses. In the perspective of communication theory, the principles provide analytical strategies that are grounded in the structure of ordinary language. They are rhetorical *topoi*, or commonplaces, which aid both everyday conversation and scientific analysis. There is no rift between the principles and those aspects of reality that they enable humans to think and talk about, because the principles are already given in people's concrete interactions with the world and with each other in communication. Wieland (1962), thus, concluded that Aristotle's principles do not involve nominalism – the position that only physical particulars are real, that these have just a name in common, and that abstract concepts such as the principles are derivative and secondary: "Aristotelian physics is not nominalist, because language itself is not nominalist" (p. 339, my translation). Language is not all that we know, but the primary medium through which we can justify saying that we do know particular things. Both mental impressions of and communicative expressions about things in the world are real.[9]

In his *Metaphysics*, Aristotle elaborated on potential and actualization, specifically the difficult notion that different manifestations of the same thing might be equally real:

> people look for a unifying formula, and a difference, between potency and complete reality. But, as has been said, the proximate matter and the form are one and the same thing, the one potentially, and the other actually. Therefore it is like asking what in general is the cause of unity and of a thing's being one; for each thing is a unity, and the potential and the actual are somehow one.
>
> (Aristotle, 2007a: n.p.)

The notion of potentiality in itself is even "indefinable," and it was explained by Aristotle through particular instances, as exemplified by one of his commentators:

8 potential and actualization

9 realism vs. nominalism

> As a man who is building is to one who knows how to build, as the waking is to the sleeping, that which sees to that which has sight but has its eyes shut, that which is shaped out of matter to its matter, the finished product to the raw material, so in general is actuality to potentiality.
>
> (Ross, 1923: 176)

In the present context, the examples indicate that Aristotle took the principles of potential and actualization to apply not just to material reality, but to reality as manifested in consciousness and communication, as well.

This difficulty – of grasping reality as a diversified set of distributed entities, each with several differentiated potential states, and of representing it in language and other means of communication – has remained the core challenge for human knowledge and communication. It is a fundamental human experience that the common objects of our natural as well as cultural environments exist in one particular state, even though this state may change as an effect of the presence of other objects – the proverbial billiard ball hitting and moving another ball. In other cases, the processes behind a change of state are less self-evident – the similarly proverbial apple falling, causing a startle, a pain, or perhaps a bright idea as to why it fell. Aristotle did distinguish two senses of potentiality, one being its ordinary meaning in Greek, namely, "the power in one thing to produce change of some sort in another. The other, in which he is mainly interested, is the potentiality in a single thing of passing from one state into another" (Ross, 1923: 176). While typically stated as dualities, then, the principles of potential and actualization presuppose some third element or instance,[10] an externally or internally induced process of change. The question is, what may account for the transformation – also within single entities, organisms, or structures – of a potential into an actual state: the "something which caused the movement from potency into actuality" (Aristotle, 2007a: n.p.)?

Whereas the process of transformation, evidently, varies for different natural and cultural domains of reality, Aristotle found the ultimate explanation for the states and changes of things in their final cause – the end that they serve in the world. In an inherently meaningful, religious universe with a presupposed purpose, actuality is assured: "God is in the fullest sense actual, since He is always what He is at any time, and has no element of unrealised potentiality" (Ross, 1923: 178). In a secular and modern worldview, the end of things – of natural objects, personal lives, or social relationships – and their transformations are often radically in question. The end, as well as the best means of achieving it, is subject to individual reflection and public negotiation through the historically available media. In media studies, it is of considerable interest to compare the potential to the actual social uses of different information and communication technologies. The unrealized potentials – as well as the unforeseen consequences – of media deserve a place higher on the research agenda than they have mostly been given.

10 a third instance

In the rest of this book, I return at different points to potential and actualization as "sensitizing concepts"[11] concerning the material, discursive, as well as institutional conditions of communication – in contrast to the kind of operational or "definitive concepts" that refer "precisely to what is common to a class of objects" (Blumer, 1954: 7). In the rest of this chapter, I relate Aristotle's principles of potential and actualization to two other turning points in the history of ideas – one cognitive, the other communicative. It is helpful to state questions regarding both individual cognition (What can I know?) and communicative practice (What can we know?) in terms of transformations or mediations between potential and actual states – the "something which cause[s] the movement" (Aristotle, 2007a: n.p.). Whereas Aristotle applied the principles of potential and actualization both to the world and to human knowledge about it, it was the latter aspect – how humans may gain actual knowledge of a potential reality – that came to preoccupy modern philosophy.

11 sensitizing concepts

Kant and other Copernican turns

The history of philosophy is frequently told with reference to a number of 'turns,' through which the mainstream of philosophy could be seen to redefine its first premises, key questions, or preferred analytical procedures. In brief overview, much ancient and pre-modern philosophy had had an ambition of accounting for reality in terms of its ontology,[12] asking 'What does the world consist of?' Aristotle and other classical philosophers assumed four main elements as constituents of the world: fire, air, water, and earth. From the seventeenth and eighteenth centuries onwards, modern philosophers restated the question in more modest terms as a matter of epistemology:[13] 'What can be known about the world?' And, during the twentieth century, much philosophy began to practice a form of linguistics, asking 'What is meant by "know" and "world"?' In one sense, philosophy had gradually retreated from the object of knowledge, into the subject as a precondition of knowledge, and further into the formal vehicles that might reunite the two sides of the philosophical equation. In another sense, philosophy increasingly recognized linguistic and other means of communication as concrete points of access to the world, vehicles of insight, and conditions of intersubjectivity. Twentieth-century media and communication research joined the turn toward the formal vehicles of information and communication, as witnessed in such traditions as cybernetics[14]< and semiotics.[15]<

12 ontology

13 epistemology

14 > cybernetics, Chapter 3, p. 43

15 > semiotics, pp. 28–30

En route to contemporary communication theory, Immanuel Kant embodied the second, epistemological turn above in his question: "What can I know?" What Kant referred to as his Copernican turn, derives its name from the Polish astronomer Nicolaus Copernicus. In *On the Revolutions of the Heavenly Spheres* (1543), Copernicus had demonstrated that the movements of the planets could be explained without assuming the earth to be the center of the system, and subsequent scholarship confirmed and consolidated a modern cosmology with the sun at the center. Kant presented his philosophical system, in the *Critique of Pure Reason* (1781/1787), as a reversal of perspective of a similar scope. As explained below, Kant sought to shift the attention of philosophers from the objects of knowledge as such, to the categories by which the human subject might come to know about the objects. What I can know about any object depends on what I am as a subject.

Placing the earth toward the periphery of the material universe, but the individual human subject still at its center, the two turns of astronomy and philosophy entered into the long and complex transition from traditional into modern forms of culture and society. The Renaissance had begun repositioning humans at the center of the universe, stimu-

16 humanism

lating humanism[16] as a widely influential program of scholarship and education (Kristeller, 1961). In the words of the pre-Socratic Greek philosopher, Protagoras, "Man is the measure of all things." Humans would serve as the reference point in understanding the other things that exist in the world – what is – and in refashioning the natural environment for human ends. The Protestant Reformation movements, moreover, had raised profound doubts regarding the legitimacy of the Church in determining what ought to be – in interpersonal and social relations. The idea that faith should be a personal matter was placed on an increasingly public agenda, in part, through the growing diffusion of print media (Eisenstein, 1979).

Kant pointed to the individual human being as the final arbiter of doubt through reason, both in a descriptive-cognitive (What can I know?) and a normative-ethical (What ought I to do?) sense. In his worldview, however, human beings were not alone at the center of the universe, which still had a purpose or final cause. Thanks to human reason, God was not in doubt. The belief in God could be regarded as a presupposition for the realization of both moral behavior and personal happiness: "God and a future life are two hypotheses which, according to the principles of pure reason, are inseparable from the obligation which this reason imposes upon us" (Kant, 1998/1787: n.p.).

If God was the final instance of reason, its first instance, to Kant,

17 transcendental categories of human understanding

was the categories[17] of human understanding. Aiming to transcend religious dogmatism, simple empiricism, as well as the skepticism challenging philosophy during his lifetime, Kant suggested that humans do have knowledge of reality, but only because they themselves furnish the necessary categories – or transcendental forms – for grasping even the most basic physical event. These categories are preconditions of human knowledge that are at once *synthetic* and *a priori* – a combination that traditionally had been labeled a contradiction in terms. They are a priori, or pre-given, because I do not infer them from what I perceive, but presuppose them as logical or meaningful structures. They are also synthetic, or composite, in the sense that they capture aspects of some phenomenon or field of interest beyond their own implicit logic or meaning. The prototypical example is cause and effect, such as billiard balls colliding and apples falling. Kant's insight was that the category of causality is neither 'out there' in entities or events, nor 'in here' in any mental analysis of what happened. Instead, it is a precondition for recognizing what is happening before our senses. The categories enable and lend shape to concrete instances of experience. They constitute interfaces between rudimentary perceptions and subsequent cognitive operations, and they enable further inquiry, for example, into the exact nature of specific causes and effects. As such, the categories make up a Janus face orienting to the object as well as the subject of understanding and inquiry. Mediating between potential worlds and actual states of mind, Kant's categories introduced a distinctive third instance to account for the individual human subject's contact with reality.

Kant's philosophical system was an accomplishment of sustained introspection. Like thinkers before and after him, Kant was trying to relate two kinds of worlds – in his terminology, *das Ding an sich* (things in themselves) and *das Ding für uns* (things for us) – on a secure foundation of categories. Like other philosophical foundations, this one proved contestable, not just through further logical inquiry, but also through radically new forms of empirical evidence. Atomic physics, notably, introduced the principle of complementarity,[18] suggesting that, at least at this level of physical reality, "the interaction between the objects and the measuring instruments . . . forms an integral part of the phenomena" (Bohr, 1958: 72). Certain things are, in fact, both particles and waves, but not in the same context of observation and measurement. Niels Bohr's colleague, Werner Heisenberg, commented explicitly on the way in which quantum physics had decisively shifted the foundation of Kantian philosophy:

18 the principle of complementarity

> Whenever we try to deduce laws from our study of atomic phenomena, we discover that we no longer correlate objective processes in space and time, but only observational situations . . . Kant could not possibly have foreseen that in an experimental realm so far beyond daily experience we could no longer treat observations as if they referred to '*Dinge an sich*' or 'objects.'
>
> (Heisenberg, 1971: 122–23)

Even more fundamentally, the theory of evolution had suggested that the very categories by which *Homo sapiens* apprehends reality remain subject to change as part of natural selection. Nature is a moving target, including this peculiar kind of animal that reflects on and speaks about its own place in it. The manifest tendency for 2,500 years of Western thinking to reiterate similar issues in different guises over and over again – realism versus nominalism, materialism versus idealism, and other 'eternal' questions of philosophy – may bear witness to an absolute, in the sense of evolutionary limit to what humans can know in common through cognition and communication. Such questions – whether the historical limitations of human inquiry follow from our evolutionary condition – cannot, in the nature of matter, be answered by members of the human species.

Kant's ambition was an epistemology of the first instance – foundationalism, not in the pejorative sense of a fundamentalism that stipulates a small set of authoritative maxims, but in the descriptive sense of carefully established first principles of inquiry. His epistemology, further, was grounded in individualism.[19] Individuals are endowed with the capacity as well as the responsibility to think for themselves and to act accordingly: "The motto of the enlightenment is therefore: *Sapere aude!* Have courage to use your *own* understanding!" (Kant, 1970/1784: 54). In comparison, Charles Sanders Peirce outlined an epistemology of fallibilism and communalism.[20] Humans, including philosophers and scientists, are bound to err, but they may arrive at reliable conclusions as members of interpretive communities, if only in the final instance. In contrast to the common metaphor of one secure foundation, which may turn out to have been built on sand, or "a chain which is no stronger than its weakest link," Peirce preferred the metaphor of "a cable whose fibers may be ever so slender, provided they are sufficiently numerous and intimately connected" (Peirce, 1931–58: 5.265). Peirce took his own position to represent yet another Copernican turn in the history of ideas.

19 foundationalism and individualism

20 fallibilism and communalism

Peircean pragmatism

Signs and interpretants

Like Kant, Peirce developed an ambitious architecture of concepts and analytical categories. In marked contrast to Kant, Peirce did not present a sequence of major syntheses of his ideas, instead leaving behind a disorganized set of contributions to logic, mathematics, semiotics (which he termed semiotic), and philosophy generally. His works are still in the process of being published in an authoritative edition (Peirce, 1982: vol 1ff.). Accordingly, his writings have invited, and might be said to require at least some measure of, prophetic interpretation[21]< (Liszka, 1998). Through edited collections and commentaries (for key texts, see Peirce, 1992–98), it is particularly Peirce's semiotics and, to a degree, his theory of science that have made their mark on the humanities and social sciences in recent decades (e.g., Colapietro, 1989; Joas, 1993; Sheriff, 1987; Singer, 1984) (for my perspective on Peirce and pragmatism in relation to media and communication research, see K. B. Jensen, 1995). A common denominator for these influences has been Peirce's broad concept of the sign. Signs are more than words, images, and other externalized notations: they are constitutive of human consciousness and the interface of subject and object.

21 > prophetic interpretation, p. 21

One of Peirce's most widely cited definitions of the sign is the following:

A sign, or *representamen*, is something which stands to somebody for something in some respect or capacity. It addresses somebody, that is, creates in the mind of that person an equivalent sign, or perhaps a more developed sign. That sign which it creates I call the *interpretant* of the first sign. The sign stands for something, its *object*.[22]

22 sign, object, interpretant

(Peirce, 1931–58: 2.228)

Peirce's premise is that perception, cognition, reflection, and communication are all mediated by signs. Signs, accordingly, come in many varieties – from basic sense impressions and simple statements, to visual narratives and computer algorithms. The objects to which signs refer are, similarly, diverse and distributed across different levels and domains of reality. Objects include physical entities, subconscious desires, and collective beliefs, all of which can be considered real. Interpretants, finally, are a form of second-order signs by which human beings orient themselves toward and interact with reality.

The interpretant is key to Peirce's thinking and its implications for communication. Importantly, the interpretant is different from the interpreter, or the human agent performing an interpretation. It is a cognitive as well as communicative category that represents one moment in an interpretive process – semiosis.[23] Interpretation, then, is not a single or unified act which, once and for all, internalizes selected aspects of external reality through an instrument of signs. Nor is the interpretant some essence 'in there' in a person's mind that depicts what is 'out there.' Neither the sign (representamen) nor the interpretant constitute secondary *representations* of a primary, brute reality of facts. Instead, reality *presents* itself and remains present to experience in different signs (Bergman, 2004: 299–309). The sign is not a boundary between *das Ding an sich* and *das Ding für uns*; it is a three-way interface maintaining our contact with reality.

23 semiosis

This triadic model of the sign[24] has come to the fore in recent semiotics as an alternative to the dualist concepts and analytical categories that were derived from the linguistic framework of Ferdinand de Saussure's (1959/1916) semiology.[25]< In the longer historical perspective, Peirce's semiotics was an attempt to bridge the epistemological divide between subject and object within one figure of thought and analysis. Building on as well as criticizing Kant, Peirce was resisting the notion that perception, as an interface or third instance, occurs through a narrow conduit of foundational categories and in a brief moment of elementary contact between subject and object. Instead, he pointed to an extended process of semiosis that involves a complex repertoire of interconnected perceptual, cognitive, and behavioral sign types. Figure 2.1 indicates how an interpretant is both a sign for further interpretation and an orientation toward objects to be engaged in action; the dotted line suggests the constitutive role of signs in relating interpreter and world. Figure 2.1, further, suggests the parallelism between individual cognition and interpersonal interaction: communicators relate both to other subjects and to objects in reality through signs. In retrospect, Peirce undertook half a communicative turn on philosophy, redefining Kant's

24 triadic sign model

25 > semiology, Chapter 3, p. 44

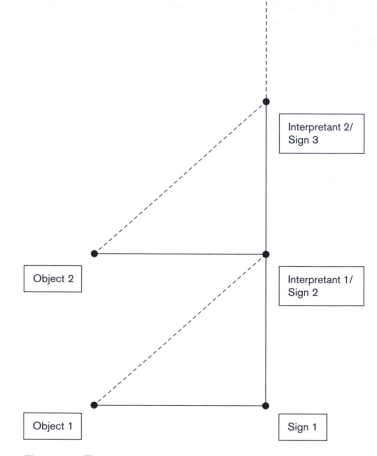

Figure 2.1 The process of meaning production

categories as signs and the process of inquiry as a communicative activity with practical implications.

Beliefs and actions

Like semiotics, pragmatism had a long genealogy in the history of ideas since antiquity (Lobkowicz, 1967), before it took shape as a recognizable tradition particularly within American philosophy, represented by three classic figures – Peirce, William James, and John Dewey – as well as other thinkers and commentators (for overview, see, e.g., Menand, 2001). At issue has been the dialectic of theory and practice[26]< – the relationship between a contemplative understanding and a concrete engagement of reality, between ethical principles and moral choices, ideologies and policies, communication and action. Notions of theory and practice have, of course, been informed by shifting historical circumstances. While Kant and the Enlightenment trusted, or required, humans to create themselves as individuals, Karl Marx became the first philosopher to

26 > theory and practice, Chapter 8, pp. 148–150

argue that "man can transform himself by transforming the *material world*" (Lobkowicz, 1967: 139). Communication and other collective efforts have structural consequences.

Peirce himself summed up pragmatism in his somewhat cryptic pragmatic maxim:[27]

> Consider what effects, which might conceivably have practical bearings, we conceive the object of our conception to have. Then, our conception of these effects is the whole of our conception of the object.
>
> (Peirce, 1986: 266)

To clarify, the key terms are 'practical' and 'conceive.' On the one hand, Peirce was trying to move away from the characteristically abstract conceptual analyses of his contemporary colleagues. Pragmatism pointed beyond a philosophy of human consciousness, and toward a philosophy of social practice. On the other hand, Peirce recognized that we only come to realize the potential practical consequences of our objects of study if we conceive of – reflect on – them in an appropriate variety of signs. In this regard, both laboratory experiments and thought experiments are called for. The practical effects of things in the world amount to differences[28]< that manifest themselves at physical, biological, social, psychological, and other levels of existence and inquiry. Formal scientific inquiry runs a course that is similar to that of informal learning. Peirce (1931–58: 5.51) even compared the process of learning from experience with teaching through practical jokes: "I don't remember that any one has advocated a system of teaching by practical jokes, mostly cruel. That, however, describes the method of our great teacher, Experience." *Erro, ergo sum.*

A key element of Peirce's pragmatism, linking the philosophical position to mundane matters, is his concept of belief. In keeping with a processual notion of semiosis and a practical notion of experience, human beliefs, to Peirce, constitute moments in the flow of consciousness toward actualization in action. Rather than being a mental representation of something, belief constitutes a readiness to act in relation to that something – a situated engagement with reality. Beliefs are not neatly bounded opinions waiting to be executed. Such a processual and differential understanding of consciousness was widespread in philosophy and science during the last half of the nineteenth century, when Peirce was writing. Whereas John Stuart Mill, the British utilitarian and liberalist philosopher, advocated this position in his influential *A System of Logic* (1843), it was the less famous Scottish philosopher, Alexander Bain, who became the central influence on American pragmatism regarding the inseparability of belief and action:

> Belief has no meaning except in reference to our actions. But Aristotle's distinction between potentiality and actuality applies. In respect of matters upon which we have no present occasion to act,

27 the pragmatic maxim

28 > difference, Chapter 3, pp. 42–47

our belief is "an attitude or disposition of preparedness to act" when occasion offers. Under civilization and education we acquire numerous beliefs of a scientific and historical kind, upon which it is not likely we shall ever have occasion to act. But the readiness is there if the unexpected occasion should arise, and the readiness constitutes the belief.

(Fisch, 1954: 419f.)

A pragmatist distinction between representation and readiness, and a priority given to the readiness, can be found in a great deal of contemporary social and cultural theory, notably Pierre Bourdieu's (1984/1979) concept of the habitus,[29] which is an embodied as well as acculturated orientation toward action, and Anthony Giddens' (1984) category of practical consciousness,[30] which, though operating below the level of conscious or explicit discourse, guide social actors in everyday life. In media and communication research, questions of belief and action have most often been stated in terms of potential and actual 'effects' – what media do to people, and what people do with media (Katz, 1959). During the last few decades, much research has addressed this interchange with reference to audiences as active participants in communication, or interpretive communities – an idea that can be traced to Peirce.

29 habitus

30 practical
   consciousness

Case study: interpretive communities

Widespread in interdisciplinary media, communication, and cultural studies, the terminology of interpretive communities suggests that meaning is not present as such 'in' media or other discourses; meaning only comes to be through the intervention of interpretive agents (for overview, see Holub, 1984). In its radical formulation, the idea is that neither the message nor the community exists prior to or outside the act of interpretation (Fish, 1979). More moderately, both humanistic and social-scientific media studies have sought to account for meaning production as a cultural process in which a potential of meaning is actualized by someone, in a context, and for a purpose. Qualitative reception studies,[31] in particular, have explored how, concretely, ordinary media users understand and appreciate various genres – regardless of what textual analysts and other experts say (K. B. Jensen, 1987). In methodological terms, studies have probed the interrelations between interpretive and sociodemographic categories of audience analysis.

The meeting of audience and medium presents an analogy to the meeting of subject and object. Peirce conceived human inquiry as a communal and, by implication, communicative activity. To begin, he distanced himself from the sort of all-encompassing doubt that had been the point of departure for modern philosophy, summed up and resolved by René Descartes with reference to an absolute certainty: *cogito, ergo sum*. Peirce rejected both the problem and the solution. Taking a position of "critical common-sensism,"

31 qualitative
   reception studies

he suggested that "this initial skepticism will be a mere self-deception . . . Let us not pretend to doubt in philosophy what we do not doubt in our hearts" (Peirce, 1958: 40). Doubts are only relevant insofar as they have practical consequences, and they must be resolved, not by individuals, but by publics:

> Unless truth be recognized as *public* – as that of which *any* person would come to be convinced if he carried his inquiry, his sincere search for immovable belief, far enough – then there will be nothing to prevent each one of us from adopting an utterly futile belief of his own which all the rest will disbelieve.
>
> (Peirce, 1958: 398)

In all human inquiry, whether formal or informal, it is the community that sanctions both reasonable doubts and their resolution through communication. Moreover, it is only in the very final instance that even the community may arrive at truth. It was the combination of these two premises – the "transindividual *unity of interpretation*" (the community) and the "*validation of experience in the long run*" (the final instance) – that Peirce took to be his own Copernican turn (Apel, 1972: 95, 100). This combination made it "possible for Peirce to escape Hume's skepticism without insisting with Kant on the necessity and universality of propositions which for the moment are accepted by experts" (p. 101), such as the categories of Kant, the expert philosopher.

Peirce's Copernican turn revolved around communication, without being articulated as a theory of communication in the contemporary sense. On the one hand, Peirce advanced an understanding of signs as media of communication about reality for practical as well as reflective purposes (particularly in his late works on semiotics, see Bergman, 2004: 242–56). On the other hand, like Aristotle and Kant before him, Peirce presupposed the existence of an inherently meaningful universe. Pragmatism was, in part, an attempt to reconcile evolutionary natural science with a religious worldview (Kuklick, 1977: 26). (Peirce was twenty years old in 1859 when Charles Darwin's *Origin of Species* was published.) Regarding the final instance of reality, Peirce relied on what philosophers call a 'counterfactual' argument:[32] Reality is what we *would* come to know if only we had infinite time for our inquiries and communications. Peirce, thus, tended to treat interpretive communities as abstract rather than operational, let alone democratic principles of inquiry. Although some commentators have associated a "logical socialism" (Fisch, 1984: xxviii) with Peirce, he also spoke vehemently against democracy and about "the ruinous effects of universal suffrage and weakly exercised government" (Peirce, 1958: 402).

The notion of interpretive communities was taken one step further in the direction of an abstract ideal by another pragmatist philosopher – Josiah Royce – who considered "communities as being logically prior to individuals" (Parker, 2004: n.p.). While advocating an absolute form of idealism, Royce devoted special attention to error as a fact of life and a constant possibility

32 counterfactual arguments

in inquiry. Clearly, we all sometimes have erroneous ideas, for instance, about where we left something, or when we agreed to meet someone. To Royce, the very possibility of error, and the capacity to recognize it, indicated that some infallible knower exists as a universal principle, even if, in any given instance, the individual mind may not be connected to this principle. "Only as actually included in a higher thought, that gives to the first its completed object, and compares in therewith, is the first thought an error" (Royce, 1969/1885: 351). Royce defined his principle with reference to Peirce's concepts of signs and communities. Whereas idealism as traditionally understood suggests that all aspects of reality are unified in one Absolute Mind, Royce understood "reality as a universe of ideas or signs which occur in the process of being interpreted by an infinite community of minds" (Parker, 2004: n.p.).

In a contemporary perspective, interpretive communities can be appreciated as social formations engaging in scholarship, public debate, and other kinds of deliberation. The communicative interchange between specialist and generalist communities of interpretation is key to the ways in which expert knowledge about various domains of nature and culture, matter and mind, is fed into society at large. Like religious beliefs, however, scientific findings as well as democratic outcomes are contingent and without guarantees. In a universe without first foundations or final instances, fallibilism acquires a stronger sense than even that implied by Peirce. His pragmatic maxim also applies to itself, so that we must ask what the process of inquiry delivers in the comparatively short run as a basis of further inquiry and subsequent action:

> 'the long run' of inquiry is meaningful only if it exhibits 'effects' now. If it does, those 'effects' will have a 'practical bearing' or a pragmatic meaning. If they do not so manifest, then we cannot permit the notion of 'the long run' to undermine the ontological significance of what is felt now.
>
> (Wells, 1996: 322)

The implications of Peirce's semiotics and pragmatism for media and communication research are summarized in Figure 2.2. The figure conceives the axes of the basic sign model as relations of information, communication, and action – which I elaborate in Chapter 3. Information articulates and makes available an understanding of reality in what will remain an essentially contestable[33]< relation between signs and objects. Communication makes information accessible for individual as well as communal deliberation. The end of communications and interpretations anticipates human actions, on natural objects, artifacts, and other human beings, from the local to the global level. Since Peirce, philosophy has taken at least two additional turns, both of which have revolved around communication, with direct implications for media studies. The iconic twentieth-century philosopher, Ludwig

33 > essentially contestable concepts, Chapter 1, p. 6

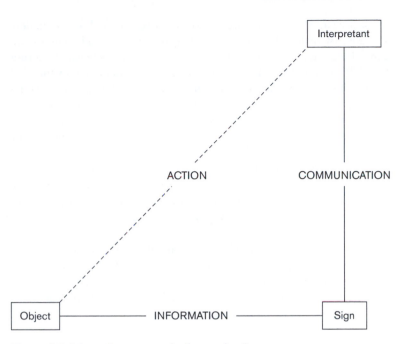

Figure 2.2 Information, communication, and action

Wittgenstein, set the agenda, not once, but twice, not just for philosophy, but for a range of disciplines and fields (Hartnack, 1965). During his second phase, Wittgenstein developed a position that resonates with both classic pragmatism and recent communication theory.

The linguistic turn

Next to Kant's Copernican turn, the linguistic turn of twentieth-century philosophy (Rorty, 1967) is among the most commonly cited shifts in modern philosophy. The terminology refers to the effort, particularly among Anglo-American analytic philosophers, to examine the structures and functions of language in great detail as a privileged way of knowing the structures of reality as well as the conditions and limitations of such knowledge. Whereas Peirce had emphasized the heterogeneity of signs, the early Wittgenstein gave priority to linguistically based and logically formulated representations of reality. In *Tractatus Logico-Philosophicus* (Wittgenstein, 1972/1921), he held that all knowledge must be founded on elementary propositions about minimal features of reality. Laws of nature as well as other types of inference and generalization should ultimately be reducible to direct observations of basic phenomena. In a sense, this position was reaching far back into the history of ideas, before Kant and his centering of the knowable world in human consciousness. The purpose of philosophy, accordingly, would be to reestablish a correspondence between the fundamental structures of reality and the

linguistic and logical structures expressing the potential human understanding of reality. In this way, Wittgenstein prepared some of the
central arguments that were developed by logical positivism[34]< during
the 1920–30s. Not least the application of such principles to history and
society, including studies of culture and communication, generated some
of the most intense debates on theory and methodology in twentieth-
century research. If only certain minimal signs are permitted, how are
we supposed to communicate about those issues of power, beauty, or
morality that so often motivate action?

The originator of positivism,[35] during the first half of the nineteenth
century, was Auguste Comte, who had been a target of criticism for
Peirce. Peirce's triadic concept of cognition and inquiry contrasted with
Comte's dualist and reductionist position:

> Comte [and other positivists] take what they consider to be the first
> impressions of sense, but which are really nothing of the sort, but
> are percepts that are products of psychical operations, and they
> separate these from all the intellectual parts of our knowledge, and
> arbitrarily call the first *real* and the second *fictions*.
>
> (Peirce, 1955: 267)

The issue, to Peirce, was *both* the processing of one kind of sign (sense
data) into other kinds (inferences and plans for action), *and* the variety
of sign types that enter into each of these stages. If reality consists in a
diversified set of distributed entities, each with several differentiated
potential states, then the attempt to arrive at a common denominator
for all of these likely will produce thin or irrelevant findings in many
domains. Or, it may force science to tap only certain features of reality.
This, in fact, was the solution hinted at by Wittgenstein in the last
sentence of his first book: "What we cannot speak about we must
pass over in silence" (Wittgenstein, 1972/1921: 151). In many cases,
however, silence is not an option. Either practical circumstances force
us to take a stand, or we find it necessary to speak out against what
others have to say.

It should be added that 'the linguistic turn' has meant different things
to different fields outside philosophy. In the social sciences, the greater
theoretical emphasis, in recent decades, on language and discourse as
constitutive elements of everyday life and social relations is sometimes
referred to as a linguistic, cultural, or narrative turn. In the humanities,
the close analysis of language and other signs and symbols, their structures and functions, had long been the methodology of choice across
historical and aesthetic disciplines. However, it was reemphasized in
twentieth-century scholarship – from early Russian formalism (Erlich,
1955) to structuralism,[36]< which became a dominant position in the
humanities from the 1960s (Culler, 1975). The common strategy of
human and social sciences has been to approach language as a formal and
modular interface with reality that lends itself to systematic inquiry – a
strategy that holds both potentials and problems. On the one hand,

34 > logical
positivism,
Chapter 7, p. 133

35 classic positivism

36 > structuralism,
Chapter 3, p. 44

structural and systemic modes of analysis promised a new kind of systematics, and an enhanced degree of precision and intersubjectivity, in the sort of qualitative scholarship that remains typical of the humanities. On the other hand, language might end up being treated as a universe unto itself, detached from the objects of research, as exemplified by poststructuralism.[37]< In addition, a narrow emphasis on verbal language as the model of inquiry would not do justice to the distinctive features of either nonverbal fine arts or popular audiovisual media. Most important, as a matter of analytical practice, the linguistic turn entailed a comparative neglect of language as a communicative practice that real people engage in within specific historical and social contexts. It is this aspect that the most recent turn in the history of ideas has brought to the fore, reconnecting with pragmatist themes of communication and community.

37 > poststructuralism, Chapter 3, p. 45

A communicative turn

The later Wittgenstein himself rejected the view of the structure of language as a mirror image of the structure of reality. Instead, he came to define language as a complex set of discursive activities – language games[38] – which are inseparable from the life forms or practices that they serve to constitute. The dictum summing up his second phase – "meaning is use" (Wittgenstein, 1953: 20e) – also provides a heading for a wider shift in recent decades within a variety of disciplines and interdisciplinary fields. Meaning inheres neither in the form of language, nor in its correspondence with reality, but in the ordinary as well as extraordinary ends to which language (and other modalities) is put by communities communicating. In philosophy, the distinction is sometimes made between knowing-that and knowing-how (Ryle, 1949): knowing *that* something is the case, in comparison with knowing *how* to engage with that something. In sum, the latest turn of philosophy has suggested a refocusing of research attention, from language as a medium of representation, to language as a resource of interaction.[39]

38 language games

39 language as representation or resource

   In the heading above, I use the indefinite article – *a* communicative turn – to suggest that, in comparison with the several Copernican and linguistic turns, the communicative turn is, at best, still in the process of being taken. Before proceeding, in the next chapter, to the place and potential contribution of media and communication research in this process, I return, in conclusion, to the three classic questions of philosophy: What does the world consist of?; what can be known about the world?; and, what is meant by 'know' and 'world'? A communicative turn may help to shift attention toward a middle ground, between first premises and final instances, literal meanings and correspondences: Which problem is at hand?; why do we want to know about its solution?; why is reality?[40] For practical purposes, as far as humans are concerned, reality affords an infinite range of potentials for common enterprise and social interaction, only some of which will ever be actualized in reflection and action.

40 why is reality?

A communicative turn, arguably, implies a pragmatic turn. At issue are the beliefs that we – as individuals, families, communities, nations, cultures, or species – are prepared to act on. Communication in public is a privileged instance of human inquiry, involving any and all citizens of a democracy – "anyone as someone"[41] (Scannell, 2000). While associated by Paddy Scannell especially with broadcasting, the terminology applies more generally. The modern media of communication address anyone who is able and willing to attend, but always in terms of some social role, cultural identity, and imagined community (Anderson, 1991). In comparison, much of the history of ideas has been engaged in attempts at defining a position of 'someone as anyone,' or a "view from nowhere" (Nagel, 1986). The record shows that first premises and final instances remain subject to error. We cannot become anyone. We can, however, communicate with anyone as someone; and we can delegate our communication to communities and institutions which would, ideally, serve everyone.

It is for this reason that the material and social conditions of communication in general, and the modern media in particular, have such strategic importance. This is why they are fought over so intensely in theoretical as well as practical contexts. Communication can be considered a synthetic a priori[42] – a precondition of knowing things in common for practical ends. Media are resources for the production and circulation of knowledge across space, time, and individuals. It is only within the last fifty years or so, however, that these issues have been associated with and assigned to a dedicated field of media and communication research. The current state of this field is the topic of Chapter 3.

41 anyone as someone

42 communication as a synthetic a priori

Differences that make
a difference

3

The art and science of media
and communication research

Differences that make a difference

The art and science of media and communication research

A conflict of the faculties

The field of media and communication research emerged at the cross-roads of several disciplines and faculties, which themselves had taken shape over a period of 200 years. In 1798, around the time of the formation of the university as a modern research institution (Fallon, 1980; Rudy, 1984), Immanuel Kant had identified a conflict among its different faculties, arguing that the humanities (the philosophical faculty), not the theological faculty, should provide the foundations for inquiry into natural as well as cultural aspects of reality within the other faculties (Kant, 1992/1798). Around 100 years ago, the social sciences gradually detached themselves from the humanities to produce new forms of knowledge about, and more professionals to administer, increasingly complex modern societies (Murdock, 2002). About 50 years ago, an interdisciplinary field of media and communication research began to take shape in response to the greatly increased role of technologically mediated communication in society, drawing on concepts and methods from both the humanities and the social sciences and, to a degree, the natural sciences. Throughout its brief history, the field has remained a site of conflict among the faculties (on the history of the field, see K. B. Jensen, 2002d; Park and Pooley, 2008).[1] Most scholars will agree in principle that *apartheid* is counterproductive to new knowledge – the difficulty is how, in practice, to avoid *imperialism* (K. B. Jensen, 1995: 141–45).[2]

This chapter addresses some of the potentials for theoretical and methodological convergence in the face of media convergence, with specific reference to the ideas of information, communication, and action. Media are vehicles of information – they make representations of and insights into reality available, as articulated in text, image, and sound. Media are channels of communication – they make information accessible to communicators, and communicators to each other. And, media are means of action – communication is performative, as it unfolds, and as it ends. While most research traditions will agree to these summary descriptions, information, communication, and action have proven ambiguous as terms, concepts, and phenomena. This comes out,

1 history of media and communication research

2 neither apartheid nor imperialism

for instance, in variations on the standard communication model that continues to inform introductory textbooks as well as cutting-edge theory development. As a bridging and sensitizing concept,[3]< I refer to difference. Classic pragmatism anticipated the more recent definition of information as a difference that makes a difference; the notion is found in natural-scientific, social-scientific, as well as humanistic communication theories, specifically cybernetics and semiotics. The mediation of difference in various domains of reality recalls what I described, in Chapter 2, as the third instance[4]< of human cognition and communication, with reference to Aristotle's principles of potential and actualization, Kant's transcendental categories, and Peirce's triadic signs. Difference offers a common figure of thought and analysis concerning key moments of transformation and transition within processes of cognition and communication. To probe the transition between communication and action in the case of digital media, I revisit the concept of interactivity, situating it in the broader context of social structuration theory.[5]< In the last part of the chapter, I examine the boundaries of communication – as a phenomenon and as a field – in terms of its upper and lower thresholds. I suggest that media are programmable in more ways than one, and that different media are programmable to variable degrees – as technologies, discourses, and institutions. Media of the first, second, and third degrees all enable communicators to consider how things might be otherwise, but in radically different ways.

3 > sensitizing concepts, Chapter 2, p. 25

4 > the third instance, Chapter 2, p. 24

5 > structuration theory, Chapter 6, p. 105

When is meaning?

> Common linguistic habits render information as an attribute of messages or data, or as the purpose of human communication – as if information were an objective entity that could be carried from one place to another, purchased, or owned. This conception is seriously misleading.
>
> (Krippendorff, 2008b: 2213)

And yet, it is a commonsensical conception of the 'content' of communication that underlies the most diverse kinds of research. Also research traditions that prefer to speak of content in terms of its meaning have tended to approach the object of study in essentialist terms, asking: 'Where is meaning?' In which material units, discursive structures, mental states, or behavioral events does meaning reside? By considering a different question – 'When is meaning?' (K. B. Jensen, 1991) – my purpose is not to evade or dissolve the issue of how, concretely, to operationalize and empirically examine the constitutive elements of communication. My aim, instead, is to recognize the categorically different forms in which information and communication manifest themselves in multiple stages and contexts of human cognition and social interaction.

As with models of human consciousness – from Aristotle to Kant, Peirce, and Wittgenstein – the authors of communication models[6]< have

6 > communication models, pp. 49–51

mostly agreed on the constituents, but have disagreed, often fundamentally, about their status and interrelations (McQuail and Windahl,
1993). Not surprisingly, different faculties have defined communication
in terms of their own specific domain of reality – physical signals
(Shannon and Weaver, 1949), discursive codes (Jakobson, 1960), or social
practices (Lasswell, 1948). Realizing the diverse aspects of communication, commentators have frequently introduced metaphors or analogies
to establish the link between reality domains and academic faculties.
One illustration is Warren Weaver's classic commentary on Claude E.
Shannon's (1948) information theory. In it, Weaver cautioned that
"*information* must not be confused with meaning" (Shannon and Weaver,
1949: 8), and that technical, semantic, and effectiveness problems of
communication should be treated as separate issues. Toward the end
of the commentary, nevertheless, he envisioned a general theory of
communication that "will surely have to take into account not only the
capacity of the channel, but also (even the words are right!) the capacity
of the audience" (p. 27). Whether or not these are the right words, is
precisely the question.

All scholarship depends on communication through words and other
signs; interdisciplinary fields, in particular, need resources for the
translation back and forth of their terminological and conceptual
repertoires. Difference[7] – a differential and relational approach to the
constituents and processes of communication – provides such a resource.
As an alternative to information as "an objective entity," Krippendorff
(2008b: 2213) pointed to Gregory Bateson's (1972: 351) definition:
"'information' may be succinctly defined as *any difference which makes a
difference in some later event*." Bateson duly noted that the world presents
an endless number of differences that might be of interest. Returning to
Immanuel Kant's point that, in a piece of chalk, as a *Ding an sich*, "there
are an infinite number of potential facts," Bateson described how only a
very small number of these facts acquire relevance as information:

> There are differences between the piece of chalk and the rest of the
> universe, between the chalk and the sun or the moon. And within
> the piece of chalk, there is for every molecule an infinite number of
> differences between its location and the locations in which it *might*
> have been. Of this infinitude, we select a very limited number, which
> become information.
>
> (Bateson, 1972: 428)

Moreover, differences manifest themselves in many shapes and forms,
such as "forces, impacts and the like . . . classically exemplified by the
heat engine, where available energy . . . is a function of a *difference*
between two temperatures" (p. 351). Out of the potentially endless sets
and sequences of states of the world – from the subatomic to the
planetary level – only some will ever be actualized. Next, an infinitely
smaller set of these differences will ever be realized as information in a
human perspective – in individual perception and cognition, and through

7 difference

social interaction. In a media user's perspective, differences take the shape, for example, of information selected and presented (or not) by the press as news; the news of the day as recommunicated (or not) to others face-to-face; and actions (or inaction) in response to news of natural disasters or upcoming political elections.

Bateson was writing in the tradition of cybernetics[8] – the science of "control and communication in the animal and the machine" (Wiener, 1961/1948) (for overview, see Heims, 1991). Cybernetics emphasizes formal descriptions of natural as well as cultural processes, which are said to share certain elementary structures of information. A further assumption of cybernetics is that such elementary structures enter into more complex differential structures, from the functioning of living organisms to the programming of information technologies:

8 cybernetics

> The very simplest perception that we can imagine, upon which, for example, the tropisms of protozoa [growth responses in, e.g., amoebas] are presumably based, must still tell the organism that there is light in that direction and not light in that other direction. Many pieces of information may be more complex than this, but always the elementary unit of information must contain at least this double aspect of asserting one truth and denying some often undefined opposite.
>
> (Ruesch and Bateson, 1987/1951: 175)

A key issue, dividing both communication theorists and philosophers, is the precise sense in which such a structure of information may be elementary or minimal: as an empirical phenomenon, as an analytical device, both, or neither. On the one hand, Bateson and other cyberneticists are heirs to Kant's insight that differences are not found 'in' objects, but are established through humans' attention to and analysis of them. On the other hand, it still seems tempting, also for cyberneticists, to assume that more complex forms of difference are made up of, or reducible to, some "elementary unit of information." Bateson's formulations suggested the existence of some kind of *Ur*-difference, or an information essence in disguise.

I treat difference on a par with Aristotle's principles of potential and actualization,[9]< as a sensitizing concept (Blumer, 1954) regarding human communication. Again, I am not pushing an anti-reductionist argument, in the sense of rejecting approaches that reduce the complexity or restate the singularity of various communicative expressions and experiences; I return, in Chapter 7, to some of the necessary methodological balancing acts. As an illustration of the general point, consider our daily encounter with digital media interfaces. Most users know that if you come close enough to the screen images, their naturalistic shapes and colors reveal themselves as large sets of small pixels. The states, both of the pixels and of their configurations, can be modified at multiple levels of software and hardware – on down (or up) to the proverbial 0s and 1s that stand for minimal states within the physical architecture of the medium.

9 > potential and actualization, Chapter 2, p. 23

Depending on one's purpose – as a user, interface designer, or programmer – certain levels and differences will be decisive, others practically irrelevant.

All differences are, in a sense, created equal. Some differences, however, are more equal than others, as far as humans and their communicative purposes are concerned.

Case study: three differences that make a difference

Gregory Bateson drew, in part, on the ideas of Charles Sanders Peirce – specifically his concept of abduction[10]< – but without crediting the influence (Bateson, 1979: 142–44; Bateson and Bateson, 1988: 37). The influences and family resemblances between the broader traditions of cybernetics and semiotics are many (Heims, 1991; L. E. Kay, 2000; Wilden, 1980). A differential and relational conception of information and communication was basic, as well, to the second founding father of semiotics: Ferdinand de Saussure (who referred to his science as semiology)[11]. In parallel with Peirce (the two thinkers were unaware of each other's work), Saussure (1959/1916: 16) had outlined a framework for studying "the life of signs within society."

A fundamental idea of semiotics is that meaning is not a quality inherent in any given sign, but an aspect of how that sign differs from other signs. Sounds, letters, and words are defined by the features that distinguish them from other sounds, letters, and words; sentences, books, libraries, and cultures can be examined as increasingly complex configurations of difference. Saussure, who was also the originator of modern linguistics[12] and structuralism, combined two insights: an understanding of all consciousness as "purely differential and negative in nature" (an idea prominent also in pragmatism and other nineteenth-century thinking), and the ancient realization that the links between speech sounds and linguistic meanings are arbitrary (e.g., Aristotle's point[13]< that different cultures use different words and writing systems). Saussure's

> novel contribution was to imagine the sound side of language on the one hand, and the conceptual side on the other, as perfectly alike in their nature and mental operations . . . two orders of difference, held together by a force that is essentially social.
>
> (Joseph, 2007: 14)

In humanistic media research and cultural studies, it was particularly Saussure's approach to verbal language as a combinatorial system that was extended to other systems of signs, including audiovisual forms of expression. In addition, cultural artifacts and practices such as fashions and foods might be considered signs or media. A structural conception of entire cultures and societies as systems of meaning,[14] further, became widely influential in

10 > abduction,
Chapter 7,
pp. 137–139

11 semiology

12 linguistics

13 > Aristotle on
language,
Chapter 2, p. 20

14 structuralism

anthropology (Lévi-Strauss, 1963/1958) and in critical variants of social science (Althusser, 1977/1965; Foucault, 1972/1969). At the same time, Saussure's systemic conception of signs has been roundly criticized for neglecting the processes of meaning production, most strongly by poststructuralist authors.

Poststructuralism (or deconstructionism)[15] questions the stability of any meaning as manifested in either consciousness or communication (for overview, see Coward and Ellis, 1977). Radicalizing the concept of difference, poststructuralists have argued that Saussure's two orders of difference are out of sync: the acoustic or material signifiers do not – cannot – provide access to any shared reality of conceptual signifieds. To make that point, the analytical strategy of poststructuralism has been to expose internal contradictions in texts and to undermine their stated intentions through close readings. Compared with other skepticist or relativist positions in Western philosophy, the grand project of poststructuralism has been to suggest, not merely that human knowledge is uncertain, or that new forms of science and scholarship are needed, but that no insight into either reality, oneself, or other minds is possible.

The key reformulation of the concept of difference came from the philosopher, Jacques Derrida (1973/1967), in his neologism *différance*.[16] The term twists the French verb *différer*, which means both 'to differ' and 'to defer.' The implication is that moments of meaning, insight, or intersubjectivity are forever delayed in a play of differences. And that, to poststructuralists, is a good thing. The argument is that any fixation of meaning is a way of exercising, or succumbing to, the power emanating from particular categories of understanding, even a form of discursive violence oppressing other worldviews. Much poststructuralist writing, accordingly, has presented itself as a critical and socially progressive enterprise, occasionally as having revolutionary potential (Kristeva, 1984/1974).

Peirce's processual conception of signs and semiosis has led some writers to suggest that he anticipated *différance*, representing both an alternative to Saussure and an ally of poststructuralism *avant la lettre*. This is in spite of the fact that, considering his pragmatism and realism, Peirce scholarship has generally dismissed such interpretations. Derrida, for one, found that "Peirce goes very far in the direction that I have called the de-construction of the transcendental signified, which, at one time or another, would place a reassuring end to the reference from sign to sign.. . .The self-identity of the signified conceals itself unceasingly and is always on the move" (Derrida, 1976/1967: 49). In his own lifetime, Peirce reacted to what he considered abuses of the term 'pragmatism' by others, renaming his own philosophy 'pragmaticism,' which, he added, "is ugly enough to be safe from kidnappers" (Peirce, 1955: 255).

Signs are never safe, however, even though some of their social uses can be regulated. A pragmatic option is to reclaim difference, and to ask, in accordance with the pragmatic maxim, which types of difference manifest themselves in communication, and what may be their practical consequences

15 poststructuralism (deconstructionism)

16 *différance*

for individual interpretations and social interactions. In order to make the abstract notion of difference do concrete analytical work, it is helpful to focus attention on the category of interpretants.[17]< True to form, Peirce developed several typologies of the interpretant that were not entirely consistent, but which can be taken to refer to stages in a process of communication (Johansen, 1985: 250f.). The three main types correspond to three moments of the communicative process, each of which can be specified – conceptually and empirically – in terms of the difference it makes for the process as a whole.

17 > interpretants, Chapter 2, p. 29

● *Discursive differences.* To refer to a range of potential meanings, Peirce spoke of the *Immediate Interpretant* – "the total unanalyzed effect that the Sign is calculated to produce, or naturally might be expected to produce" (Peirce, 1958: 413). Media discourses have more or less predictable and foreshadowed interpretations. This was indicated, for instance, in Stuart Hall's (1973) encoding-decoding model of communication,[18] which assumes that the discursive structure of a given media message 'prefers' or suggests a particular interpretation to the audience. To exemplify, an advertisement is supposed to promote some product or service, even if readers may resist or negotiate this meaning. Both the preferred and other possible readings can be analyzed as a set of discursive differences or relational structures. Importantly, these structures lend themselves to multiple theoretical conceptions – as 'information' or 'meaning' – and to empirical study in different research traditions.

18 encoding-decoding model of communication

● *Interpretive differences.* Compared with Saussure's systems of difference, Peirce emphasized processes of interpretive differentiation. Compared with poststructuralism, Peirce pointed to specific moments at which particular meanings manifest themselves as actual. The *Dynamic Interpretant* is a "direct effect actually produced by a Sign upon an Interpreter of it" (Peirce, 1958: 413). In Hall's (1973) model, examples of interpretive difference would be negotiated and oppositional decodings of advertisements as, perhaps, everyday entertainment or capitalist propaganda (but also dominant decodings that take commodities or their associated lifestyles to heart).[19] In other theoretical vocabularies, the research question might focus on brand recall following exposure to the advertising in question, or the relative cost of reaching a particular number of potential consumers via different media (CPM).

19 decodings – dominant, negotiated, oppositional

● *Performative differences.* The third type – the *Final Interpretant* – addresses an end point or phase change of interpretation. It was commonly described by Peirce in counterfactual terms[20]< as "the effect the Sign *would* produce upon any mind upon which circumstances should permit it to work out its full effects" (Peirce, 1958: 413). Additional subtypes are Emotional, Energetic, and Logical Interpretants, and an "ultimate logical interpretant" that constitutes a habit-change or

20 > counterfactual arguments, Chapter 2, p. 33

a "modification of a person's disposition or tendency, when actuated by certain desires, to respond to perceptual conditions by conduct of a certain kind" (cited in Johansen, 1993: 165). In a pragmatist vocabulary, the outcome of interpretation is a predisposition to act in particular ways, for example, buying or boycotting advertised goods. Communication translates into action, which may take the form of inaction.

Although Peirce, as noted, did not devote much attention to the diverse social contexts in which interpretations are made and take effect, his account of these phase changes – discursive, interpretive, and performative differences – speaks directly to the communicative practices by which cultures and societies are continuously reproduced. As I suggested in Chapter 2, Peirce's three-way model of the sign captures the analogy between individual interpretation and communicative interaction: a stage of interpretation corresponds structurally to a turn of communication (Figure 2.1). The model also highlights the interdependence of information, communication, and action as aspects of both interpersonal relationships and macrosocial structuration (Figure 2.2). It is the disciplinary definition and operationalization of information, communication, and action that has occupied so much theory development within media and communication research from the 1940s onwards.

Information into meaning

Since Warren Weaver's admonition to communication researchers not to confuse information and meaning (Shannon and Weaver, 1949: 8), the field has been at work to spell out the relationship between the two concepts. Informational difference, negatively defined, emerges as a positive experience of meaningful presence and social contact. In a sense, the whole of meaning is more than the sum of information.[21] The more analytical question has been how to define and parse the elements of communication. What are the degrees of freedom that apply to the selection and combination of these elements in remarkably flexible, yet distinctively patterned ways?

21 the whole of meaning is more than the sum of information

In Figure 3.1 (K. B. Jensen, 1995: 50), I identify four ideal-typical conceptions of meaning. The figure compares different ways of operationalizing what most research traditions consider as the messages, contents, or texts of communication. On the one hand, the constituents of meaning may, or may not, be understood as a predefined or fixed inventory. (I refer to the constituents as units *and/or* events in order to allow for different emphases on either the products or the processes of communication.) On the other hand, the combinatorial structures may, or may not, be assumed to make up a predefined or fixed range of message types – narratives, arguments, and other generic formats.

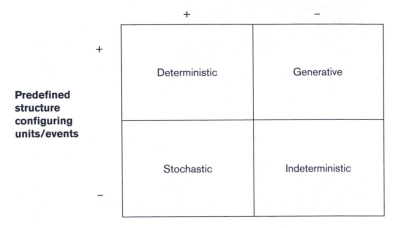

Figure 3.1 Four models of meaning

At one end of the spectrum, a *deterministic* model assumes that the outcome of predefined inventories and structures is a law-like configuration of what can be thought and said. Few researchers will advocate a strong version of this position; communication represents a measure of indetermination in human experience and social interaction. Nevertheless, research traditions, to varying degrees, have noted how biological and technological circumstances precondition communication. At a biological level, physical and mental capacities present enabling as well as constraining conditions of human cognition and communication (Capella, 1996). At a technological level, different media extend human capacities, but in biased ways[22]< (Innis, 1951), facilitating some forms of expression and experience above others.

22 > biases of media, Chapter 4, p. 64

At the other end of the spectrum that is suggested by Figure 3.1, an *indeterministic* model implies that there are, in effect, no boundaries to what might be thought or said. A strong version of the position is found in poststructuralism,[23]< which holds that the differential structure of information will forever undermine any closure around particular meanings. Some accounts of interpretive communities[24]< (Fish, 1979), similarly, have suggested that texts are essentially empty and open to individual and situated projections of meanings. More moderately, institutional senders (artists, film directors, popular composers, etc.) can be seen to selectively realize cultural tradition, as inflected through their own biography and historical context, just as individual receivers actualize more or less unique meanings in their personal encounters with media.

23 > poststructuralism, p. 45

24 > interpretive communities, Chapter 2, p. 32–34

The other two ideal-types of meaning are representative of the two relatively separate mainstreams of the current field of media and communication research, namely, quantitative variants of social science and qualitative forms of humanistic scholarship. This familiar divide is especially noticeable when it comes to the 'contents' or 'texts' of communication. The *stochastic* type, prominent in social-scientific methodologies, is typified by quantitative content analysis:[25] "the objective, systematic, and quantitative description of the manifest content of communication" (Berelson, 1952: 18). The analytical procedure serves to establish the probability distributions of certain communicative vehicles or content units – words, propositions, images, evaluative statements, and so on – within a sample of messages. Given, first, a predefined range of content units and, second, a set of analytical categories for coding them, the immediate research question is how this multitude of elements enter into differential and relational structures. The more interesting implication is that such configurations within radio newscasts, television series, or online chat sequences carry worldviews: their constituents are selective, and their combinations tell certain stories rather than others. A main contribution of the content-analytical tradition (Krippendorff, 2004) has been to keep a tab on representations of reality in the media, documenting and questioning the most widely accessible forms of information about public events and issues.

> **25** content analysis

The *generative* model of meaning, finally, grows out of the humanities, and is characteristic of qualitative studies of media and other texts as discourses[26] (Wetherell *et al.*, 2001). Literary theory and aesthetics since the Russian formalism of the early twentieth century (Erlich, 1955), and linguistics since the rise of transformational grammar (Chomsky, 1965), share the insight that a relatively few 'deep structures' generate an immense, even infinite variety of 'surface structures' in the case of both single sentences and stories the length of books or feature films.[27] As predefined matrices, deep structures are at once very general and highly adaptable. Accordingly, they yield many variations, for instance, of bedtime stories or advertisements, whose basic themes and structures might otherwise be considered identical. They keep the attention of children and consumers, not because either group is immature or gullible, but because that is the structure of meaningful information.

> **26** discourse studies

> **27** deep and surface structures

To sum up, each ideal-type of message or discourse analysis taps certain aspects of the differential structures of information and meaning – they are all necessary contributions to a diverse and applicable field of media and communication research. Scholars regularly remind their students that the *how* of research depends on the *what* and the *why*: the appropriate methods of data collection and analysis depend on the given domain and issue of empirical inquiry. It is only by recognizing the full range of discursive differences constituting communication that research will be in a position to analyze and assess any interpretive and performative differences that may follow.

Communication – between transmission and ritual

The foundational question of the field has been: "Who / Says What / In Which Channel / To Whom / With What Effect?" (Lasswell, 1948). The question might have been: who shares what with whom, in which processes of interaction? The root sense of communication is to share, and to make common (Peters, 2008). Implicit in these different formulations are two models of communication that have been treated as antithetical for at least 30 years.

28 transmission
model vs. ritual
model

The distinction between a transmission model and a ritual model[28] of communication was foregrounded by James W. Carey in a 1975 benchmark article (J. W. Carey, 1989b/1975). According to Carey, the US mainstream of social-scientific media studies had taken as its premise a transmission model emphasizing the transfer of information from senders to receivers within a centralized system of mass communication. The backdrop was the pivotal role of information and communication, and of related research activities, in an emerging social infrastructure that depended on new means of regulating itself through intensified surveillance and registration (Beniger, 1986). The functional or dysfunctional impact of media on individuals, their attitudes and behaviors, was placed high on the research agenda: mass-mediated violence and propaganda were feared; advertising, for the most part, favored. One implication of the transmission model seemed to be that the media are mechanisms which are somehow separate from society – means for either positive or negative ends. Media may have effects, or they may not.

Carey's ritual model, in contrast, suggested that media necessarily have effects: communication is a sharing of meaning and a condition of community. Rituals are never empty. Returning to pragmatism, Carey quoted the philosopher, John Dewey: "Society exists not only by transmission, by communication, but it may fairly be said to exist in transmission, in communication" (J. W. Carey, 1989b/1975: 13f.). Communication, accordingly, should be considered a constitutive ingredient of, and a mediating factor between, human agency and social structure: "a symbolic process whereby reality is produced, maintained, repaired, and transformed" (p. 23). While Carey's work has been most influential in the USA, his ritual model resonates with much European humanistic media scholarship on texts as the concrete vehicles of social and cultural ritual. In a redevelopment of the ritual perspective, Newcomb and Hirsch (1983) suggested a cultural forum model

29 media as cultural
forum

of communication.[29] The most popular and widely accessible media in a culture, represented in their article by television, could be understood as a forum in the classic sense of an arena for articulating and negotiating common concerns: "in popular culture generally, in television specifically, the raising of questions is as important as the answering of them" (p. 49). (On the internet as a cultural forum, see K. B. Jensen and Helles, 2009.) Still, an important issue is who gets to deliberate on the answers, and how: who is in a position to transmit what to whom in the course of the ritual process of the forum?

While it is easy, as always, to exaggerate the extent to which new technologies may be changing old practices of communication, digital media at least suggest a new perspective on the concepts of transmission and ritual. Like other media, they make information accessible to people, and people accessible to information providers. In advertising jargon, both television audiences and internet users are attractive to commercial and political interests as eyeballs. Unlike earlier media, networked media allow a critical mass of people to become senders – to both raise and answer questions, one-on-one and collectively, synchronously as well as asynchronously, introducing new forms of interpretive and interactive difference, as they become eyeballs for one another. On the internet, social actors themselves constitute open-ended sources of information,[30] or dynamic databases of sorts. Digital technologies make information available and accessible on a different order of magnitude and in new structures of transmission and ritual – for better or worse.

30 **communicators as open-ended sources of information**

Societies exist by transmission as well as in ritual. Whether pushed or pulled, information is transmitted; rituals motivate transmissions. The current task of communication theory is to conceptualize the shifting configurations of communicators and messages, and their mutual accessibility in digital media. Interactivity with media anticipates inter-actions between people. Communication is a particular constellation of interactivity and interaction.

Performativity and interactivity

Performing possible worlds

Compared with transmission and ritual, or information and meaning, categories of human and social action have been less central to theory development in the field of media and communication research. Action has, most commonly, been understood as input to or output from a process of communication. On the input side, editorial decisions and legislation condition what is communicated; on the output side, com-munication feeds discursive and physical behaviors by the audience. In order to return action to the center of theory development, it is useful to specify three aspects of the general relationship between communi-cation and action.

First, all human actions can be considered communications in their own right.[31] They may be intentional statements, or incidental behaviors with which others associate meaning, or they may belong to the considerable grey area in between the two. At the intentional end of the scale, the terrorist attacks on the United States on September 11, 2001, were, in one sense, acts of communication – the loss of life and the material destruction accomplished a symbolic purpose. Toward the incidental end, we continuously communicate with each other through clothing and other visual appearances, body sounds, and general conduct. Indeed, any object, event, or action in the world might be considered a medium of communication, because humans are forever ascribing mean-ing to their cultural as well as natural environments (Ruesch and Bateson, 1987/1951: 6). As one student of Gregory Bateson, Paul Watzlawick (1967: 49), put it, humans "cannot *not* communicate."[32]

31 **action as communication**

32 **humans cannot *not* communicate**

Second, all communication is as a form of action;[33] it occurs in a context and for a purpose. Saying something means doing something.

33 **communication as action**

This was the central insight of speech-act theory (Austin, 1962; Searle, 1969). Speaking to others about the weather, or mutual acquaintances, or recent events, is a way of maintaining and modifying social relations. The performative conception of language has influenced current human and social sciences profoundly as part of their pragmatic and communicative turn.[34]< They stand on the shoulders of the later Wittgenstein (1953), who came to understand language, not as a mirror image of reality, but as a set of language games or discourses that, in Carey's (1989b/1975: 23) terminology, produce, maintain, repair, and transform reality. Language games are played for real and incessantly, and they are inseparable from the life forms, or social practices, that they serve to constitute. In the classic pragmatist formulation, "if men define situations as real, they are real in their consequences" (Thomas and Thomas, 1928: 572).

Third, communication anticipates action.[35] Communication is a self-reflective, recursive form of action: it addresses actions that communicate and communications that enact. Communication explores the relations between what is, and what could be – what has been referred to, in several fields of study, as possible worlds.[36] Many different realities are conceivable, as exemplified by science fiction and so-called counterfactual historiography describing what might have happened if key historical events had taken a different turn (Hawthorn, 1991). Only some of these realities, however, are possible in either a material or a logical sense, as examined by philosophical logic (Divers, 2002; Kripke, 1980) and literary theory (Ryan, 1991). For communication theory, one particularly interesting account of such multiple realities came from the philosopher and theorist of science, Karl Popper, who counted three worlds. World 1 refers to the domain of physical objects or states; World 2 is the world of consciousness, mental states, or behavioral dispositions to act. Linking such 'external' and 'internal' worlds, World 3 covers "the world of the objective contents of thought," whether scientific or poetic (Popper, 1972a: 106).[37] As a communicative coin of exchange, World 3 includes fictional, normative, and other contestable accounts of reality in the full range of media.

Popper's scheme bears a strong family resemblance to Peirce's three-part model of semiosis or meaning production: the 'external' Object, the 'internal' Interpretant, and the mediating Sign. Popper, however, only became aware of Peirce's philosophy late in his career (Chauviré, 2005: 209); he, further, gave priority to World 1 as a bottom-line of brute reality. What the two thinkers shared, nevertheless, was an understanding of both cognition and communication as more than brief moments of elementary contact with the natural environment and with other human beings, including *their* possible worlds. Communication maintains possible worlds in common – *and* over time, depending on the available media. Immanuel Kant (1998/1787: n.p.) also had noted that time is primary as a category of human reason:[38] "Time is the formal condition a priori of all phenomena whatsoever. Space, as the pure form of external intuition, is limited as a condition a priori to external

34 > a communicative
turn, Chapter 2,
p. 37

35 communication
anticipates action

36 possible worlds

37 Worlds 1, 2, and 3

38 time as the
primary
transcendental
category

phenomena alone." (The category of time, further, provided one inter-face between classic American pragmatism and European continental philosophy. Both the work of William James (1981/1890) and of Henri Bergson (2005/1907) highlighted the relationship between the flow of human experience and the flow of events in the world.)

At the juncture of traditional philosophical logic and modern tech-nologies, the digital computer refocused attention on time as a condi-tioning factor of what comes to be known in the first place. "Adding time to propositional logic, which is limited to stating facts, creates an algorithmic language, capable of describing processes and essential to programming computers . . . anything that can be stated logically can be converted into an algorithm and hence becomes computable" (Krippendorff, 2008a: 1156).[39] By adding time to logic, computing has served to produce not just new quantities of information, but qualitatively different ways of rendering and engaging reality, for example, within atomic physics and genetics. Current knowledge of subatomic reality and the human genome – and actions on both – would be inconceivable without digital computers.

39 logic + time = computing

Not all human issues and options, however, lend themselves to formal logic or computing. As noted by Jürgen Habermas (1971/1968: 137) in his criticism of Peirce's logical conception of inquiry,[40]< "it is possible to think in syllogisms, but not to conduct a dialogue in them." Like an algorithm, human communication is executed over time. Unlike algorithms, communicative interactions are not generally subject to a central perspective or procedure, or a common logic. All the computers on the grid of the internet cannot compute the pros and cons of a possible design for the future of the internet into a conclusion. The possible worlds of communication emerge across space, as well, and through the intervention of distributed social actors – through interactivity. While often used as a buzzword, which some researchers would prefer to discard altogether (Aarseth, 2003), the concept of interactivity helps to clarify the relationship between communication and action, not just in the case of digital media.

40 > Habermas on Peirce, Chapter 8, pp. 153–156

Interactivities

As currently associated with computing, the idea of interactivity derives from the sociological concept of interaction between human agents – face-to-face, but also indirectly at various levels of the social structure.[41] Parliaments and stock exchanges interact. Most basically, an analogy is suggested between human–human and human–machine exchanges. Originating in the era of batch processing, when technical staff could check the preliminary results of a run on a mainframe computer and then modify it in so-called interactive mode (J. F. Jensen, 1999: 168), interactivity has come to refer to the way in which ordinary users operate computers in a sequentially structured manner (for overview, see Kiousis, 2002; McMillan, 2002). As imported into media and communication research, the terminology has been ambiguous: the field has aimed to

41 interactivity and/ vs. interaction

account both for people's interactivity with media and for their interaction with each other through media. Communication is that unique form of interaction by which human actors negotiate their common social structure, depending on the media at their disposal.

Before turning in coming chapters to the various more or less interactive characteristics of new (and old) media, it is useful to briefly relate interactivity and interaction to two other key concepts of social theory: agency and structure (Giddens, 1984). As I elaborate in Chapter 6, media and communication have tended to remain blindspots of social theory. Figure 3.2 suggests the interdependence of medium, agency, and structure:[42] I take the category of medium to be on a par with agency and structure, a constituent of all social interaction, including face-to-face as well as technologically mediated contact, in a three-way configuration (on Giddens and Peirce, see Collins and Hoopes, 1995). The terminology of Interactivity 1, 2, and 3 reemphasizes the interdependence of three constitutive dimensions of social interaction and the communicative aspect of each:

42 medium, agency, and structure

● *Interactivity 1* is what computer scientists, and ordinary computer users, typically refer to as interactivity: clicking on a web link, entering a message into a chat service, or 'shooting at the enemy' in a computer game. Here, interactivity amounts to sustained selectivity from a preprogrammed range of options. It corresponds, in important structural respects, to the turn-taking[43]< of an ordinary conversation (Sacks *et al.*, 1974). Mass media, as traditionally

43 > turn-taking and other communicative transitions, Chapter 5, p. 100

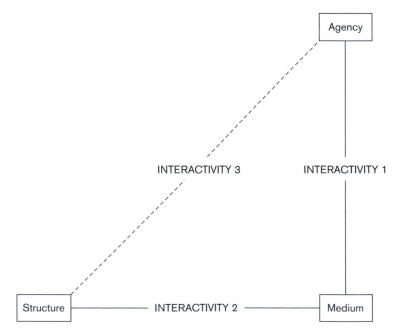

Figure 3.2 Three types of interactivity

understood, offer more limited interactivity in this regard: selecting a radio station, turning to the sports section of a newspaper, and checking in advance whodunit on the last page of a crime novel. All media, however, require measures of navigation, attention, and interpretation by users in order to access the available information.

- *Interactivity 2*, next, refers to the relationship between media and other institutions within the social structure. Depending on theoretical perspective, and on the communicative genre in question, media can be said to perform the role of a watchdog or Fourth Estate (Cater, 1959) vis-à-vis the powers that be. In a wider sense, media constitute a cultural forum (Newcomb and Hirsch, 1983) in which alternative social systems and entirely other possible worlds may be articulated. In a historical and cross-cultural perspective, a central question is whether and how basic technologies are shaped into media with such potentials. In Chapter 4, I take up the issue of the relative determination of society and culture by technology, and vice versa.

- *Interactivity 3*, finally, addresses the relationship between the social structure and its constituent actors and interests, from the individual citizen to national political establishments and global corporations. The myriad actors that make up society interact at a distance and over time; communication lends orientation and meaning to the process, providing a sense of where single actions might fit into a larger whole. The classic example is citizens' involvement in political democracy, parties, and popular movements through the media of the public sphere.[44]< A recent example is telemedicine: doctors interacting with, diagnosing, and treating their patients in private, virtual consultations. The human body and the body politic both depend on communication to reproduce and modify themselves.

44 > the public sphere, Chapter 6, pp. 111–114

The upper and lower thresholds of communication

Given the ubiquity and pervasiveness of media and communication in social interaction, the questions suggest themselves: what is *not* communication, and what is *not* a medium? The history and etymology of 'media' provide part of an answer. The *Oxford English Dictionary Online* (OED) (accessed January 5, 2006) reports that while classical Latin *medium* referred to some middle entity or state, in postclassical Latin and in British sources from the twelfth century onwards, medium and media came to denote the means of doing something. On the one hand, a medium might be understood as a more or less incidental presence, linking various phenomena in the actual world, or joining this world to other possible worlds, as in animism and spiritualism. In the kind of inherently meaningful universe that Aristotle, Kant, and Peirce inhabited, the whole world is a medium. Illustrations range from the ancient idea of the music of the spheres (J. James, 1995) (a contemporary parallel is 'DNA music,' generating musical syntheses from DNA sequences (Gena and Strom, 2001)); through the Great Chain of Being in medieval Christian cosmology (Lovejoy, 1936), in which everything had its divinely sanctioned place, and which could be read about in the Good Book (or, for the vast majority, listened to at church) and read off from the Book of Nature; to recent varieties of pantheism of the sort that Gregory Bateson increasingly emphasized in his writings (Bateson, 1979; Bateson and Bateson, 1988).

On the other hand, in a modern sense, a medium is a particular kind of resource that is adopted and developed for purposes of human action which are mostly intentional and always contestable.[45] The world, life, I have no inherent meaning. In a modern understanding of media, further, the OED distinguishes two aspects – medium as an artistic modality, material, or technique; and medium as a channel of mass communication – both of them from the mid-nineteenth century, when a general idea of communication began to take hold (Peters, 1999). This dual notion of media as expression or ritual and as transmission is the historical legacy of the field. It was not until the 1960s, however, that 'media' came into general use as a term covering diverse technologies and institutions of social interaction across space and time (Scannell, 2002: 194), as examined by a specific academic field of study.

The definition and delimitation of media and communication can take inspiration from the equally interdisciplinary field of semiotics.[46]< Umberto Eco (1976: 19–28) asked what makes up the upper and lower thresholds of semiotics (see also Eco, 1999). At a lower threshold, signs and other vehicles of communication relate to natural conditions and processes – sound waves and electrical signals, their reception by humans as stimuli, as well as genetic and neurophysiological structures. All these conditions of human communication might themselves be examined as information in Bateson's (1972: 351) sense of differences that make a difference. At an upper threshold, media and communication blend into cultural artifacts, practices, and institutions, for example, the tools by which humans transform the natural environment and the commodities through which we conduct our economic exchanges. In between these upper and lower thresholds, communication represents a character-istically human bandwidth of deliberation with a view to coordinated action.

Historically, the thresholds of communication have been shifted by new technologies and new social institutions – by the available and accessible media. At the lower threshold, silicon chips enabled comput-ing and communication on a new order of magnitude. At the upper threshold, the internet as an institution moved from the military, via the scientific, into the commercial domain of social activity, thus becoming a generally accessible medium of public communication (Abbate, 1999). As media are invented and developed, they are adapted – programmed – for certain anticipated purposes. Once in place, they remain pro-grammable, each in distinctive ways and to variable degrees, by admini-strators, regulators, and users.

45 media as incidental presences or intentional resources

46 > semiotics, p. 44

Programmable media

Media are programmable, not only in the familiar sense of coding machine-executable files, but as flexible resources of human expression and social interaction. Media are different in *kind* from other tools and from commodities, genes and stimuli; different media offer different *degrees* of programmability with respect to the information, communication, and action that they mediate. In this book, I emphasize communication as the relaying of categorical information that can be recognized *as information*, and which can be recategorized – restated, responded to, or reprogrammed – in the course of communication. Communication, further, serves to recontextualize information. Recontextualization[47]< occurs both when arguments or narratives are exported to other contexts of relevance, and when other contexts are imported to contradict or relativize an argument or narrative in a present context. Through communication, information travels in and out of contexts of action. Most important here, information can be reprogrammed and remediated across different material media and sensory modalities – books and computers, verbal language and moving images.

47 > recontextualization, Chapter 2, p. 21

The common theme of the three chapters in Part II is the potentials of new, digital media – their specific programmability and interactivity, and their implications for communicative practices in contemporary society. The chapters return to the three paradigmatic, complementary conceptions of media that I noted at the beginning of the present chapter: media are, at once, material vehicles, discursive or modal forms of expression, and socially regulated institutions that facilitate and frame interaction:

- *Materials*. A medium is matter which – in a particular, programmed, historical form – enables expression and interaction. Sound recordings, from the 1870s, made possible the preservation of speech and song as part of a cultural heritage which, until then, had disappeared into the air. From the 1910s, recorded sound became mobile with the introduction of portable gramophones (Nott, 2002: 33–43). From 1979, people wearing a Walkman could create soundscapes that were at once mobile and private (Bull, 2000; Gay *et al.*, 1997). Today, users of cell or mobile phones are able to move in and out of various private and public, material and virtual worlds.
- *Modalities*. It is through programmable forms of expression and experience – speech, song, still and moving images – that different material media enable human communication. Such modalities are, on the one hand, grounded in biology, in the human senses. On the other hand, the modalities have been subject to millennia of differentiation and cultivation. We engage media discourses, not as general modal or perceptual differences, but as conventional genres. Novels, radio serials, music videos, and virtual worlds all invite us to interpret the content on offer in historically and culturally specific ways.

48 > institutions-to-
    think-with,
    Chapter 6, p. 104

● *Institutions.* Media are distinctive and historically variable institutions in society – programmable institutions-to-think-with.[48]< Through media, individuals and collectives are in a position to describe and reflect upon themselves and their place in society and the world at large. Writing, print, and electronic media each extended cultures in space, and sustained empires and nation-states over time. Media and communication research, at present, is witnessing – and seeking to understand – another transitional moment in media history.

The three aspects of media are explored, in turn and in further detail, in Chapters 4–6. I should clarify in advance that each of the media of three degrees – the human body enabling communication face-to-face; the technically reproduced means of analog mass communication; and the digital technologies facilitating interaction one-to-one, one-to-many, as well as many-to-many – is taken up in each chapter. In order to compare and contrast these different media forms, and to probe the idea of media convergence, the structure of the presentation is not one type of medium per chapter, but one aspect of all three media types per chapter; Figure II.1 lays out the structure of the argument. I should also emphasize that I employ the typology of media of three degrees as a heuristic tool in a pragmatist vein – as a fallible systematic with a history and a purpose. My aim is to develop a framework for conceptualizing and analyzing an emerging media environment. Digital media and networked communications pose the greatest challenge to the field of media and communication research since its founding half a century ago.

Media of three degrees

part II

	Materials – Chapter 4	Meanings – Chapter 5	Institutions – Chapter 6
Media of the first degree	Human bodies; artistic and writing utensils; musical instruments; etc.	Speech; writing; song; musical performance; dance; drama; painting; etc.	Local and regional organizations, relying on oral, scribal, and hybrid forms of interaction
Media of the second degree	Analog information and communication technologies: printing, photography, telegraphy, telephony, film, radio, television, etc.	Technically reproduced, enhanced, and separated forms of representation and interaction	Local, national, regional, and transnational organizations, relying on print and electronic forms of interaction
Media of the third degree	Digital information and communication technologies: stand-alone and networked computers; intranets; internet; mobile telephony; etc.	Digitally processed, enhanced, separated, and simulated forms of representation and interaction	Local, national, regional, transnational, and global organizations, relying on networked forms of interaction

Figure II.1 Media of three degrees

Media matters

4

The material conditions of communication

Media matters

The material conditions of communication

Determination in the first instance

The media of communication occupy a middle ground between material and immaterial reality. Printed pages, celluloid strips, electromagnetic signals, and bit streams are all material phenomena. At the same time, different material media provide access to a wide variety of actual, possible, and barely imaginable worlds. Being programmable in distinctive ways, digital media have invited more or less radical claims that the boundaries between material and immaterial reality may be shifting in fundamental ways. Research addressing such boundaries ranges from the largely failed attempts since the 1950s to program a general sort of artificial intelligence (for overview, see Boden, 1996; Partridge, 1991), via an early mainstream of new-media studies embracing cyberspaces, cybercultures, and cybersocieties (Bell and Kennedy, 2000; Benedikt, 1991; Jones, 1998), to cultural criticism projecting a cyborg future and a posthuman era of life (Haraway, 1991; Hayles, 1999). Digital computers might even be thought to dissolve the distinction that René Descartes had referred to, at the outset of modern philosophy, between *res extensa* (extended matter) and *res cogitans* (thinking matter).[1] In certain respects, media extend thinking matter.

This chapter reconsiders the material conditions enabling and constraining communication through different media. Despite the extraordinary flexibility of digital technologies, they lend themselves, like any tool or technology, to certain social uses, and not others. Matter matters.[2] It seems necessary, by way of introduction, to reemphasize this premise, because media and communication research has tended, in recent decades, to shy away from issues of determination, perhaps partly to distance itself from early and still popular notions of strong and direct effects, partly under the influence of an underspecified social constructionism[3] across the social and human sciences (for a critical discussion, see Hacking, 1999). Research might reasonably be expected to answer, or at least clarify, questions of whether, in the final instance, media shape society, or vice versa.

A reformulation of that question was suggested by one of the founders of cultural studies in Great Britain, Stuart Hall (1983), who introduced a distinction between determination in the final instance and determination in the first instance. In a reappraisal of Marxism, he questioned

1 *res extensa, res cogitans*

2 matter matters

3 social constructionism

a tendency for a great deal of critical theory to take for granted that, ultimately, it is the economic bases of society that determine how humans live their lives and make their history. Hall proposed a reversal of this analytical perspective. While recognizing that the prevailing economic and other material conditions establish certain outer limits to human agency and social interaction, he underscored the relative indetermination and variability of how, for example, technological inventions are put to social uses. Technologies have unforeseen, even unforeseeable consequences.

To illustrate, text messages (sms)[4] have been a key factor in the diffusion of mobile telephony around the world over the past decade (Castells *et al.*, 2007). This is in spite of the fact that such messages were apparently first thought of as a one-way service, so that operators could page customers about voice messages waiting for them, not as communication between subscribers (Gow and Smith, 2006: 55). Neither the technical potential (which had to be realized and refined) nor the general profit motive (which is a given in market economies) will explain the current prominence of text messaging – the first killer application of mobile communication. The social practice of texting was technologically (and economically) determined, but only in the first instance.

In Aristotle's terms, a material potential had to be actualized in a social form.[5]< In Bateson's terms, the specific way in which it was actualized made a difference,[6]< for subscribers' everyday interaction and for service providers' profits. Determination in the first instance implies a differential or negative conception also of the material bases of communication. New technologies draw new lines between the possible and the impossible, but they do not predict what precisely becomes possible. Social applications must be exacted from matter; they are recognized, redeveloped, and "culturally invented" (Carroll, 1988: 143) in a protracted and incremental process – clay into tablets, metal into types, electromagnetism into broadcasting. Given the material resources and cultural inventions of different historical epochs, certain forms of expression, representation, and interaction have been possible, others impossible.

The material conditions of communication are, evidently, outside the control of any individual human being. The perceptual, cognitive, and interactive capacities of my body, while cultivated through socialization and education, are the limits of my communications. My body is my "general medium for having a world" (Merleau-Ponty, 1962/1945: 146). The extensions of human capacities into diverse technologies (McLuhan, 1964), in turn, are collective accomplishments that circumscribe and embed the individual as second nature. Technologies stake out particular windows of opportunity for collective deliberation and collaboration. Like humans, material media have been socialized and acculturated – programmed – over time.

In the first section below, I review the characteristics of three prototypes of material media – humans communicating in the flesh, classic mass media, and digital information and communication technologies.

4 text messaging (sms)

5 > potential and actualization, Chapter 2, p. 23

6 > difference, Chapter 3, p. 42

Focusing on their current configuration, I highlight the migration of communicative practices across different material media. Digital media recall the early finding that mass communication typically involves a two-step flow (Lazarsfeld *et al.*, 1944) from technological media via embodied opinion leaders into social groups. The current media environment may be understood in terms of a three-step flow.[7] In the middle portion of the chapter, I specify the transformation of matter into media with reference to three main concepts: affordance, emergence, and momentum. Matter affords or allows for diverse uses in representation and interaction. Matter emerges as specific stable and shared resources of communication. And, once established as a medium, matter acquires a momentum of its own. In the last section of the chapter, I briefly consider contemporary culture as an emerging as well as a transitional media environment, pointing toward media of a fourth degree.[8] Digital media are becoming ubiquitous; they make both information and other people accessible almost anytime, anywhere. Digital media are also increasingly pervasive; integrated into common objects and artifacts, natural and cultural environments, they may no longer be recognized as media. Also as embedded in other stuff, however, media are material forces with consequences.

Material media of three degrees

Medium theory

Medium theory is the research tradition that has given the most sustained attention to the material conditions of human communication. In summary, medium theory poses the question: "What are the relatively fixed features of each means of communicating and how do these features make the medium physically, psychologically, and socially different from other media and from face-to-face interaction?" (Meyrowitz, 1994: 50). Incorporating historical as well as anthropological perspectives, studies have examined how a given material medium supports certain kinds of communication, while rendering others impossible or unlikely. In a wider sense, research has explored how different media may give rise to shifting forms of consciousness and culture. Form carries meaning or, in Marshall McLuhan's (1964) words, "the medium is the message."[9] A key insight of McLuhan's mentor, Harold A. Innis (1951; 1972/1950), was that the extension of empires, religions, and other social formations in space and time, geographically and historically, is explained, in large part, by the communicative resources that have been available to them. In particular, Innis (1951) suggested that a given medium manifests a "bias"[10] toward either time or space. Examples include stone tablets, whose inscriptions last a long time, but do not travel well, as opposed to papyrus and paper, which support the administration of distant provinces, but which are vulnerable to destruction and to appropriation by oppositions for purposes of social change.

7 > three-step flow, pp. 71–74

8 > media of the fourth degree, pp. 80–82

9 > the medium is the message, Chapter 5, p. 84

10 biases of media

Medium theory was, in part, a product of media history. "What we can say of 'the media' is that the sense in which it is commonly used today – and by now it is a commonsense term and part of everyone's ordinary usage – is no older than the early 1960s" (Scannell, 2002: 194). The coming of 'new,' electronic media, especially television, stimulated reflection on the very idea of media. In an authoritative overview appearing just before the public breakthrough of the internet in the mid-1990s, Joshua Meyrowitz (1994) divided (media) history into oral, scribal, print, and electronic cultures. Digital media reopen the discussion of how many periods there have been in media history[11] (for overview, see Finnemann, 2008) – a discussion that involves the interrelations between technologically mediated and embodied communication, as well. Whereas Meyrowitz (1994: 50) implicitly took "face-to-face interaction" to be an unmediated bottom line of communication, to which each "medium" was to be related, it seems necessary, fifteen years on, to ask what is the medium of face-to-face interaction.

11 how many periods of media history?

In the perspective of the history of various material instruments, media constitute a unique set of resources extending the human body in diverse contexts of action – tools, technologies and, most recently, metatechnologies.[12] "Tools can be made and used by individuals working alone and make it possible to process matter or energy in single steps" – from stone axes to pens. Technologies, such as the printing press or radio, "require a number of people to work together," and they "make it possible to link several processing steps together in the course of transforming matter or energy." As such, technologies enabled industrialization and other material infrastructures of modernity. Metatechnologies, finally, are informational or digital. They:

12 tools, technologies, meta-technologies

> vastly expand the degrees of freedom with which humans can act in the social and material worlds . . . enabl[ing] long processing chains, . . . great flexibility in the number of steps and the sequence . . . an ever-expanding range of types of inputs and . . . an essentially infinite range of outputs.

In addition, meta-technologies "are social, but enable solo activity within the socially produced network" (Braman, 2006: 56–57).

To illustrate a necessarily brief argument about the three degrees of media, I refer to various kinds of sound media – speech, music, public and private soundscapes – and their place in essentially multimodal contexts of communication (see further K. B. Jensen, 2006). While traditionally neglected compared with visual forms of communication (radio has been the Cinderella of media studies (Scannell, 2002: 198)), sound has been coming back in style with mobile phones, mp3 players, online radio stations, and ambient everyday environments (Bull and Back, 2003; Nyre, 2008). Whereas my discussion holds implications for the periodization of media history, my main purpose is to compare and contrast the present media environment with past media environments.

Bodies and tools – the first degree

In the perspective of the history and theory of communication, human beings can be understood as media. The human body is a versatile material platform, hosting speech, song, dance, drama, painting, and creative arts generally – capacities that are cultivated into competences by children as well as professional artists. In itself, the human body is a necessary and sufficient material condition of communication;[13] our bodies become productive and receptive media of communication through socialization and acculturation. In comparison, tools – writing utensils or musical instruments – are neither necessary nor sufficient, but extend the human body and its communicative capacities in significant ways. Media of the first degree – human bodies and their extensions in tools – externalize accounts of actual as well as possible worlds,[14]< and enable each of us to communicate with others about such worlds for both reflective and instrumental purposes.

Embodied communication is perhaps most commonly associated with speech and oral interaction. The everyday conversations that join family and friends, neighbors and coworkers, into groups and communities are key to all social life. Face-to-face interaction, however, comprises diverse modalities of expression. We encounter other people as audiovisual media and in multimodal communication:[15] we cannot *not* be heard and seen (Watzlawick *et al.*, 1967: 49). And, our tools and artifacts create more or less durable mediascapes (Appadurai, 1996) and soundscapes (Schafer, 1977). One historical example is so-called rough music, as studied by the historian E. P. Thompson (1991: 467–538) in eighteenth- and nineteenth-century England, which had parallels in other European countries and in the United States. If an individual or a family had offended the rest of a community, it was a common practice to name and shame them by chanting, shouting obscenities, and banging pots and pans. And, rough music is not entirely a thing of the past: On March 11, 2005, BBC World News reported that authorities in Andhra Pradesh, India, had sent groups of drummers to tax evaders' houses to make them pay up (http://news.bbc.co.uk/1/hi/world/south_asia/4397907.stm, accessed July 4, 2005).

Verbal language, nevertheless, constitutes a privileged modality – in evolutionary, psychological, and social terms.[16] Language relays categorical information that can be recategorized – restated, responded to, reprogrammed – in ways that no other modality can. As noted by the linguist, Émile Benveniste (1985/1969: 236), "the signs of society can be interpreted integrally by those of language, but the reverse is not so. Language is therefore the interpreting system of society." Speech interprets images, but images rarely interpret speech, except in the odd aesthetic experiment.

For most of human history, of course, bards or singers of tales were the only media around – singular and localized archives of information and means of communicating a cultural heritage. The literature on non-literate, prehistoric societies describes oral cultures as context-bound and

13 the human body as a necessary and sufficient condition of communication

14 > possible worlds, Chapter 3, p. 52

15 humans as audiovisual media

16 language as privileged modality

present-oriented (Goody and Watt, 1963; Ong, 1982; Scribner and Cole, 1981). Far from labeling these as inferior, medium theory does suggest that primary orality – a state of culture that is "totally untouched by any knowledge of writing or print" (Ong, 1982: 11) – is incompatible with a sense of a historical past, and of a different future. (This is in contrast to a secondary orality, which Ong (1982: 11) associated with the spoken word of broadcasting, and a tertiary orality that may be emerging with digital media.)[17] In a primary oral culture, communication is an expression and an event in context, rather than a representation and a resource across contexts.

[17] **orality – primary, secondary, tertiary**

In a comparative perspective, I include writing[18] with media of the first degree. To be sure, manuscripts supported vast and complex economic, political, and scientific systems for millennia, by fixing information as knowledge and facilitating the reflective production of ever more knowledge. As constituents of communicative practices, however, manuscripts depend on multistep flows of social interaction. Because copies are precious and few, they will be distributed in an extremely selective fashion to central individuals within established institutions. Such individuals – priests, generals, literate servants, and so on – will pass on even more selective and contextually adapted information with oral commentary within dedicated organizational hierarchies. The point is not only that social hierarchies may restrict public access to information (and to the literacy required) – which has notoriously been the case throughout history. Nor is it merely that the copying of manuscripts is laborious and subject to error, which limits access to precise and applicable information. Rather, in a scribal culture, communication remains an expression and an event that is primarily enacted in local contexts by embodied individuals. Even a utopian state that would encourage and financially support the literacy of its people, and their copying of as many manuscripts as possible for as wide a group of other readers as possible, would require sheer human labor on a scale that makes anything approaching equal access to the culturally available information inconceivable. Mass communication is not a potential of the medium of writing.

[18] **writing**

In unsentimental terms, Joshua Meyrowitz (1994: 54) noted that the comparatively inefficient forms of reproducing and distributing writing made it "a transitional cultural form." Writing by hand, of course, remains as a major cultural practice. Writing is integral to upbringing and education; to much drafting of texts in political life, business administration, and scholarship; and to communication with one's intimates and, importantly, oneself through notes. In news studies, reference is sometimes made to source media (Ericson *et al.*, 1987: 41) – oral interviews, scribbled notes, printed press releases, and so on – all of which feed into what is reported as news in media of the second and now third degrees. As media of record, and of interaction within and between the main institutions of society, however, embodied individuals and written texts were superseded by a second degree of media.

Technologies – the second degree

19 'the mass media'

20 technical
reproduction of
communication

21 aura

22 > anyone as
someone,
Chapter 2, p. 38

Until quite recently, it was still common to refer to 'the mass media'[19] – media that distribute the same, or similar messages from a few central senders to many distributed receivers. The philosopher, Walter Benjamin (1977/1936), famously defined mass media in terms of their technical reproduction and dissemination, specifically of artworks, but with implications for other communicative practices, as well.[20] Whereas Benjamin focused on photography, film, and radio, I take media of the second degree to include the various analog technologies – from printed books and newspapers to film, radio, and television – all of which took shape as one-to-many media institutions and practices of communication. Their common features were, first, one-to-one reproduction, storage, and presentation of a particular content. Second, media of the second degree radically extended the potential for dissemination of and access to information across space and time, irrespective of the presence and number of participants.

Benjamin noted a specific ambiguity that arises from reproduction. On the one hand, it results in the loss of what he termed aura:[21] the sense of uniqueness and, perhaps, transcendence that has traditionally been associated with fine art – paintings or sculptures, for instance – and with actors or musical performers appearing on stage. Present artifacts and singular actors mediate an absent reality, and thus appear larger than life. (Also other human beings – anyone[22]< – could be said to carry an aura, as informed by their biographies and shared histories, and as appreciated by intimates, friends, or strangers in a chance meeting. This, however, was not Benjamin's original point.)

On the other hand, technical reproduction represented a major civilizational advance. When artworks and other cultural products are divorced from their unique, but local origins, they afford many more uses by many more people. Reproduction entails a shift of emphasis in the understanding of art, from singular expression to social communication. Accordingly, Benjamin (1977/1936: 390f.) concluded, art need no longer be subordinated to religious and other ritual uses:

> for the first time in world history, mechanical reproduction emancipates the work of art from its parasitical dependence on ritual. To an ever greater degree the work of art reproduced becomes the work of art designed for reproducibility . . . the total function of art is reversed. Instead of being based on ritual, it begins to be based on another practice – politics.

"Designed for reproducibility": reproduction is not an incidental, but a planned activity with social implications. Two classic examples – books and newspapers – suggest the point. Books, pamphlets, and other printed formats could be considered a necessary (though far from sufficient) condition of Renaissance and Reformation (Eisenstein, 1979). Newspapers, in turn, served as material vehicles in political revolutions and in the formation of nation-states (Anderson, 1991; Habermas, 1989/1962). Print media were at once impersonal and public, potentially outside the reach of the auratic leaders of religious and political establishments. The printing press, thus, facilitated the modern understanding of religion as a personal matter, and of politics as a public matter.[23]

Compared with the printing press, technologies for recording and disseminating sound[24] came late to media history, from the 1870s onwards (for overview, see Millard, 1995). For the first time in human history, sound events – from song and other musical performances, to political speeches, to natural environments – could be preserved as part of the cultural heritage. Sound became constitutive of the central mass media of the twentieth century: radio, film (from 1929), and television. Moreover, analog sound technologies contributed to new kinds of soundscapes,[25] in private and in public. In shops as well as in workplaces, an important and underresearched ingredient of urban life has been muzak (see, e.g., Barnes, 1988; Lanza, 1994). In the home, radio broadcasts and recorded music came to compete, in different social groups, with piano recitals and community singing. With several radio, television, and stereo sets per household, private listening increasingly equaled personal listening. From the 1960s, the transistor radio made music, news, and other genres accessible on the move.

It should be noted that multistep communication remained the order of the day in print and electronic cultures. For one thing, access to printed materials in different historical and cultural settings has remained severely limited by the economic means of potential readers, low literacy levels, and living conditions generally. For another thing, reading as a communal activity – reading aloud – has remained a significant cultural practice (Boyarin, 1992). In a critique and redevelopment of Eisenstein's (1979) classic study of the role of printing presses and books in the Reformation, Pettegree (2005) showed how both processes of reading and of converting to a new faith were public activities involving singing, preaching, drama, and visual images, as well. Furthermore, readers themselves became writers, adding comments or 'marginalia' (Jackson, 2001), perhaps alongside those of others already appearing in book margins (anticipating user tags[26]< in digital media), and taking notes for later inclusion in letters.[27]< And, in the case of broadcast audiences, the new reception studies from the 1980s documented how audiences, in addition to actively interpreting media content, collectively engage media as part of their own communicative practices in context (Lull, 1980; Morley, 1986; Radway, 1984). Whereas face-to-face and mass communicative practices have long been intertwined, digital media have lent new material forms to their links and networks.

Meta-technologies – the third degree

The digital computer reproduces and recombines all previous media of representation and interaction on a single material platform of hardware

23 religion as personal matter, politics as public matter

24 sound recording

25 soundscapes

26 > user tags, Chapter 5, p. 93

27 > letter writing, Chapter 6, pp. 121–122

28 meta-media

and software. At the beginning of the era of personal computers, Kay and Goldberg (1999/1977), accordingly, described computers as meta-media.[28] As means of expression, digital media join text, image, and sound in some new and many old genres, as inherited from mass media as well as face-to-face interaction: narratives, debates, games, and so on. As modes of interaction, digital media integrate one-to-one, one-to-many, and many-to-many forms of communication. The central example of media of the third degree remains the networked personal computer. At the same time, mobile telephones and other portable devices are becoming equally important access points to the internet, and already account for much of the diffusion of the internet in some parts of the world, notably South-East Asia and Japan (Castells *et al.*, 2007).

With meta-technologies, communication has come full circle to the sort of interactive and multimodal forms of interchange that characterize face-to-face settings. With mobile phones, technologically mediated speech has become a much more prominent component of everyday life in the coordination of public as well as private affairs. Online computer games, further, exemplify the integration of different auditory and visual modalities, not just in the representation of a game world, but in the coordination of the gameplay, for instance, through continuous spoken interaction between multiple players (Jørgensen, 2007). And, the sense of being virtually present in some literally absent world may translate into a sense of engagement with public events and issues. One example is the Sonic Memorial project that commemorates the events of September 11, 2001. In addition to presenting sounds from the neighborhood around the World Trade Center, the site includes interactive functionalities so that visitors may themselves "add a sound" (http://sonicmemorial.org, accessed July 15, 2009) (E. L. Cohen and Willis, 2004).

Digital technologies in general, and the internet in particular, invite research to refocus studies from media to communication, and to clarify the relationship between the two categories. One material medium may support several different communicative practices; some communicative practices travel well between media; and certain familiar practices come back in style when new platforms become available, as illustrated by text messaging (sms).[29]< Not least when envisioning the potentials of new media, both research and policy have commonly returned to certain basic modes of communication: the Athenian forum, the Habermasian (1989/1962) dialogue, or the online wisdom of Web 2.0 crowds (Surowiecki, 2004). The niches of different digital media for various communicative purposes are still in the process of being established (Kim *et al.*, 2007; Ramirez *et al.*, 2008). In the next section, I present a typology and an empirical study of six basic forms of communication, as they relate to digital media (K. B. Jensen and Helles, 2009).

29 > text messaging (sms), p. 63

Case study: three-step flow

Figure 4.1 lays out and exemplifies six communicative practices that are found in media of all three degrees. Along one dimension, the figure distinguishes between synchronous and asynchronous communication. Time is of the essence in communication: there is a world of difference between talking to a family member on the telephone and listening to the message s/he left on one's answering service, or between watching a sports competition live on television and streamed the next day on the web. The point is not that synchronous communication is preferable to the asynchronous version, or vice versa, but that both forms are flexible means of expression and interaction for different social ends. A love letter might be valued more highly than a brief encounter with the beloved; a printed drama lends itself to reflection and contemplation that is impossible in a theater or in front of any screen.

Along the other dimension, Figure 4.1 refers to the number of participants in a given communication and the nature of their interaction: who gets to say something to how many? It is, not least, the cells at the top and at the bottom of the figure that have generated special interest in connection with digital media. In the case of one-to-one communication, the extraordinarily rapid diffusion of mobile telephony has raised questions, for example, about changes in the forms and uses of verbal language (Baron, 2008) and about the maintenance of strong and weak social ties to intimates and acquaintances, respectively (Ling, 2008). Ordinary media users talk and text on the move to become and remain members of families and networks, societies and cultures.

In comparison, the future of many-to-many communication still appears an open question, at least as society-wide practices of coordinating politics, economy, and culture. This is in spite of the undoubted early success, for instance, of specific collaborative achievements such as Wikipedia; of open-source programming and peer-production initiatives (Benkler, 2006; Von

	Asynchronous	Synchronous
One-to-one	email, text message	Voice, instant messenger
One-to-many	Book, newspaper, audio and video recording, Web 1.0 / webpage, download	Broadcast radio and television
Many-to-many	Web 2.0 / wiki, blog, social network site	Online chatroom

Figure 4.1 Six communicative practices

Hippel, 2005); of personal, professional, and corporate blogs (Rettberg, 2008; Schmidt, 2007); and of social network sites (Boyd and Ellison, 2007). Many-to-many communication simply has few historical precedents. Examples include, for synchronous communication, a marketplace and a sports stadium and, for asynchronous communication, graffiti and community notice boards. In the case of organizations, movements, and communities such as political parties, labor unions, cultural interest groups, and so on, newsletters and other media have traditionally served as internal communications involving a limited membership and its leadership around specified issues. The understanding of mass communication as a two-step flow (Lazarsfeld *et al.*, 1944), similarly, emphasizes the integration of one-to-many with one-to-one – or few-to-few – interactions. Digital media at least suggest "the Babel objection" (Benkler, 2006: 10) – that everyone may end up speaking, with no one listening.

The empirical study below aimed to produce a baseline of information about the range of communicative practices that an average media user engages in. The survey included three basic sets of questions: one on *media uses*, including newspapers, radio, television, audio and video players, telephony, and the internet; a second set on respondent *values* in a variety of domains, including politics, family life, shopping, work, leisure, and faith; and a third set of questions registering standard *demographics*. In addition, the questionnaire referred to a variety of internet genres: email, online shopping and banking, file sharing, blogging, and so on.

Data collection was conducted online in the summer of 2008; the early diffusion and high penetration of the internet in Denmark made a web survey an efficient and reliable research instrument in this setting. The present analysis examined a reduced data set (N = 1425), whose size corresponds to earlier comparable studies, and which displays a distribution on the relevant demographic variables that approaches the Danish population as a whole (see further K. B. Jensen and Helles, 2009). In overview, Figure 4.2 indicates the intensity with which respondents reported engaging in each of the six prototypes of communication on a scale from 0 to 1.

- *Synchronous one-to-one (S11).* Aristotle noted that humans are talking animals; with modern communicative extensions (McLuhan, 1964), we keep on talking, not necessarily more, but in different circumstances and changing configurations. This is borne out by a mean of 0.609 for this practice. The mobile phone, in particular, has made ubiquitous communication and the microcoordination (Ling and Yttri, 2002) of our daily lives possible to a remarkable extent.
- *Asynchronous one-to-one (A11).* Perhaps surprisingly, the mean for asynchronous interpersonal communication – 0.869 – tops that of the synchronous equivalent. It is plausible, first, that text messaging is an especially convenient means of microcoordination: people arrange their shared lives in an out-of-sync everyday, and the arrangements remain accessible for later reference on their small screens. Second, text

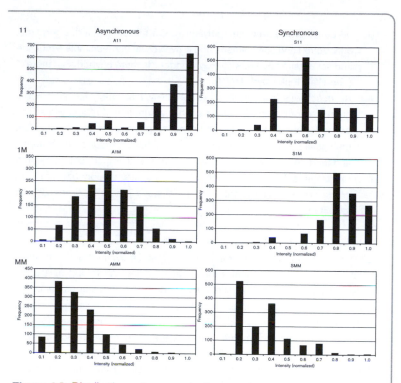

Figure 4.2 Distributions of communicative practices

messaging is relatively inexpensive because it takes up little bandwidth. Talking may be cheap, but texting is cheaper.

- *Synchronous one-to-many (S1M).* Good old-fashioned push broadcasting can be considered an integrated element of the everyday lives and cultural practices of the general public. The mean – 0.779 – approaches that of asynchronous one-to-one communication. Whereas interactive and user-controlled forms of communication have frequently been described as preferable, even as ways of liberating audiences from mass media, it can be not only entertaining, but also engaging and informative to go with the flow (Williams, 1974).

- *Asynchronous one-to-many (A1M).* In comparison, asynchronous mass communication lets the audience go for what they (think they) like or need. This applies to newspapers and traditional web pages, but also to recorded audiovisual material, whether downloads, time-shifted television, or rented films and programs, which might be thought of as the special events of everyday media culture. Especially when recording and renting, pulling requires a certain effort, which may help to explain the somewhat lower mean in this case – 0.435.

- *Synchronous many-to-many (SMM).* Both of the many-to-many varieties represent lower perceived intensities of use, in this first case a mean of 0.285. On the one hand, the self-generated flow of a chat session might be considered particularly attractive. On the other hand, it requires, again, effort and commitment, and it involves an unpredictable sequence and set of participants, who may wonder, "Is there anybody out there?" (*The Wall*, Pink Floyd, 1979).

- *Asynchronous many-to-many (AMM)*. This last variety has attracted a great deal of public as well as scholarly attention in recent years. The political arena of blogging, the economic potential of peer production, the social relations of network sites – all have generated both hopes and fears. Available here are self-selected and, in part, self-generated fora of interaction for all manner of subcultures and subpublics. At least in the present survey, such communicative practices produced the lowest mean – 0.264.

In sum, the study indicated that at least Danish web users in 2008 would talk, text, and flow their way through everyday life; they may be less inclined, so far, to engage in communications many-to-many. While preliminary, the findings begin to delineate a research agenda that reemphasizes communication above media (see further K. B. Jensen, in press). Media convergence is perhaps best examined with reference to the communicative uses that people make of different media – their conceptions of what each medium can do for them, at what level of intensity; the time, effort, and money that they are willing to spend on each; and their flows across various media in three or more steps of communication.

From matter to media

Affordances

The currently emerging digital media environment presents a special case of the general question underlying medium theory, namely, how material potentials become actual media. Both the simplest of tools and the most sophisticated of meta-technologies are made rather than found. Compared with inherent biases,[30] the notion of affordances underlines the ongoing social and cultural programming of media. This perspective has become more obviously relevant with meta-technologies than in the case of the analog media that Innis (1951; 1972/1950) examined.

30 > biases of media, p. 64

The concept of affordances was developed by the psychologist James J. Gibson (1979) to underscore the dynamic interplay between humans and their natural environment. Humans are constituents of nature. Although we commonly say that we *have* a body, we also *are* a body[31] (Merleau-Ponty, 1962/1945: 174). Affordances are, on the one hand, properties of nature that humans refer to and depend on; on the other hand, such properties only manifest themselves relative to particular organisms. Trees hold different affordances for birds, cats, and humans. Humans are distinguished, in part, by the manner in which we both select

31 humans both have bodies and are bodies

from and modify trees and any other affordances that we encounter, individually and collectively. Walking in a wood, I can use a branch that has fallen from a tree as a seat, or I may move it to serve as a makeshift bridge across a stream. In a feature film, the rear end of a car will provide seating for two heroes catching their breath and planning their next move; later, several cars can serve as a bridge as they jump in coordinated pursuit of the villain inside the truck up ahead. Making the film, and streaming it online, depends on an additional variety of material affordances and human competences.

In human interactions with the environment, there is a decisive difference between objects that we find, with identifiable affordances, and objects that we make, presenting affordances that are developed in more or less complex and collaborative sequences. One illustration comes from a famous scene in the film, *2001: A Space Odyssey* (Stanley Kubrick, 1968). A hominid, having just used a bone as a weapon to kill another hominid from a competing band, throws the bone into the air and, there, it dissolves into a spacecraft hovering above the earth. Certain kinds of made objects are special in the extent to which they envelop humans as environments – spacecraft and cars, for example. Films and other media of communication are a unique kind of enveloping tool insofar as they may represent bones, cars, spacecraft, and any number of natural and cultural objects, making them available for individual consideration and social deliberation. The affordances of media are both general and programmable.[32]

Gibson's (1979) concept of affordances has influenced a number of research traditions and fields, including communication studies and social psychology. One difficulty of applying it has been the definition of affordances as more or less explicit and conscious. To what degree, and in what sense, do people realize the existence of an affordance before or while taking advantage of it? In the area of interface design, Donald A. Norman's (1990) early accounts of the affordances of computers were influential, but left unclear the difference between "real and perceived affordances."[33] In later writings, Norman aimed to clarify this distinction: "What the designer cares about is whether the user perceives that some action is possible (or in the case of perceived non-affordances, not possible)" (www.jnd.org/dn.mss/affordances_and.html, accessed July 15, 2009) (see further Hartson, 2003). There is clearly little point in a designer insisting that an affordance is 'really' there if users do not perceive it; in this regard, the customer is always right. Nevertheless, Norman's distinction remained ambiguous. Perceiving links or buttons on a computer screen may, or may not, mean being conscious of the various steps of navigating them; users may, or may not, be able to communicate about or justify these steps; and they may, or may not, be able to specify and articulate alternatives – to themselves or others. Gibson (1979: 134) himself noted that perceiving and using something is not the same as being able to classify it.

This phenomenon – of doing without knowing – has been referred to in social and cultural theory, variously, as tacit knowledge[34] (Polanyi,

32 **general and programmable affordances**

33 **real and perceived affordances**

34 **tacit knowledge**

35 > practical
    consciousness,
    Chapter 2, p. 32

36 > habitus,
    Chapter 2, p. 32

1962), practical consciousness[35]< (Giddens, 1984), and the habitus[36]< orienting an individual's social interaction (Bourdieu, 1984/1979). The insight that these literatures share is that information and communication point forward in time to action. Affordances – of nature as well as of media – enable us "to go on" (Wittgenstein, 1953: no. 154) (see also Winch, 1963/1958: 24–33, 59). In some cases, but far from always, I am able to make explicit, reflect on, and communicate with others about how and why I go on. In communication, I am able, further, to elicit the tacit knowledge that others have of the situation at hand, and I can question what they do, what they *say* they are doing, and how, in fact, they go on. In doing so, I accept or decline some of the affordances for social interaction that they present to me, whether face-to-face or by technological mediation.

The social aspect of affordances has been examined, as well, within psychology. The concept recalls classic questions of nature and nurture: to what extent, and in what ways, are various cognitive affordances of the human body inherited through evolution or cultivated in society? To address such issues, research on social affordances has emphasized studies of cognition and interaction in real-life settings – the natural environment and everyday social contexts (for overview, see Valenti and Good, 1991). Laboratory studies, by their very design, isolate humans from their natural and, simultaneously, social habitats. The naturalistic credo was suggested by one book title: *Cognition in the Wild* (Hutchins, 1995). And, the wild includes other people. Even though Gibson (1979) had highlighted "the visual perception of the unpopulated environment," his approach "was intended to embrace the complexities of social interaction as well," as suggested also by "Gibson's early writings in social psychology" (Valenti and Good, 1991: 80). One of the most important and complex affordances of the natural environment for humans is –

37 other humans as
    affordances

other humans:[37]

> The richest and most elaborate affordances of the environment are provided by other animals and, for us, other people . . . Behavior affords behavior, and the whole subject of psychology and of the social sciences can be thought of as an elaboration of this basic fact.
>
> (J. J. Gibson, 1979: 135)

One very elaborate affordance of other people is that they speak, and that they speak to us. It is through speech and other communication that we find out what other people are able and willing to afford us in other respects. Equally, it is through communication that we discover how, collectively, we may make the most of nature's affordances. In our ecological niche, other humans are both unavoidable and indispensable media. As a species, and as cultures and societies, humans have extended themselves in shifting communication technologies (McLuhan, 1964). However, it is only quite recently that communication studies have begun to apply the concept of affordances, likely in response to the manifest similarities of embodied and computer-mediated communication.

Hutchby (2001), for one, sought to specify the affordances of the internet and of mobile telephones, while at the same time questioning a tendency in historical and sociological studies of technology since the 1980s to exaggerate not just the material flexibility, but also the ad hoc interpretability of both software and hardware (for overview, see Biagioli, 1999). Not everything goes at the material interface of communication. The question is how and why some material affordances, and not others, emerge as media.

Emergence

The term emergence refers to a process whose end state is different in kind, unpredictable, even inconceivable from the opening state of its constituent elements. In common parlance, the whole turns out to be greater than the sum of its parts. Emergence concerns some of the most basic and, by definition, interdisciplinary issues of scholarship. Even if the institutional division of labor between various natural, human, and social sciences has meant that different fields typically attend to different domains of reality, the interfaces between domains constitute the input, output, and boundary conditions of each. In the domain of physical reality, reference is sometimes made to the 'butterfly effect'[38] – the possibility that a butterfly moving its wings might ultimately elicit a natural disaster on the other side of the earth (Gleick, 1987: 9–31). In a social domain, 'cyberspace'[39] (W. Gibson, 1984) is the collective product of innumerable local acts of communication on a similarly staggering scale. Media history is ripe with examples of how the social uses of a technology have changed markedly over time, or have taken an entirely unexpected turn. The mechanical phonograph, before emerging as a music player for the mass consumer market, was thought of by Thomas Edison as a machine for the recording of dictated letters to be typed in businesses. Early telephone services included subscription to transmissions of concerts, lectures, and news for the general public – as a medium of mass rather than interpersonal communication (Winston, 1998: 51–64).

Emergence, its scope and relevance as an explanatory concept, in strong or weak versions, remains debated (for one overview, see Sawyer, 2004). In the context of communication theory, the notion suggests at least two points. First, the upper and lower thresholds of communication[40]< represent boundaries on the order of magnitude that is implied by emergence. Neither microscopic nor macroscopic entities of nature communicate, but innumerable configurations of material reality, within human bodies and their technological extensions, condition all our communication. Cultures and nations, equally, do not communicate, but their constituent parts do, in the shape of heads of state, tourists, and media imports/exports. The literature on emergence commonly refers to boundaries and transitions between four separate levels of reality – physical, biological, psychic, and social.[41] On the one hand, the mechanisms and functions of each level must be understood in terms of a distinctive local logic; on the other hand, events and pro-

38 butterfly effect

39 cyberspace

40 > upper and lower thresholds of communication, Chapter 3, p. 55

41 physical, biological, psychic, and social levels of reality

cesses at one level translate and carry over to other levels. The inter-relation between the last two levels – psyche and society – holds special degrees of freedom, or a "continuous mutual conditioning and inter-dependence between emergent psyche and sociality" (Emmeche *et al.*, 2000: 15). Put more simply, humans and societies shape and reshape each other on biographical and historical time scales, bounded by the physical and biological preconditions that they share. The interaction between psyche and society is the domain of communication.

Second, it is a distinctive feature of communication that it can reshape its own conditions – its media. Different material media afford different kinds of modification. Films, in the late 1890s, were one attraction at traveling variety shows and other entertainments, presenting fact as well as fiction (Altman, 2004; K. Thompson and Bordwell, 2003: 13–22). During the first decades of the twentieth century, it gradually found its cultural form or profile – fictional feature films of a certain length, as shown to the public for a fee at a given time and place, and enabled by centralized systems of production, distribution, and exhibition. Today, film can increasingly be considered a piece of software, appearing on diverse material platforms, distributable and modifiable, in principle, like any other type of digital file (Klinger, 2006). In digital media, moreover, local users can modify not just individual files but also, to an extent, the very system of communication – its form as well as its content (Finnemann, 2005). The point was brought home on a grand scale by Tim Berners-Lee's public posting in 1991 of the protocols and principles that, in a comparatively short time span, grew into the World Wide Web[42]< (http://groups.google.com/group/alt.hypertext/msg/395f282a67 a1916c, accessed July 15, 2009). Less grandly, but as importantly, the daily interactions of internet users, and of diverse interest and pressure groups – from business, civil society, and the public sector – serve to maintain and modify the internet as a technical as well as a social organization.

42 > the World Wide Web, Chapter 5, pp. 91–94

Networked communication suggests an extension of Elihu Katz's (1959) motto for media studies: ask not only what media do to people, but also what people do with media. The additional question is what people do to change media as they find them, in order to do something different with them.[43] Digital media restate the question of effects, consequences, and momentum.

43 what people do to change media, in order to do something different with them

Momentum

The effects of media on individuals' attitudes, emotions, and behaviors are, without question, the one issue that has been most frequently addressed by research (for overview, see K. B. Jensen, 2002a, 2002b). It is also a question that is continuously raised in public and policy debates, and which motivates a good deal of funding and legitimacy for the field. In comparison, the structural and longterm conse-quences of media have seemed more difficult to state in research-able terms – despite important contributions on the diffusion[44] of media in various cultures and social groups (Rogers, 2003); on the 'domestication'[45] of new media into households and other settings

44 diffusion

45 domestication

(Haddon, 2004; Helle-Valle and Slettemeås, 2008); and on the shifting configurations of 'new' and 'old' media at different historical times (Briggs and Burke, 2005; J. B. Thompson, 1995; Winston, 1998). Research on other kinds of technologies holds valuable implications regarding the systemic consequences of new media.

In an important contribution to the history of technology, Thomas P. Hughes (1983) examined the introduction of electricity into Western societies during the period 1880–1930. Lighting in the home, in the workplace, and in the street provided a general condition for a more secure and comfortable way of life; electricity remains a precondition of modern media, from printing presses to web servers. Hughes (1983) referred to "technological systems,"[46] rather than to technologies as delimited objects or artifacts. Technological systems constitute second nature, enveloping people and framing the projects that they undertake together. Once in place, such systems acquire what Hughes called momentum – an inertia with an almost glacial force. This momentum is explained less by the size or complexity of the system in itself than by its integration with other social institutions and practices. Electricity plants and digital networks take time to plan and build; they also require substantial economic investment and public planning, typically preceded by political debates and legislative processes. Access to light, water, communication, and other necessities of life pose ideological questions, and the answers will be socially binding. Accordingly, the consequences of new media are best examined not as events, but as processes that take effect over time.

In the standoff between technological determinism and social constructionism, Hughes (1983) sought to identify a middle ground. He was particularly careful to distinguish the different phases of transforming a material resource into a technological system. In a later article, he suggested that a social-constructionist perspective may be well suited to capture some of the malleability of 'young' technological systems, whereas the function of 'mature' systems is better explained by a moderate technological determinism (Hughes, 1994). Determination should be approached as a layered and accretive process with multiple causal agents – what other fields of inquiry have referred to as overdetermination.[47] The concept was introduced by Sigmund Freud in *The Interpretation of Dreams* (1911/1900) to indicate how the events of an ordinary day will mix with long gone and perhaps repressed experiences in the contents as well as in the forms of one's dreams. Transferring Freud's concept to critical social theory, Louis Althusser (1977/1965) was questioning the economic determinism of traditional Marxism. In line with Stuart Hall's (1983) reference to determination in the first instance,[48]< Althusser underscored the relative autonomy of political and cultural practices in shaping social developments. Determination in the first instance suggests a general scope of indetermination in the transformation of matter into media; overdetermination begins to identify the various material, discursive, and institutional factors that enter into the process to create its momentum.

46 technological systems

47 over-determination

48 > determination in the first instance, p. 62

The momentum of media can be attributed, in large measure, to their ubiquitous and pervasive nature. Communication is embedded in any and all of the practices and institutions that make up culture and society; different media have afforded the emergence of different types of cultures and societies – oral, literate, and digital. In his classic account of the relationship between technological innovation and modern civilization, *Technics and Civilization* (1934), Lewis Mumford highlighted the encompassing and enveloping nature of what he called "technics":

> For note this: mechanization and regimentation are not new phenomena in history: what is new is the fact that these functions have been projected and embodied in organized forms which dominate every aspect of our existence. Other civilizations reached a high degree of technical proficiency without, apparently, being profoundly influenced by the methods and aims of technics . . . The Chinese, the Arabs, the Greeks, long before the Northern European, had taken most of the first steps toward the machine . . . They had machines; but they did not develop "the machine."
>
> (Mumford, 1934: 4)

For Mumford, modern humans live inside "the machine." By analogy, we live inside the (latest generation of) media. But, media are neither separate nor simulated realities. Media and communicative practices are constitutive means of access to actual as well as possible worlds, our conditions "for having a world" (Merleau-Ponty, 1962/1945: 146). Mumford (1934: 4) was emphatic about the uniqueness of modern technics. Similarly, contemporary research, in various ways, has described current society as a unique information society (Bell, 1973; Castells, 1996; Porat, 1977). All historical societies, however, have depended on communicative resources, and might be considered information or media societies[49] (Finnemann, 2008). Speech, writing, and printing all held and still hold momentum. Media of the third degree, while still emerging, may prove a transitional form.

49 one or several
information
societies

A fourth degree

For some time, another generation of digital media – beyond a Web 1.0 of homepages, banner advertisements, and directories; also beyond a Web 2.0 of social network sites, sponsored links, and tags – has been referred to in terms of their ubiquity and pervasiveness (for overview, see Greenfield, 2006; Lyytinen and Yoo, 2002). Information technologies everywhere, in everything, and for everybody have been the commercial and policy buzzwords. While the preferred terminologies still vary, the common assumption is that future digital media will become categorically different from their current form of work stations, laptops, and mobile devices:

> Ubiquitous computing (ubicomp) is a postdesktop model of human–computer interaction . . . in which information processing has been thoroughly integrated into everyday objects and activities. As opposed to the desktop paradigm, in which a single user consciously engages a single device for a specialized purpose. In the course of ordinary activities, someone "using" ubiquitous computing engages many computational devices and systems simultaneously, and may not necessarily even be aware that they are doing so.
>
> (http://en.wikipedia.org/wiki/Ubiquitous_computing, accessed June 5, 2009)

The originator of the idea of ubiquitous computing,[50] Mark Weiser (1991), contrasted ubiquity with virtuality. Early versions of virtual media environments during the 1980–90s were based on a model of 'the world *in* a medium' – one local, stationary, and multimodal interface, including goggles, gloves, and a treadmill that enabled the user to enter a separate, virtual reality (for overview, see Levy, 1993). In contrast, ubiquitous computing embeds multiple media interfaces in diverse natural objects, artifacts, and social settings – 'the world *as* a medium.'[51] The development has also been referred to as the coming of "the internet of things" (ITU, 2005). Compared with the graphic user interfaces that helped to make the computer a popular medium, research has begun to refer to organic user interfaces[52] (Vertegaal and Poupyrev, 2008). Here, the basic metaphor of the interface shifts from one of a tool to one of skin or membranes (Rekimoto, 2008: 40). Simultaneously, hardware systems are moving "beyond silicon"[53] (Munakata, 2007) toward even more miniaturized and physically integrated bases of computing, for instance, at the chemical and atomic levels. At the intersection of hardware and humans, life support systems and implants are examples of media as body parts. At the very least, digital media enable significantly more location-dependent and personalized communication; ubiquitous access to other communicators in image, text, as well as sound; and more actions at a distance, in a physical as well as a social sense, in ways that are still waiting to be imagined and realized.

In a future perspective, mobile, ubiquitous, and pervasive media will require another reassessment of the very idea of communication, specifically its upper and lower thresholds. In what sense do humans communicate with digitized artifacts and with the rest of material reality, for instance, through the Global Positioning System (GPS) and other Geographical Information Systems (GIS)? Cognitive science has described the bandwidth of human cognition and communication with reference to so-called basic-level categories[54] (Lakoff and Johnson, 1999), whose yardstick is the human body. We have, and are, a particular neurophysiological structure that taps into certain levels of reality, and not others. We have access to things that are about our size and within the reach of our senses: luminous surfaces and loud music, but not infrared radiation or the echoes of the Big Bang (although digital

50 ubiquitous computing

51 the world as a medium

52 organic user interfaces

53 beyond silicon

54 basic-level categories

technologies can transform the Big Bang to our bandwidth, www.astro. virginia.edu/~dmw8f/index.php, accessed July 15, 2009). Beyond the

55 > transcendental categories of human understanding, Chapter 2, p. 26

transcendental categories of human reason[55]< as stipulated by Immanuel Kant, basic-level categories enable humans to think and speak about what is up and down, in and out, before and after, both literally and metaphorically in terms of who is up or down in a society, in or out as far as a subculture is concerned, first or second in a sports competition or an online auction. The "metaphors we live by" (Lakoff and Johnson, 1980), while determined in the first instance by the human body, are extended in tools, technologies, and meta-technologies. We make sense, both of communication and of its thresholds and limits, from within a human bandwidth that we express in discourses, genres, texts, images, and sounds – which are the focus of the next chapter.

Media meanings

5

The discourses, genres, and
modalities of communication

Media meanings

The discourses, genres, and modalities of communication

The medium was the message

1 the medium is the message

2 form trumps content

3 > meta-media, Chapter 4, p. 70

4 function trumps form

One of the most familiar statements about media, in research as well as in public debate, remains Marshall McLuhan's (1964: 23) "the medium is the message."[1] While open to interpretation, the point of his dictum was that various historical media have been the source of characteristic worldviews above and beyond their concrete messages about and representations of reality. Form trumps content.[2] Specifically, McLuhan suggested that twentieth-century audiovisual media had challenged previously dominant literate perspectives on the world from within "the Gutenberg galaxy" (McLuhan, 1962). With digital media, we may have entered an "internet galaxy" (Castells, 2001). The legacy of McLuhan is the insight that media lend form to cultures and societies: media program the meanings that cultures and societies ascribe to themselves in communication.

Marshall McLuhan could not have anticipated the sort of meta-media[3]< (A. Kay and Goldberg, 1999/1977) that digital technologies came to enable. When suggesting that the content of each new medium is another, older medium – "the content of writing is speech, just as the written word is the content of print, and print is the content of the telegraph" (McLuhan, 1964: 23–24) – he was implying that the characteristics of one medium are imported more or less wholesale into the form of the next medium. In comparison, digital media are characterized, not least, by their modularity and by their selective recombination of the constituents of older media. The medium is no longer the message in McLuhan's original sense – the message of digital media is all previous media, and then some. His general insight, however, still holds: different forms of expression afford different contents of individual experience as well as of social interaction. Meanings emerge in the meeting of form and content – in the discourses, genres, and modalities of communication.

In this chapter, I address the relationship between discursive forms and communicative functions. Qualifying McLuhan and current digital aesthetics, I suggest that function trumps form.[4] Media are resources of communicative interaction, before they are forms of representation or objects of contemplation. The first section considers how different media remediate – reproduce as well as reconfigure – the basic modalities of human communication: speech, song, writing, still and moving images. Media of the third degree are the source of an unprecedented variety of linguistic and pictorial forms, and of a corresponding diversity of contextual functions. To specify the interrelations between text and context, the second section revisits the concept of intertextuality. I use the case of search engines to illustrate how texts make sense in relation both to other texts and to their contexts of use. The third section introduces the concept of meta-communication – communication about communication, about the status of the information being exchanged, and about the roles of the communicators. Whereas meta-communication is an aspect of any communicative practice in any medium, digital media enable distinctive kinds of meta-communication that reconfigure the forms, the contents, as well as the functions of communication. In the fourth and final section, I consider the end of communication as concrete discursive structures. In communication, we navigate media and interact with other people, taking turns and ending communication. Media of the third degree present a distinctive resource for both communicative turn-taking and transitions to other social interaction.

Media and modalities

Marshall McLuhan's dictum might have been, in a less catchy phrase, "the modality is the message." While deeply influenced by Harold A. Innis' (1951; 1972/1950) account of media as material and economic infrastructures with implications for "political power and control, McLuhan focused more on the ways in which new media experiences lead to perceptual shifts, such as a changing ratio of the senses" (Meyrowitz, 2008: 2801). Modalities[5] constitute an intermediate category between the material and discursive vehicles of communication. Occupying a middle ground of communication – beyond matter, before meaning – they are general registers of expression and experience: affordances of the human senses vis-à-vis the environment (on the biology and psychology of sense perception, see Sternberg, 2009: 254–70 and passim). Whereas everyday language distinguishes five main senses – sight, hearing, smell, taste, and touch – communication studies traditionally have focused on the functions of sight and hearing in mediation and social interaction, even while recognizing, for example, the role of touch in interpersonal communication and the occasional experiment integrating smell into cinema (Smell-O-Vision, 1960; Odorama, 1981). In practice, the emphasis of research has been on linguistic and pictorial modes of communication.

> 5 modalities

Given the extensive reconfiguration of analog media within digital media, one may ask: How many modalities are there? How many could there be? With reference to face-to-face interaction, one representative overview distinguished between a vocal-aural and a visuo-spatial modality, subdividing the latter into gesture, gaze, and body posture, and the former into lexico-syntactic, vocal, and prosodic channels (Stivers and Sidnell, 2005) – all depending on the particular research issue and, hence, the appropriate granularity of the analysis. In the course of media history, different technologies have served to separate and recombine these channels in a wide variety of ways. Face-to-face interaction is inherently multimodal; we are each other's multimedia.[6]< Literacy required readers to focus their vision into a communicative gaze on texts. Cinema and television, in time with sound and color, recreated important aspects of the "vivid present" of everyday perception (Schütz, 1962/ 1945). Digital media, in turn, have reintegrated elements of face-to-face interaction into technologically mediated communication, in addition to reproducing or simulating media of the second degree. The point is not that media could reshape the human senses, but that shifting historical technologies have made manifest – actualized – additional potentials[7]< of the human body for communication, productively and receptively. Tools, technologies, and meta-technologies have enabled cultures and societies to discover, cultivate, and institutionalize new ways of communicating.

The modalities of human communication share at least three distinctive features. First, they are programmable, lending themselves to an infinite number of variable representations and interactions. Second, they are translatable, even if certain elements and layers of meaning may be lost in translation. Third, modalities can be remediated, or transposed between material media. Different technologies have allowed for a reprogramming and translation of particular modalities – the reproduction, enhancement, separation, and simulation of communicative forms and functions. At the same time, technologies have rejoined and mixed different modalities – from illuminated manuscripts (with decorated initials and miniature drawings), via illustrated magazines and sound film, to multimodal virtual reality applications.

Programmability

As outlined in Chapter 3, media are programmable in several respects.[8]< Modalities constitute highly general resources for formulating very specific understandings of events and issues for any number of practical purposes in innumerable contexts. At the individual level, a very large proportion of the verbal utterances that an ordinary human being makes every day are unique, as documented by so-called corpus linguistics (Halliday *et al.*, 2004) (which examines large data sets of how people actually speak and write, rather than how they ought to pronounce or spell words). We are all sophisticated programmers of verbal expression and interaction. At the cultural level, pictorial representation, for instance, in the case of maps, has been refined and adapted to diverse uses in discovery, warfare, and public administration (Ehrenberg, 2006). Maps also serve as means of reflection concerning the place of individuals, societies, and the human species as such in some universal order (Mukerji, 2006). Most recently, technologies such as the Global

6 > humans as multimedia, Chapter 4, p. 66

7 > potential and actualization, Chapter 2, p. 23

8 > programmability, Chapter 3, p. 57

Positioning System (GPS), as implemented in cars and mobile phones, have enabled individual users to overlay maps on their everyday environments and, thus, to program their way towards geographical locations and points of cultural or personal interest.

Translatability

Different modalities make different aspects of reality accessible for deliberation, interaction, and intervention. A picture says a thousand words; a few words can articulate an insight that no picture could ever capture. On the one hand, modalities might be considered untranslatable, as suggested by the Italian adage: *traduttore, traditore* (translator, traitor!). On the other hand, both individuals and institutions constantly engage in translation between modalities. Parliamentary speeches are transcribed for the record. Novels are adapted as feature movies for the cinema that, next, become available for private viewing on smaller screens. With mobile phones, spoken commands may be replacing the visual identification and typing or tapping of a contact number: a speech act[9]< literally makes the call.

9 > speech-act theory, Chapter 3, p. 52

Remediability

Fine arts and aesthetic theories have traditionally been the fields exploring and expanding the communicative potentials of materials and modalities, as suggested by the common reference to 'mixed media'[10] in art museums. The idea of a *Gesamtkunstwerk*, developed by the composer Richard Wagner in an 1849 essay on "Art and revolution" (http://users.belgacom.net/wagnerlibrary/prose/wagartrev.htm, accessed July 15, 2009), held out the promise of reintegrating the theater, music, and visual arts of ancient Greek drama. In modernist art, the combination of media took on added significance as part of an aesthetic of ruptures[11] or breaks. These would follow, in part, from the confrontation of several media in one artwork or the presentation of everyday artifacts and natural objects as art. If the formal compositions of art present unresolved, even unresolvable, perspectives on reality, they might prompt radically new insights; they might, in addition, cultivate a longer-term readiness on the part of readers or spectators to change their viewpoints. In due course, aesthetic radicalism might entail political radicalism, stimulating people to collectively reconstruct, or revolutionize, culture and society. By defamiliarizing past and present, modernist art proposed to make the future new. In this vein, an advocate of the avant-garde Fluxus movement, Dick Higgins (2001/1965), introduced a notion of 'intermedia.' While crediting an 1812 use of 'intermedium' by the British poet Samuel Taylor Coleridge, Higgins stressed the aesthetically innovative and socially transgressive potential of artworks that articulate their messages in the interstices of different media forms.

10 mixed media

11 aesthetic of ruptures

In media and communication research, a more common terminology has been one of 'remediation,'[12] frequently in the uncontroversial sense that new media derive some of their forms and contents from old media,

12 remediation

but sometimes with a more specific theoretical and ideological commitment. Also digital media might be thought to make consciousness and culture new in distinctive ways. In 1999, Jay David Bolter and Richard Grusin published their widely cited volume, *Remediation: Understanding new media*, which outlined a framework for analyzing the reconfiguration of both traditional arts and old mass media within digital media. Here, media history was told in terms of the ebb and flow of two complementary principles: immediacy (media as mirrors of reality) and hypermediacy (media as opaque interfaces questioning the status of reality as depicted). In insightful analyses of, for instance, digital photography and graphic user interfaces, the authors showed how immediacy and hypermediacy mesh in most artworks and media forms. As suggested by the key terms, however, the book conceived media basically as representations of the world – texts – rather than as resources for communicating about and acting in social contexts. Moreover, like much other digital aesthetics, the authors were inclined to draw far-reaching conclusions about the impact of digital representations on recipients, for example, in terms of a "remediated self" (Bolter and Grusin, 1999: 230, 236), extrapolating from general forms of expressions to general psychological and social consequences (for a critical discussion, see K. B. Jensen, 2007).

For most people most of the time, media use is not an aesthetic practice of representation or contemplation. Media are means to mostly mundane ends of communication. Media place texts in contexts that are, simultaneously, discursive, material, and social. With digital technologies, it has become more manifest how texts and contexts enter into networks of social activity. Textual networks, however, have been a central topic of scholarship since the early twentieth century. What started out as a framework for grasping certain distinctive features of written fiction, proved applicable to other media and genres, and to textual artifacts as well as communicative practices.

Is there a text in this network?

Texts and intertextuality

In a famous book title, the literary theorist, Stanley Fish (1979), quoting a student, asked, *Is there a text in this class?* His provocative and influential suggestion was that texts – meaningful discourses – are not found in classrooms, libraries, or any other location. Instead, texts have a virtual existence in the minds of their readers and in readers' dealings with each other as interpretive communities.[13]< Moreover, the meanings of texts as well as their boundaries – what is (not) part of a given text – will remain open to interpretation by additional readers and other interpretive communities. Fish's suggestion was provocative because it sought to deconstruct the traditional conception of texts within the humanities as delimited objects of immanent analysis, interpretation, and introspection,

13 > interpretive communities, Chapter 2, pp. 32–34

typically regarding unique artworks with an aura[14]< transcending historical time (Benjamin, 1977/1936). His suggestion also proved influential, in part, because it extended and radicalized the redefinition of texts, meaning, and information as relational structures that had been gaining currency in twentieth-century semiotics (and cybernetics). Readers and other communicators have a stake in, and could be considered a part of the text, along with its explicit or implicit cross-references to other texts. All the while, a broader understanding of 'texts' as any vehicle of meaning,[15] including images, conversations, and artifacts, became the norm in twentieth-century scholarship on communication and culture.

Deriving from classical Latin *texo* (to weave, to construct) and *textum* (fabric as well as speech and writing), the term 'text' highlights the process in which a content of ideas is given form: it is in-formed. To be sure, the classical traditions of rhetoric (Kennedy, 1980) and hermeneutics (Ricoeur, 1981) had approached texts as composite structures of meaning in layers, webs, and circles. What theories of intertextuality[16] came to insist on was the transience of texts – in contrast to any transcendent content or form. Neither a literary work nor any other message could be considered a site of essential or stable meaning. Texts make sense, not in themselves, but in relation to other texts. The seminal contribution had come from the Russian literary scholar Mikhail Bakhtin and his circle in the early decades of the twentieth century (Bakhtin, 1981). His most basic concept concerning the relationship between different literary works – dialogism – was translated as intertextuality by Julia Kristeva (1984/1974). Among other things, she reemphasized the structural point of semiotics[17]< that signs are defined in relation to other signs. By extension, texts acquire their meaning as part of a network of texts, past as well as present. Texts are momentary manifestations of a general textuality; texts selectively articulate a cultural heritage. A culture could be understood as the most complex instance of intertextuality.

This line of argument, on the one hand, suggests that all texts – all human acts of communication – are created equal, at least as a working hypothesis. The task of research, accordingly, would be to establish how specific texts with particular origins and trajectories feed into cultural patterns and social structures. On the other hand, ironically, the bulk of intertextual studies have looked for interrelations among a small and select category of texts. Through formal and thematic readings of literature, visual arts, film, and television, research has identified a wide variety of explicit and, more commonly, implicit references to other texts, for instance, metatextual relations hinting at the historical origins of key cultural symbols, or paratextual relations between a novel and its cover text (Genette, 1997/1982). It is particularly striking that intertextual studies mostly have given no empirical attention to readers or audiences. Presumably, they are the interpretive agents who establish the links between the nodes of textual networks.

The shift of analytical focus from delimited texts toward discursive practices – and from media to communication[18]< – has been a long time coming. In part, it has been the response of the academy to a changing

14 > aura, Chapter 4, p. 68

15 text – any vehicle of meaning

16 intertextuality

17 > semiotics, Chapter 3, p. 44

18 > communication and/vs. media, Chapter 1, p. 14

media environment. As long as the legitimate objects of analysis remained a comparatively few canonical or prototypical works summing up and disseminating cultural tradition, it might seem natural to study intertextuality with reference to such texts only. With mass media, certainly on the scale witnessed in the industrialized world over the course of the twentieth century, that approach became increasingly untenable. Mass-mediated texts are the products of a meticulously planned, systemic kind of intertextuality; mass media anticipate their audiences as more or less willing partners in intertextuality across time, media, and genres. By the 1980s, also humanistic studies of media as texts had come to devote more explicit attention to their audiences in qualitative reception studies (for overview, see K. B. Jensen, 2002b).

From primary texts to hypertexts

In an important contribution, John Fiske (1987) distinguished two aspects of intertextuality: horizontal and vertical.[19] The horizontal dimension refers to the traditional understanding of intertextuality in literary theory as a transfer of meanings across historical time – over decades and centuries – as preserved in the metaphors, characters, styles, and so on, of both fine arts and popular media. Vertical intertextuality, in comparison, focuses attention on the media system that circulates themes, issues, and agendas in a shorter time frame – from minutes to months. Importantly, the vertical dimension includes audience members as media in their own right, who may respond to or debate both the contents and the forms of mass media texts among themselves.[20]< To specify the process circulating meaning in society, Fiske identified three categories of texts.[21] Primary texts are carriers of significant information or insight in their own right – not necessarily aesthetic masterpieces or trend-setting media products, but privileged texts, nevertheless. To exemplify, if the primary text is a new feature movie, the secondary texts will consist of studio publicity, reviews, and other criticism. The tertiary texts are audiences' conversations and other communications about the movie – before, during, and after a visit to the cinema. Figure 5.1 lays out the two axes of intertextuality.

Research has explored the trajectories of texts across media, audience groups, and time periods. Studies have examined, for instance, James Bond (Bennett and Woollacott, 1987) and the Batman (Pearson and Uricchio, 1990) as cultural icons that have provided sounding boards for political as well as existential reflections. Methodologically, the process of intertextual meaning production has been examined through, for instance, oral history interviews and analyses of the creations of fan cultures (Lewis, 1991). In the case of television, viewers can be seen to shape their own intertextual sequences by selecting and combining (parts of) programs, preannouncements, and commercial breaks from multiple channels in the flow[22] of given viewing session (K. B. Jensen, 1994). However, as suggested by the terminology of primary, secondary, and tertiary texts (Fiske, 1987), research on mass-mediated intertextuality has tended to still approach the entire process of communication from the

19 intertextuality – horizontal and vertical

20 > humans as media, Chapter 4, p. 66

21 texts – primary, secondary, and tertiary

22 television flow

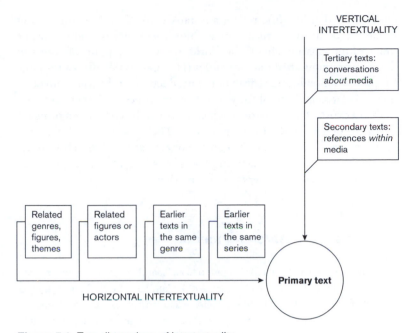

Figure 5.1 Two dimensions of intertextuality

perspective of texts, as if meaning flowed from a relatively few mass media, perhaps via other media and texts, and on to audiences.

Digital media, from the outset, invited research on the distributed processes in which users interact both with texts and with each other through texts (Aarseth, 1997; Bolter, 1991). With digital technologies, intertextuality became an explicit and operational set of structures – hypertextuality[23] – typified by the familiar hyperlinks that relate the elements of various computer-mediated texts and applications. Links make explicit, retrievable, and modifiable what might have remained a more or less random association in the mind of either sender or receiver. Fully fledged hypertexts can be organized and marked up both for creative purposes of interactive story-telling and for instrumental purposes of indexing, searching, and combining items of information (Nelson, 1965). Like other 'texts,' hypermedia[24] mix visual, auditory, and alphabetic modalities of communication. A click on a news headline activates a video clip; a click on a photograph brings up a text box or a spoken commentary.

The World Wide Web is the most massive example, so far, of a multi-modal hypertext, appropriately named to suggest the weaving of texts in a worldwide network. While some commentators, once again, have claimed that hypertextual representations of social reality would tend to be aesthetically innovative and socially transgressive (e.g., Landow, 1997), the more pertinent research question is how, in actual practice, users approach and apply this wealth of texts and their constitutive elements. In addition to their browsers and graphic user interfaces, web users depend on a distinctive kind of intertextual resource – search

23 **hypertextuality**

24 **hypermedia**

25 search engines

engines[25] – that identify, relate, and rank texts. Search engines bring home the point that texts are much more than representations of, or items of information about, the world; the web is a point of access to diverse communicative functionalities (Herring, 2004: 30) – a resource for political mobilization, distributed production, and cultural involvement. As far as millions of daily searchers are concerned, there are texts in the network. The question is which texts will be considered primary, in which contexts, and for what purposes? The answer depends not only on users' search terms, but also on the organization of search engines, and on the intertexts, metadata, and algorithms that link service providers with searchers, and searchers with each other.

Case study: searching media

To be precise, what are mostly referred to as 'search engines' are web search engines (for overview, see Halavais, 2009; Hargittai, 2007). Search engines include a variety of digital retrieval systems that facilitate access to information also in stand-alone databases and on personal computers; an example of this last type is the Spotlight feature of Apple's MAC OS X operating system, which identifies search terms in different file types, so that I may trace, for instance, my own writings on search engines, the sources that I relied on, and the advice that I received from colleagues by email.

Beyond household names such as Google, Yahoo!, and MSN, there exists a great variety of web search engines. First, they are differentiated by language (including national or regional variants of the 'same' service). In the People's Republic of China, the most popular search engine is Baidu (www.baidu.com/, accessed July 15, 2009), which is also a major global player, ranking third in share of searches after Google and Yahoo! in December 2007 (www.comscore.com/press/release.asp?press=2018, accessed July 15, 2009). In Europe, the practical as well as symbolic implications of search were suggested by the French–German Quaero initiative to develop a 'European' search engine with multilingual (and multimedia) functionalities (www.quaero.org/modules/movie/scenes/home/, accessed July 15, 2009) (Machill et al., 2008: 599). Second, there is a wealth of specialized search engines that address different areas of social activity. In the case of Refugees United, search acquires an existential meaning: this particular search engine "provides refugees with an anonymous forum to reconnect with missing family" (www.refunite.org, accessed July 15, 2009).

26 > climate change, Chapter 1, pp. 7–10

Web search engines provide pre-structured access to information for living. A few basic searches regarding climate change,[26]< as addressed in Chapter 1, suggest some general implications of searching as an intertextual process (www.google.com/, accessed February 21, 2008). For the text string "climate change," The Top 20 results, which searchers will typically give a certain weight, included, first, official sites of national and international entities, such as United Nations agencies, and, second, 'green' or environmentally concerned voices. In comparison, the Top 20 for the string "global warming" produced a mixture of 'green' and 'skeptical' positions, including organizations arguing against the reality of global warming, or advocating different cost–benefit strategies than, for instance, internationally coordinated limits on carbon dioxide emissions. Also in the case of internet domain names, naming implies at least attempts at framing: www.globalwarming.net represents a 'green' position, featuring an Extreme Event Index, while www.globalwarming.org advances a 'skeptical' position under the motto, "reasoned thinking comes from cooler heads" (accessed February 21, 2008).

Search and ye shall find, depending on your search terms. Results depend, moreover, on the structure of search engines and on the skills of searchers. As noted by an early contribution to the still limited research on web search engines, search algorithms normally remain proprietary information, so that the premises of any given search are difficult to assess (Introna and Nissenbaum, 2000). Also the digital media literacy[27]< of users is in question: one study concluded that "users have only the basic skills required to use search engines; this is exacerbated by search engines' lack of transparency" (Machill et al., 2004: 321). In one respect, search engines open up the web. In another respect, searches close in on and around particular items of information and communicative relations. Like communication, searching ends.[28] < Closure is facilitated by metadata[29] – data about data.

Metadata, briefly, concern the origins, characteristics, and trajectories of any given piece of information, understood as data (see, for instance, the international Dublin Core initiative, http://dublincore.org/, accessed July 15, 2009). While referring, in principle, to any kind of data, in any medium – for the present book: its title, author, date, publisher (and company webpage), ISBN number, contents, index, and so on – metadata are key to digital communication systems. The codes in question document which items of information are available, which ones are accessed, by whom, at what time, in which formats and, perhaps, in which combinations, sequences, and contexts of use. ('Image searches,' incidentally, are still performed on linguistic and other associated metadata, rather than on visual data as such.) Crucially, metadata are documented in and of the operation of search engines (and other digital systems), and they are fed back into the system. Also on the web, you cannot *not* communicate (Watzlawick et al., 1967: 49); my search anticipates your search, and vice versa.

Metadata are commonly associated with technical and legal aspects of centralized system maintenance, copyright administration, security clearance, and so on. In principle, however, the senders or providers of both data and metadata include anyone in a networked communication system: companies that specialize in 'search engine optimization,'[30] tweaking the system to deliver favorable results for their clients, as well as ordinary users who add so-called 'folksonomic'[31] (as opposed to taxonomic or expert) tags to content and share them via dedicated websites such as Delicious (http://delicious.com/,

27 > media literacy, Chapter 6, p. 121

28 > the end of communication, Chapter 1, p. 5

29 metadata

30 search engine optimization

31 folksonomy

32 code is law

accessed July 15, 2009). Clearly, the capacity of different types of users to send, receive, and apply metadata for their own purposes depends on their technological and economic resources; the potentials of search, further, depend on the political and legal frameworks that regulate the coding of communication at the national and international levels. As summed up by Larry Lessig (2006), in a digital communication infrastructure, code is law.[32]

Also in other media, code – conventional and institutionalized uses of discourse – is law in specific ways. Metadata have functional ancestors in media of the first and second degrees that hold important implications for media of the third degree. We constantly communicate about whether and how we would like to communicate with each other. We cannot *not* meta-communicate.[33]

33 we cannot *not* meta-communicate

Meta-communication in three degrees

The first degree

34 meta-communication

The key formulations regarding meta-communication[34] came from Gregory Bateson, who was examining contexts of face-to-face inter-action. Departing from work in anthropology and psychiatry, he suggested that "human verbal communication can operate and always does operate at many contrasting levels of abstraction" (Bateson, 1972/1955: 150), above and beyond the exchange of literal information. Taking a standard example from logic – 'the cat is on the mat' – Bateson noted that this proposition carries a denotation[35]< that refers to an actual state of affairs: the position of a furry four-legged organism in space (on a mat that we can point to) and time (is, not was). Apart from such denotations, people introduce, first, meta-linguistic information into their interactions, for example, to clarify that they may mean the word 'cat' to include tigers. Second, they also meta-communicate about their relationship as communicators, "e.g., 'My telling you where to find the cat [tiger] was friendly,' or 'This is play.'" Not only does communication thus operate at several levels at once; "the vast majority of both metalinguistic and metacommunicative messages remain implicit" (p. 151) and must be inferred from their 'context' – in a discursive, material, or social sense. In another publication, Bateson added that "a majority of propositions about codification are also implicit or explicit propositions about relationship and vice versa" (Ruesch and Bateson, 1987/1951: 209). The meaning of what we say to each other implies the meaning of our relationship.

35 > denotation, p. 97

Because communication operates at several levels at once, it is ripe with potential conflicts regarding what people are actually saying to each other and, not least, why. Bateson (1972/1956: 173–98) showed how schizophrenic disorders can be understood in communicative terms as the outcome of a "double bind"[36] in which a person is unable to resolve

36 double binds

several conflicting levels of communication. Of course, most people, most of the time, are remarkably good at mastering such communicative complexity. We recognize that 'this is information' (a signal of something else), and that 'this is *this* kind of information' (a message in a specific modality and code, with a particular reference to reality and a likely relevance for us in context). We establish and adjust our communicative relationships, relying on conventional forms of expression, turn-taking, and role-playing. In doing so, we establish contexts that are both psychologically and socially real, what Bateson described as frames[37] (Bateson, 1972/1955: 157). The concept was developed further by Erving Goffman (1974) to suggest how frames are continuously observed or broken, modified and replaced, in social interaction. Media studies have later used the concept of frames to explain how audiences make sense of texts with reference to other texts and to their contexts of use (K. B. Jensen, 2002a: 149–50).

37 frames

Like Goffman, Bateson remained focused on embodied interactions in local contexts. However, his two aspects of meta-communication – codification and communicative relationships[38] – are constitutive of mass and network communication, as well. Technologies and meta-technologies transport texts across contexts, and frames across social settings.

38 codification and communicative relationships

The second degree

Mass media address their audiences at a distance: hail, fellow, well met! (Hartley, 1982: 87). To establish a communicative relationship among absent partners – a contract of sorts – they depend on genres:[39] discursive conventions of expressing and experiencing a particular subject matter. The concept comes with a long history since Aristotle's *Rhetoric*; it has lent itself to spoken, written, print, and electronic forms of communication; and it has remained a central analytical category within literature, aesthetics, and other humanities. Recent research has witnessed a revived interest in genre across the humanities and social sciences, simultaneously as a discursive and a social phenomenon (Bawarshi, 2000; Miller, 1984, 1994; Yates and Orlikowski, 1992). Genres include not just epic, dramatic, and lyrical formats, but job interviews and online dating, as well. Genres constitute frames of interpretation and interaction, including scripts for social action at a later point in time, beyond the moment of communicative exchange.

39 genres

One of the founders of British cultural studies, Raymond Williams (1977), usefully identified three aspects of any given genre:

- *Characteristic subject matter* (e.g., the 'public' content of news, the 'private' content of fiction);
- *Formal composition* (e.g., narrative or didactic forms of expression in texts, still or moving images);
- *Mode of address* (e.g., the anticipated relevance of an advertisement or a public-service announcement for an audience).

Genres are discursive forms with social functions. They signal the nature of what is being communicated and the kinds of social relationships that are being maintained – the two aspects of Bateson's conception of meta-communication. Unlike both the classic transmission and ritual models of communication[40]< – but like linguistics and semiotics – Bateson and cybernetics helped to bring the micromechanics of communication to the fore. Complementing cybernetics, linguistics and semiotics has contributed additional models that help to describe, in more fine-grained detail, how meta-communication works at the level of discourse and genre.

40 > transmission and ritual models of communication, Chapter 3, p. 50

The classic example of a linguistic-semiotic model of communication was presented by the linguist and literary critic, Roman Jakobson (1960). Compared with the two aspects of meta-communication that Bateson noted – codification and communicative relationships – Jakobson identified an entire set of communicative functions. His model of the constituents of any communicative exchange, and of the corresponding functions, is laid out in Figure 5.2. The implication of the model was that all discourses bear traces of all these constituents of communication – sender, message, and receiver; channel, code, and context – to varying degrees and in shifting configurations. Addressing a classic question in poetics – is there a special poetic language? – Jakobson concluded that there is, instead, a poetic function of language, and that this function is manifest in many other genres, for instance, advertising. Poets, while inviting people to ponder what might be the 'message' of their poems (poetic function), also address their readers (conative function) about some possible world[41]< (referential function). Web banner advertising, in its turn, relies liberally on the poetic function in order to address internet users about the merits of specific commodities that will be sold and consumed in the real world.

41 > possible worlds, Chapter 3, p. 52

In empirical terms, Jakobson (1960) stayed closely focused on discursive forms. While extrapolating to their communicative functions, his analysis explicitly bracketed the social origins and consequences of

Constituents		
Addresser	Context Message Contact Code	Addressee
Functions		
Emotive	Referential Poetic Phatic Metalingual	Conative

Figure 5.2
Jakobson's (1960) model of communication

either forms or functions: "the question of relations between the word and the world" (p. 19). Other humanistic scholars have been more adventurous, seeking to model the common experience that we all listen for tones of voice and choices of words to get the points that others are making – their codes and the communicative relationships that they afford us. Faced with media that communicate at a distance and in additional modalities, audiences read between the lines of texts and the frames of images.

Departing from Louis Hjelmslev's (1963/1943) linguistics, Roland Barthes (1973/1957) suggested that meaning is produced in layers that build up as worldviews or mythologies. Technically speaking, the expressive form (signifier) and conceptual content (signified) of a word, image, or statement, in combination, articulate a denotation or basic meaning. Next, the two sides of this first sign jointly make up the form of a second-order sign, whose content is connotation (Figure 5.3);[42] and connotations further enter into cultural configurations with social implications. To take Barthes' most famous example, a magazine cover with an image of a young black man in a uniform saluting the French flag becomes the expressive form of a further ideological content, namely, that French imperialism was not a discriminatory system. Barthes' critical point was that this two-tiered mechanism of meaning production serves to naturalize certain worldviews, while silencing others. In later work, Barthes (1970: 13–16) reversed the perspective, suggesting that denotations are not foundations or points of departure, but preliminary end points of meaning production: relatively stable textual moments within a continuing intertextual process. In both perspectives, however, connotations are neither private nor idiosyncratic constructs, but social facts that are reproduced in communication and become real in their consequences.

In Bateson's terms, connotations can be understood as codifications – the meta-linguistic aspect of meta-communication. Connotations are codes that accumulate as representations, frames of interpretation, and views of the world. At the same time, codes inscribe communicators into social relations, as recognized by both Bateson and Barthes. Paralleling his model of connotations, Barthes identified another model which begins to capture some of the distinctive communicative relationships that digital media establish and maintain.

42 denotation and connotation

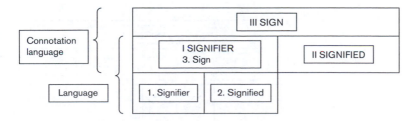

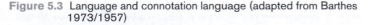

Figure 5.3 Language and connotation language (adapted from Barthes 1973/1957)

The third degree

Roland Barthes' use of Louis Hjelmslev's original terms and formal concepts was, at best, debatable. Nevertheless, his appropriation of Hjelmslev's basic figure of thought became massively influential in analyses of contemporary culture and communication, and has proven its relevance as a prophetic[43]< interpretation of a classic (Liszka, 1998). Being a twentieth-century linguist, Hjelmslev approached languages as systems – systems of communication and second-order systems that either build on or describe such systems. Barthes' accomplishment was to apply this logic to communication as a practice and a process: connotation languages can be examined not only in the analytical rearview mirror, but as they are articulated and take effect. Barthes, further, included other modalities than spoken and written language into his analysis of the several levels of meaning production.

In Hjelmslev's definition, connotation languages and meta-languages[44] have different, but complementary relations to their common reference point, which is first-order language – 'language' as commonly understood. Connotation languages, on the one hand, build on language, and are themselves second-order languages or vehicles of communication, as exemplified by Barthes' myths. Meta-languages, on the other hand, describe language: they are not languages in themselves, but languages about languages, for instance, syntactical or semantic descriptions of the English language. Figure 5.4 lays out the principle of meta-languages. Compared with Barthes' first model (Figure 5.3), the figure inverts the interrelation between signifier and signified at the second level. The connotations add to the codification of the content; the meta-constituents configure the social relationships that communicators enter into with reference to this content. A linguist, for one, takes the analyst's rather than the user's stance vis-à-vis language.

Hjelmslev had qualified his typology by making an antecedent distinction between scientific and non-scientific languages. Meta-languages would be scientific languages, defined by their formal operations (but presumably accessible, above all, by expert users of language, such as linguists). In some media and modalities, however, meta-languages are informal and accessible to anyone. As in the case of Barthes' prophetic interpretation of Hjelmslev, I propose to treat meta-languages, not merely as analytical systems, but as practices of

43 > prophetic vs. priestly interpretations, Chapter 2, p. 21

44 meta-languages

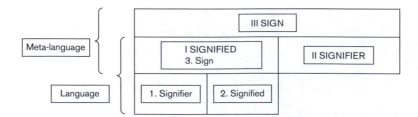

Figure 5.4 Language and meta-language (adapted from Barthes 1973/1957)

communication, as well – meta-communication. Ordinary users of digital media effortlessly employ a wide variety of such meta-languages: they customize their own profile at a social network site; they tag the blog entries of others; they forward a news story to a friend from a website via an embedded email service; and they pull a later push of information to themselves through an RSS feed (Really Simple Syndication).

Digital media facilitate interactivity,[45]< not only with information, or with other communicators about the denotations and connotations of the information at hand, but also with the interfaces and systems of communication. Users customize their own access points to the internet, and they may affect its infrastructure, to a degree, by participating, for instance, in open-source innovation (Benkler, 2006; Von Hippel, 2005). The potential uses and systemic consequences of such meta-communication in digital media are still being discovered. Here, I briefly note three issues for further research.

45 > interactivity, Chapter 3, pp. 53–55

First, web search engines[46]< present a prototypical example of meta-communication: they codify information and enact communicative relationships. Depending on the coded structure of the available information, I gain access to it (or not) *as* information and as *this* kind of information with some contextual relevance. I further establish a communicative relationship, not necessarily with identifiable individuals or institutions, but with a distributed resource of communication. In and of my search, I both provide input to and reconfigure the system, however minimally. My meta-communication prefigures subsequent communications both by myself and by others, whether searching for more information or interacting about, and perhaps acting on, the outcome of our searches.

46 > search engines, pp. 92–94

Second, also in other digital applications, users enter information into the system, more or less willingly and knowingly. Depending on technical and legal frameworks, such information remains available and accessible. The contents and forms of digital media, but also their uses and some of their contexts – the communications as well as the information – lend themselves to data mining (Han and Kamber, 2006). This is in contrast, of course, to most face-to-face interaction, which literally disappears into the air, but also to mass media use, which traditionally has been sampled and documented for dedicated purposes of research, development, and marketing. Most meta-communication in any medium moves below the communicators' radar of awareness. However, meta-communication is not necessarily or permanently beyond the upper or lower thresholds of communication.[47]< In digital media, a wealth of data and metadata are documented in and of their use. Citizens' and consumers' meta-communication is of obvious interest to big governmental brothers and little commercial sisters, who may treat it as information, communicate about it, and act on it.

47 > upper and lower thresholds of communication, Chapter 4, p. 55

Third, digital media transport both texts and contexts across space and time. By responding to the ring tones of mobile telephones and logging onto conference systems, users introduce additional communicative relationships into existing contexts. They do so in several modalities, sometimes as a matter of choice: with 3G mobile phones, users can decide whether or not to look at each other, or to show and tell, while conversing at a distance. Television introduced moving images (and sounds) of public events into the private sphere of the home (Meyrowitz, 1985); mobile telephones have recontextualized private conversations within public spaces (e.g., Humphreys, 2005). The larger issue is presence[48]< – in a physical, social, as well as psychological respect – as examined by a growing body of research (Biocca *et al.*, 2003). Media of the third degree are particularly rich sources of experienced co-presence and coordinated action at a distance.

48 > presence,
Chapter 6, p. 109

The vocabularies of meta-communication and meta-media[49]< have separate origins. Meta-communication is a constitutive function of any communicative practice in any medium. In comparison, 'meta-media' (A. Kay and Goldberg, 1999/1977) represent an ad hoc conceptualization of new, digital media with reference to their integration of old, analog media technologies and institutions. Also the discursive forms of digital media remain moving targets. As vehicles of communication and meta-communication, however, they share two basic features with the discourses of both first- and second-degree media: communicators take turns, and they make transitions to action, whether of a consensual or conflictual nature.

49 > meta-media,
Chapter 4, p. 70

Turns and transitions

We navigate the material and modal interfaces of different media – books as well as mobile telephones – in order to gain access to information and to other communicators. To get your point, I listen to your speech sounds and watch your gestures. To update myself on national events, I turn the pages of my morning newspaper, and change the channels on my radio and television sets. To monitor the state of the world, in the public sphere and my own private sphere, I daily surf the web at regular intervals and exchange text messages with my partner. In my communication, I take turns with people as well as with other media.[50] Navigating different media, we make ourselves accessible for communication, and gain access to other communicators and possible worlds.

50 turn-taking – with
people and with
other media

The approach to communication as turn-taking was developed by conversation analysis[51] from the 1970s onwards (Sacks *et al.*, 1974; Wetherell *et al.*, 2001). While the focus in linguistics and discourse studies has been on the turns that speakers take in, for instance, question–answer sequences and other interpersonal interactions, the concept applies more generally to communicative practices in other media. Newspaper articles, feature films, and websites all constitute turns, as do headline glancing, visits to the cinema, and responses to a quickpoll about the news of the day or a new film release. Turns feed more turns, whether in the same or different media. We return for an update of the news the next day, or go to compare a news item with another source on the same day; we look out for the next release by our favorite film director; and we engage in discussions about world events

51 conversation
analysis

or Academy Award winners by instant messaging or face-to-face. One of the main things that people do with media is communicate about them. They do so in turns, sequences, three- or multistep flows[52]< – within and across media.

52 > three-step flow,
Chapter 4,
pp. 71–74

In computer-mediated communication as in conversation, turn-taking depends on its purpose and context – what the turns are about and why they are taken. Different genres involve different structures of turn-taking. In a classic stage drama, conversational turns are embedded in the players' action, while the audience, at least today, is expected to take long, silent turns of involvement and immersion. Historical research suggests that, before 1800, the convention was for audiences to give priority to speaking with others in the hall, rather than immersing themselves in an individualized, interior experience of the communication taking place on the stage (J. H. Johnson, 1995). Today, readers can decide to read literary classics in brief installments that are sent daily to their computer or mobile device (http://dailylit.com/, accessed July 15, 2009). In an online computer game, the distributed players' sustained interactivity with each other, and with non-player characters, is a condition of possibility of the genre – interactivity is the name of the game. The individual players' turns, moreover, decide their completion of levels and, hence, their social identity and standing within the game. In modern urban living, brief mobile phone conversations at the end of a workday coordinate who shops for an evening meal, and who picks up the children from daycare, just as e-banking sessions during a lunch break or the free time of evening serve to pay the family's monthly bills.

In the larger scheme of things, the exchange of minimal items of information and the performance of rudimentary acts of communication produce, maintain, repair, and transform social institutions (J. W. Carey, 1989b/1975: 23): families, banking, theater, popular entertainments, and other components of contemporary society. We cannot *not* take turns communicating;[53] we also incessantly make the transition from communication to other social interaction. Media and communicative practices serve to join human agency and social structure – which are the focus of the next chapter.

53 we cannot *not*
take turns
communicating

Media institutions

Between agency and structure

6

Media institutions

Between agency and structure

Institutions-to-think-with

As part of an anthropological perspective on how the members of a culture communicate, Claude Lévi-Strauss referred to objects-to-think-with.[1] Especially animals that are part of the cultural diet can become means of classifying and, thus, coming to terms with reality. It is not so much that they are "good to eat," but that they are "good to think (with)" (Lévi-Strauss, 1991/1962: 89). In a different culture, the same animal or natural object may mean something else, it may be prepared in a different manner, or it may not be considered good to either eat or think with. Also artifacts – from stone tools to oil paintings – serve as more or less programmable tokens of meaningful interchange. In comparison, contemporary media constitute institutions-to-think-with (Douglas, 1987) – highly differentiated and widely distributed material and modal infrastructures that enable reflection and interaction across space and time. Cultures and societies program their media, which, in turn, program them.

Media are a distinctive kind of institution-to-think-with. Compared with other institutions of analysis and reflection – sciences, arts, or religions – media are, in a positive sense, the lowest common denominators of culture and society. They do not require specialized skills or talents of a scientific or artistic nature for interaction and deliberation to occur. Nor do they presuppose the existence of transcendent possible worlds to which only certain privileged texts, individuals, or procedures provide access. Media address and involve anyone as someone[2] (Scannell, 2000) in communication about the ends and means of society, increasingly across time and space.

While referring to the biases of media toward either time or space,[3] Innis (1951; 1972/1950) suggested that the two biases are complementary, and "he believed that a balance between these biases optimized the social good, but was seldom achieved in history" (Blondheim, 2008: 2287). To clarify the relationship between time and space, communication necessarily occurs in time. As noted by Immanuel Kant, time takes precedence over space as a category of human reason and, by implication, in communication.[4] We cannot all speak at the same time. Nor can we, as individuals, think of everything at once. We can, however, take turns communicating, and we can delegate the capacity to deliberate among ourselves. With technologies and, later, meta-technologies has come a

1 objects-to-think-with

2 > anyone as someone, Chapter 2, p. 38

3 > biases of media, Chapter 4, p. 64

4 > time as primary category of human understanding, Chapter 3, p. 52

decisive set of resources for communication and deliberation across space, synchronously as well as asynchronously. As institutions in their own right,[5] the media belong to modernity (J. B. Thompson, 1995).

5 media as institutions in their own right

In this chapter, I first situate media in relation to a classic dualism of the social sciences: agency and structure. How is it that the sum of self-interested individual actions reproduces comparatively coherent and stable social systems? To overcome the dualism, contemporary social theory mostly recognizes a duality or dialectic of agency and structure. I introduce communication – a duality of communication – into the equation. Communication enables moments of reflection regarding both the micro and the macro structures of society. To illustrate the role of communication in the process of maintaining society, I consider the place of mobile phones in daily life – in work and leisure, in public as well as in private. The middle part of the chapter broadens the perspective and situates media among other institutions of modern society, as laid out in Jürgen Habermas' model of the public sphere. Importantly, this influential model provides both a map of modern society and an imagined framework regarding its origin, development, and possible future. At issue since the eighteenth century has been the right to communicate. Media of the third degree reactualize the question of what that right entails, including the right in some instances *not* to send or receive information.

The duality of communication

The duality of structure

The idea of a duality of structure, while specifically associated with the work of the sociologist Anthony Giddens (1984), sums up a common insight from more than a century of social sciences and cultural studies. Human agency is not the manifestation of an individual free will, nor is social structure a set of external constraints on individuals' actions. Instead, societies are structured by, and they simultaneously structure, the myriad interactions that individuals, groups, and institutions incessantly engage in. Subjects and social systems – agency and structure[6] – are each other's enabling conditions. To exemplify, the press consists of its structural properties – its economic, legal, and technological permanence – *and* of the diverse distributed actions of journalists, advertisers, regulators, and audiences. Like other institutions in society, the press, and the media as such, are reenacted day by day.

6 agency and structure

Media and communication, surprisingly, have been comparative blindspots of social theory, including Giddens' summative framework (for discussion, see, e.g., K. B. Jensen, 1995; Silverstone, 1999; J. B. Thompson, 1995). This is in spite of the central distinction that Giddens also makes between social interactions that are technologically mediated and those that are not – what he terms system integration and social integration, respectively. Social integration refers to local, embodied, face-to-face interaction; system integration is "reciprocity between actors or collectivities across extended time-space, outside conditions of co-presence" (Giddens, 1984: 377) – which depends on media technologies. Equally, communication remained a missing link of Giddens' (1979) double hermeneutics:[7]< reinterpretations of society – by scholars and (other) social actors – occur and take effect in communication. As indicated in Chapters 2 and 3 (Figures 2.1 and 3.2), I approach media as a category on a par with agency and structure. Communication mediates structure and agency.[8]

7 > double hermeneutics, Chapter 1, p. 11

8 communication mediates structure and agency

Communication accumulates as culture[9] that is remembered, archived, and disseminated, depending on the historically available media. Culture lends meaning both to the social structures emanating from the past and to the human actions shaping the future. Culture is itself an essentially contested concept[10]< (Gallie, 1956). Cultural norms and institutions serve to legitimate and prefer certain forms of agency and some social structures above others. This is in spite of the modern notion of culture, as articulated by Johann Gottfried Herder in *Ideas for a Philosophy of the History of Mankind* (1784), namely, that all humans have and share culture, and that they are both united and differentiated by their cultural practices. Humans cultivate distinctions[11] that, over time, solidify as self-explanatory structures and forms of agency (Bourdieu, 1984/1979). Media and communication research is heir to not just one, but two great cultural divides.

9 communication accumulates as culture

10 > essentially contested concepts, Chapter 1, p. 6

11 distinction

The great cultural divides

After the great divide is the title of a book by Andreas Huyssen (1986), who noted that, with mass media, high and low cultural forms increasingly came to appear side by side, influencing and, to an extent, merging with one another. With digital media, the interlinking of different cultural formations has been intensified. Both authors and audiences can engage fine art and popular culture on the same media platform. In addition, media of the third degree have returned a second great divide to center stage: the distinction between culture as finished products and as open-ended processes of communication. Through meta-technologies, cultural products – from photographs to videogames – are embedded in one-to-one and many-to-many processes of interaction, online and offline. On top, meta-technologies facilitate a continuous modification of both the products and the processes of culture. High as well as low cultures, as digitally remediated, lend themselves to being ripped, mixed, and burned (Bowrey and Rimmer, 2002).

Already in the 1950s, while the field of media and communication research was taking shape, an interdisciplinary research review had noted as many as 164 definitions of culture (Kroeber and Kluckhohn, 1952). In practice, two main conceptions have informed both research and public debate. On the one hand, culture constitutes a world apart,[12] typically in the shape of representations of reality in artworks. In fine arts and aesthetic theories, culture has traditionally been understood as

12 culture as extraordinary realm

the site and source of privileged and extraordinary insights or, in Immanuel Kant's (2004b/1790: n.p.) words in the *Critique of Judgment*, "disinterested delight." In the modern period, with secularization and democratization, the very idea of eternal or universal insights became dubious. Nevertheless, certain select expressions and representations might still be said to qualify, in the words of the cultural critic, Matthew Arnold, as "the best which has been thought and said in the world" (Arnold, 2003/1869: n.p.).

On the other hand, culture is part and parcel of the world of practice.[13] Pervading human consciousness and social interaction, it amounts to what a later cultural critic and theorist, Raymond Williams (1975/1958: 18), called "a whole way of life." Culture is constitutive of all the ordinary things that humans say to and do with each other, our artifacts and our habits, products as well as processes.

13 culture as ordinary practice

The two definitions of culture underlie and inform the two great divides. The high–low divide, for one, assumes that privileged insights derive from privileged works, institutions, and individuals – the genius philosopher or singular artist – rather than from a division of labor within cultural industries, let alone a mass of ordinary people. The product–process divide, further, has mostly given priority to 'works': culture as delimited and fixated for contemplation and introspection, rather than as recreated and redeveloped in communication. Together, the two divides suggest a descending scale of quality and legitimacy – from the unchanging classic to a mass of individuals fancying the latest fad.

The divides provided the wider cultural context for a much publicized controversy over the relative merits of Wikipedia and the *Encyclopedia Britannica*,[14] which followed the publication of a study showing the two reference works to be of comparable quality (Giles, 2005). Beyond the particular study (and the obvious interest of each side in either endorsing or questioning its premises and findings), the general theoretical as well as ideological issue was the relationship between knowledge as product and as process. What are the appropriate procedures of moving from analysis to synthesis, deliberation to conclusion, and communication to action? Who is in a position – individually and collectively – to present certified knowledge in public? Can crowds generate wisdom (Surowiecki, 2004)? In a pragmatist terminology, the question is which beliefs people will be prepared to act on, during and at the end of communication.[15]

14 Wikipedia vs. Encyclopedia Britannica

15 > belief as readiness to act, Chapter 2, pp. 30–32

Time-in culture and time-out culture

Communication is both in and out of time – it oscillates between moments of reflection and moments of action. In the case of both expert and lay knowledge, high as well as low culture, communication reflects on structure and anticipates agency. Different media and genres enable different kinds of reflection and action.

As an illustration, consider the world of sports. In basketball and (American) football, coaches can call for a time-out – an interval – to discuss strategy with their teams. While temporarily suspending the game, the time-out occurs within and addresses the total time-in of the game. By analogy, media use and other cultural practices – visits to operas and museums, web surfing and television viewing at home, or music listening en route to either type of activity – establish a time-out. While suspending other activities, in whole or in part, the communication still takes place within the flow of everyday life and with reference to families, markets, parliaments, and other social institutions. As analytical categories, time-in and time-out culture suggest several dimensions along which communicative practices vary. The production of meaning may be more or less integrated into or separate from other activities in context; its form may be relatively innovative or routinized; its function may be experienced as comparatively ordinary or extraordinary; and the meanings being expressed and experienced may present themselves either as resources inviting, even requiring immediate action, or as accounts of past or future events. Time-out culture prefigures, time-in culture configures social interaction; the mediating element is communication.[16]

16 communication prefigures and configures action

The duality of communication has taken many different shapes, depending on the affordances of the available media technologies and their social organization and regulation as institutions-to-think-with. Historically, time-out and space-out have gone together in dedicated public arenas: theaters, museums, concert halls, tivolis, and cinemas. Radio and television also began as one-set-per-household media in the dedicated space of a central room in the household. Digital media have shifted the lines of division and transition between time-in and time-out, space-in as well as space-out, by radically extending the accessibility of both information and other communicators, anytime and anywhere. In addition, digital media potentially accelerate the process of communicative turn-taking.[17]< This is true of the private coordination of family life, but also of the public negotiation of, for example, political scandals (J. B. Thompson, 2000). Most important, digital media facilitate the immediate translation of communication into action at a distance,[18] from the coordination of grocery shopping to the closing of million-dollar business deals. Mobile media are a case in point.

17 > turn-taking, Chapter 5, p. 100

18 action at a distance

Case study: what's mobile in mobile communication?

Communication maintains social relations across time and space, most recently through the small digital devices that a dramatically growing number of people around the world carry with them wherever they go (on the social uses of mobile media, see Castells *et al.*, 2007; Goggin, 2006; Katz and Aakhus, 2002; Ling, 2004, 2008) (on technological aspects, see Gow and Smith, 2006). Regional terminologies suggest different notions of how these devices relate to space – to local communicators; to the global technology connecting them; and to the movement of both information and communicators (Ito *et al.*, 2005: 1). In Japan, they are *keitai* (something you carry with you), an everyday artifact that remains close to your body. In North America, they are cell phones, terminals that exchange signals across a grid of technically defined cells. In Europe, they are mobile telephones, unfixing the location from which individuals may speak with and text to each other. What, indeed, is mobile in mobile communication?

Until the invention of the telegraph and subsequent electronic media, "transportation and communication were inseparably linked" (J. W. Carey, 1989a: 15). Any communicative interaction required the movement and physical presence in local space of humans, manuscripts, books, magazines, or newspapers. Depending on historical perspective, media have been mobile for millennia – in the form of perambulating humans, in time holding manuscripts and other writing surfaces disseminating fact as well as fiction. For centuries, print media have spread information and entertainment across and between countries and continents, first to relatively small and specialized groups, later to mass audiences. And, for decades, visual and auditory representations have been reproduced and distributed, synchronously and asynchronously, through sound recordings, cinema, and broadcasting. What's new about so-called mobile media is their integration of multimodal communication into everyday life in increasingly localized and individualized ways. What's mobile about mobile communication is not so much the particular device, the general technology, or the individual user, but the contexts in which they come together in communication.[19]

It is useful to distinguish between three general aspects of mobility – spatial, temporal, and contextual (Kakihara and Sørensen, 2002). Spatial mobility, first of all, refers to the shifting locations of objects, people, and symbols in space. Temporal mobility, next, concerns the flexible ways in which people interact with the many different elements of their environment, including other people, over time. As suggested by the anthropologist, Edward T. Hall (1959), both individuals and cultures may be relatively monochronic or polychronic: when multiple events and activities call for attention, one may engage them either sequentially or simultaneously, single-tasking or multitasking. Contextual mobility, finally, captures the extent to which entire configurations of social relations move about – contexts come and go. Communication transports contexts of meaningful interaction across space and time, and communicators bring contexts with them from place to place, as virtually present in their minds. Digital media enable a new degree of contextual mobility, first, because they further blur the line between experienced presence[20] and absence (Biocca *et al.*, 2003). With 3G mobile telephony and online video conferencing, I can see and hear not just my conversational partners, but their local contexts, as well. (For an early account of experienced presence and proximity in landline telephony, see Wurtzel and Turner, 1977.) Second, these absent settings are included in my potential contexts of action, more immediately and directly so through digital media.

Like media, contexts are at once material and immaterial phenomena. Humanistic scholarship has traditionally emphasized this point by approaching

19 mobile contexts

20 experienced presence

21 > intertextuality,
Chapter 5,
pp. 88–92

contexts literally as con-texts or inter-texts.[21]< Increasingly, social sciences and studies of human–computer interaction have also approached contexts simultaneously as physical locales and interpretive frames. In one of his analyses of everyday contexts, Erving Goffman (1971) identified three varieties of what he called "territories of the self." Fixed territories, first, are at once geographical and legally regulated; they include fields, yards, houses, and so on. Situational territories, second, are more transient, and emerge from the time-bound uses that people make of a particular place; Goffman mentions examples such as park benches, restaurant tables, and hotel rooms. The third

22 egocentric
territories

type is egocentric territories,[22] which have limited extension and represent very private spaces, for example, pockets and purses, but also personal means of expression such as diaries and letters. An obvious recent candidate for this last type of territory is the mobile phone. As encapsulated in everyday artifacts,

23 transitional
objects

egocentric territories constitute transitional objects[23] (Winnicott, 1971), akin to a child's bear or blanket, and they enable their holders to enter a time-out, in-between worlds, or liminal realms of reality (V. Turner, 1967). Whereas Goffman, as usual, stayed with contexts of co-presence, certain egocentric artifacts provide access to absent others. Media are, by definition, egocentric as well as other-directed.

Mobile telephones constitute an institution in the individual's pocket. Mobile in hand, I access useful information, sometimes from other communicators in

24 > multi-step flow
of communication,
Chapter 4,
pp. 71–74

a multistep flow:[24]< updates on traffic congestion and train delays, or the price of an everyday commodity at different stores. Thus informed, I go on communicating with my significant others (Mead, 1934), microcoordinating when I may arrive (late) for a business appointment, and negotiating best buys for my family on the fly – before enacting appointments and purchases. At the end of the day, I will have participated in the maintenance of both self and society – the socialization of myself and the institutionalization of society.

The right to communicate

Positive and negative rights

Institutions are the most durable constituents of a society – the family, the legal system, the press, and so on. Yet, unlike family homes, court buildings, and newsrooms, institutions are elusive entities that exist nowhere and everywhere – virtual forms with real functions.[25] In

25 institutions –
virtual forms with
real functions

different political, economic, and cultural domains, institutions serve to regulate the interaction between the individual and the collective according to certain recognized and enforced principles – civic and human rights. Media institutions – and the right to communicate – are special insofar as, ideally, they enable anyone to address any other social institution or right, its status and legitimacy. Current media institutions are the historical outcome of an ongoing struggle to both define and exercise the right to communicate.

Rights come in two main variants – positive and negative. The distinction was noted by Jürgen Habermas (1989/1962: 226) in his classic account of the public sphere with reference to the notoriously ambiguous concept of freedom. While some political philosophers have emphasized a negative definition (freedom *from* state interference into the affairs of individuals), others have given priority to a positive definition (freedom *to* expect or demand certain provisions and services from the collective). The modern period was inaugurated by a negative definition of freedom when, from the eighteenth century, the new middle classes asserted their rights vis-à-vis the authority of the state. A positive redefinition of rights, involving substantial economic regulation and social services along Keynesian principles, followed world crises in the late nineteenth century and particularly during the 1930s. And, positive rights recently reappeared on an international political agenda with the financial and economic crises gaining momentum in 2008.

Over the span of three centuries, the modernization of society[26] can be understood as the (preliminary) outcome of a negotiation of positive and negative rights in three main respects:

26 **modernization of society**

- *democratization and bureaucratization* of the institutions and practices of political representation and government;
- *industrialization and capitalization* of the material economy, along with a growing division and rationalization of labor, leading into variable phases of market competition, incorporation, imperialism, and conglomeration;
- *secularization* of the cultural forms of expression and experience, including the securing of niches for non- or anti-religious reflexivity, and the recognition of popular alternatives or complements to the fine arts.

In each case, media have been general conditions of specific processes and developments – as means of political organization and argument; vehicles of advertising and instruments of business administration; and forms of cultural expression and innovation. Compared with pre-modern institutions-to-think-with – religious, aesthetic, or scientific – modern media have a general brief: they address and assess the delegation of agency to other institutions in society, on behalf of and in the (contestable) public interest. Also the media themselves have been subject to a negotiation of positive and negative rights on the part of individuals and collectives. The right to communicate was collectively imagined and socially invented as part of a blueprint for the institutional structure of modern society.

Media as institutions

Jürgen Habermas' (1989/1962) public-sphere model[27] (Figure 6.1) continues to offer a valuable framework in which to examine the relationship between media and other social institutions – as part of a system of interconnected, yet relatively autonomous spheres (for review and

27 **the public-sphere model**

	Society		State
	Private sphere	Public sphere	
	Intimate sphere	*Cultural public sphere*	
Object	Religion, sexuality, emotion, friendship, etc.	Preaching, art, literature, music, etc.	The (agencies of the) state ensure(s) the material infrastructure, overall economic stability, law enforcement, and regulation of conflicts by economic, coercive, legal, and ideological means
Institution	Family	Organizations, clubs	
	Social sphere	*Political public sphere*	
Object	Private economic activity, production and sale/purchase of commodities, including labor	'Politics' and 'the economy,' including social issues	
Institution	Private enterprises and stores	Parliamentary organs, representing political parties, and the press	

Figure 6.1 The public-sphere model (adapted from Habermas, 1989/1962; Mortensen, 1977)

discussion, see Calhoun, 1992; Mortensen, 1977; Negt and Kluge, 1993/1972). The figure notes, to the right, the state agencies that establish and enforce the material, legal, and other infrastructural conditions of social interaction, ultimately with recourse to their monopoly on the use of physical violence. To the left, private economic enterprise unfolds in the social sphere, while the intimate sphere represents the domain of personal and family life. The mediating element of the entire system is the public sphere, comprising the main political and cultural institutions-to-think-with, including the press as a Fourth Estate. Although this is frequently neglected in the Anglo-American literature on Habermas, the public sphere has two components, one political, the other cultural.[28] Habermas showed how the cultural public sphere of literary journals and *salons* served, in part, as a precursor and a training ground for political deliberation and debate in a contemporary sense. In its consolidated form, the public sphere came to address two relatively separate agendas

28 political and cultural public spheres

through different genres: crudely, the 'individual' issues of culture and arts through fiction, and the 'collective' issues of politics and economy through factual genres.

Historically, the public sphere had a proactive function in asserting the economic and political rights of individuals in their confrontation with a feudal order (negative rights). Once in place, the public sphere also acquired a reactive function, negotiating the terms of cooperation among citizens, and between private citizens and the state (positive rights). The model, thus, represents a dual construct – an actual as well as an imagined reality of structure and agency. On the one hand, the public-sphere model locates media on a structural map of society with other institutions: markets, parliaments, and state agencies are all real and effective. The issue, both theoretically and normatively, has been the exact nature of the interrelations between these institutions. Just as, in pre-modern societies, monarchies, religious authorities, and patrons of the arts enabled and constrained cultural expression in decisive ways, current media, evidently, are governed as much by an economic logic as by a spirit of democratic dialogue.

On the other hand, the public-sphere model represents a plan of action – it is neither a neutral organizational chart nor a simple instance of false consciousness. Cognitivist theories of human consciousness have suggested how basic categories of understanding are grounded in and shaped by physical and biological circumstances: we carry the body in the mind (M. Johnson, 1987). By the same token, we carry society in the mind[29] as a set of predispositions to act in particular ways in relation to specific institutions. Because the public-sphere model informs the inter-actions of everyday life, it is reproduced, for better or worse, as common sense or hegemony (Gramsci, 1971) – "a sense of absolute because experienced reality beyond which it is very difficult for most members of the society to move, in most areas of their lives" (Williams, 1977: 110).

29 society in the mind

Media of the second degree opened up a virtual sphere of interaction and deliberation across physical and social space. "All experience is local . . . We are always in place, and place is always with us" (Meyrowitz, 1989: 326). Given the right media, however, communication and action can both be global. In Habermas' (1989/1962) original account, the public sphere was conceived as the ideal-type of an ideal forum in which the rational interaction of equal citizens in nation-states would serve to define the common good and the appropriate ways of achieving it. From the outset, both Habermas and other commentators (e.g., Sennett, 1974) deplored the contemporary decline of the ideal. A common figure of thought has been the re-closing of the public sphere because of pressures from either side, what Habermas had referred to as a refeudalization[30] of society. An intensified commercialization of the mass media and strategic alliances between the state and private business, as exemplified by the post-1945 US military-industrial complex, arguably conspired to silence important issues and voices of public discourse.

30 refeudalization

Amid cultural pessimism as well as optimism, the last two centuries have witnessed a tug of war, first, along the horizontal dimension of the private, public, and state spheres of social activity and, most recently, along its vertical dimension, as well. Over the *longue durée*, this is the period that the historian, Eric Hobsbawm (1995: ix), dubbed the long century of 1789–1914 (from the French Revolution to the First World War), and the short century of 1914–91 (up until the collapse of the Soviet Union, which Castells (1999) also examined under the heading of the "end of millennium"). In different national and cultural contexts, a key issue has been the balance between market-driven and publicly administered means of communication. During the short twentieth century, European-style public-service broadcasting[31] was a case in point: to what extent could public service be had for private money (Lund, 2001: 41) from a commercial press, and to what extent were public-service television and radio stations needed to deliver correctives and complements? With the growing centrality of transnational outlets – in wholesale as well as retail media – the debate was extended to international arenas, for instance, concerning the possibility and desirability of a New World Information and Communication Order (MacBride, 1980). In a mass-media infrastructure, information becomes accessible, for most public purposes, within centralized cultural fora[32]< (Newcomb and Hirsch, 1983), bounded by states and markets.

Within a networked infrastructure, the vertical dimension of the public-sphere model becomes more salient in national as well as international arenas. Communication flows more easily across the boundaries traditionally (in modernity) separating personal and family life from work settings, 'politics' from 'culture,' and individual nation-states from each other. To be sure, the implications are far from clear; current research is studying media and communication history in the making. Neither the printed books of the late 1400s nor the newspapers of the early 1700s were very precise predictors of the manifold uses to which these media have been put in subsequent centuries. In a present perspective, however, media of the third degree can be seen to facilitate distinctive kinds of communicative agency.

Communicative agency

The commonly recognized role of information and communication as strategic resources across different spheres of contemporary society has been reflected in shifting terminologies. First, the "control revolution" of 1880–1930 (Beniger, 1986) – the formation of an entire social sector of opinion polling, advertising and public relations, and organizational bureaucracies – facilitated the self-regulation of various other sectors in the face of growing complexity.[33] Second, an information society or economy (Porat, 1977) is normally said to have taken shape after 1945.[34] As elaborated by the sociologist, Daniel Bell, in *The Coming of Post-Industrial Society* (1973), a majority of the work force in advanced industrial societies was now engaged in immaterial labor; theoretical knowledge had become a central ingredient also of material production; and the coordination of social systems increasingly depended on mediating technologies. Third, and most recently, a network society,[35]

31 public-service broadcasting

32 > media as cultural forum, Chapter 3, p. 50

33 the control society

34 the information society

35 the network society

as diagnosed by Manuel Castells (1996), may be emerging that preserves the economic model of capitalism while embedding it in a new digital infrastructure – a transition from industrial capitalism to informational capitalism. While debated (Webster and Dimitriou, 2004), Castells' framework highlights a shift *from information as a resource* of material production *to communication as a process* orienting and maintaining diverse sectors of society. This is suggested by Castells' notions of spaces of flows, timeless time, and a culture of real virtuality. Separate physical spaces of social activity are linked in real time; local times are subsumed under global flows of interaction and exchange; and our sense of reality comes to include present as well as absent individuals and contexts. It is not so much that we encounter virtual realities in exceptional instances of media use, but that a substantial proportion of all social interaction is technologically mediated and embedded – which does not make it any less real. Also virtual realities can be real in their consequences.[36]<

Along the vertical dimension of the public-sphere model, networked forms of communicative agency challenge three different boundaries. First, at the juncture of the social sphere (business) and the intimate sphere (personal and family life), new forms of material and immaterial production[37] have been emerging. Benkler (2006: 3), for one, has suggested that the core of the predominant modes of production is being affected by the combination of a global information economy, the wide availability of cheap communication technologies with excess capacity, and proliferating networks of non-market, non-state collaboration. In earlier critiques of Habermas' model, feminist scholars rightly noted a tendency, not just to overlook the de facto exclusion of women from the public sphere from the outset, but also to bracket labor being conducted in the home, overwhelmingly by women (Fraser, 1992). Digital media reopen debates on the definition, organization, and control of human labor. While it is easy to exaggerate and romanticize what Alvin Toffler had referred to, almost thirty years ago, in *The Third Wave* (1981: 11), as the rise of the "prosumer," reconciling the roles of producer and consumer, digital media supply general tools of communicative agency for innovation, development, financing, collaboration, distribution, and so on, also outside the information sector proper (Von Hippel, 2005).

Second, the boundary between the political and cultural public spheres was in question from the outset, and has appeared increasingly porous. As an illustration, users may approach comedy shows such as *The Daily Show with Jon Stewart*, as available also online (www.thedailyshow.com/, accessed July 15, 2009), on a par with other sources of news (Feldman, 2007). A comparative content analysis of *The Daily Show* and US network television news, in fact, found the "substantive information" of the two program types concerning the 2004 presidential election campaign to be the same (Fox *et al.*, 2007).

The social theorist, David Harvey (1989: 38), described the events of '1968'[38] as a comparatively recent indicator that the lines of division between the 'political' and the 'cultural,' and between 'public' and 'private' domains of life, have been shifting. The very idea of a 'counterculture,'

36 > we have always been virtual, Chapter 1, p. 15

37 new forms of material and immaterial production

38 1968

and of 'anti-authoritarian' attitudes implied opposition to the 'structure' of society in a distinctive and expanded sense, just as oppositional 'agency' came to be exercised in a greater variety of contexts and formats, from issue-centered 'movements' to 'happenings' with open-ended meanings. Also, developments involving formal as well as informal institutions of knowledge contributed to a more egalitarian conception of relevant and legitimate information. For example, an unlikely alliance of counter-culture, cybernetics, and cold-war research communities depending on collaborative practices of inquiry, fed into a utopian cyberculture (F. Turner, 2006). Whereas the media, as usual, were messengers, rather than prime movers, of events, "the whole world [was] watching" (Gitlin, 1980): both activists and general audiences would encounter previously separate social issues and actors side by side in a mass-mediated cultural forum (Newcomb and Hirsch, 1983). In a networked public sphere, such interlinking is accelerated and articulated in comparable agendas and modes of address. Business corporations seek to strengthen their legitimacy by addressing the general public not merely as customers or clients, but as citizens, through corporate social responsibility, ethical accounting, and ecological initiatives. State agencies justify themselves to the public in a vocabulary of customer service. Political parties and non-governmental organizations (NGOs) alike must build and maintain constituencies whose members conceive of themselves in a hybrid of economic, cultural, and ethnic identities. And, at least some audiences, some of the time, come to act as senders as well as receivers of information about the definition of 'political' and 'cultural' agendas and issues.

The third column of the public-sphere model – the (nation-)state – mostly remains firmly in place. The system of nation-states had been inaugurated by the Westphalian peace of 1648, and was variously implemented in the following centuries. A world economic system had begun to take shape already from the sixteenth century, at first centered in Western Europe. However, unlike other such historical systems – for example, in the Middle East and China – this economic infrastructure did not develop into an empire or political entity (Wallerstein, 1974: 348). Nations took shape as delimited geographical units and cultural formations – imagined communities (Anderson, 1991) – as supported by newspapers and novels as well as by maps, museums, and the census. With an intensified globalization of economy and politics in recent decades, nation-states enter into transnational alliances,[39] such as the European Union (EU) and the North American Free Trade Agreement (NAFTA), and they negotiate their coexistence in assemblies, courts, and agencies inside and outside the United Nations. During the same period, civil society[40] organizations have reasserted themselves as a third sector of political, economic, and cultural activity beyond states and markets (for overview, see Edwards, 2004). A transnational public sphere, however, has yet to emerge (Fraser, 2007).

Individuals as well as collectives will assert and reserve certain rights of communication for themselves – from the local to the global level – in response to the potentials of the media that be. The right to

39 transnational alliances

40 civil society

communicate is technologically and historically variable, and is currently being contested in relation to several powerful institutions of national and international society.

Some rights reserved

Sending and receiving

The key principle of the Creative Commons[41] movement – "some rights reserved" as opposed to "all rights reserved" – lets "authors, scientists, artists, and educators easily mark their creative work with the freedoms they want it to carry . . . making it easier for people to share and build upon the work of others" (http://creativecommons.org/, accessed March 25, 2009). While devised as an alternative regimen of copyright, the principle applies more generally to the social uses of information in any communicative practice. Most simply, the right to communicate is exercised in minimal acts of sending and receiving information. Digital media, however, restate the question of what it means to 'send' and 'receive' – intentionally or not – in communication as well as meta-communication.

One of the first elaborate models of networked communication suggested the complexity of this question beyond the familiar sender–receiver axis of the classic communication models.[42]< In their typology (Figure 6.2), Bordewijk and Kaam (1986) identified four main types of communication. The matrix distinguishes, on the one hand, between central and distributed control over an available information base and, on the other hand, between central or distributed control over the access to particular items of information. The most familiar types are 'conversation' – face-to-face interaction, but also real-time online dialogue (e.g., chat and conferencing) – and 'allocution' or mass communication, whether in asynchronous print or synchronous broadcast media. In addition, 'consultation,' while typified today by searching and retrieving information from websites or online databases, also applies to encyclopedia and libraries. Finally, 'registration' refers to the documentation of users' acts of communication: what they access, how they react, where they come from, and where they go next. Because this last type of

41 Creative Commons

42 > classic communication models, Chapter 3, pp. 49–51

	CONTROL OF INFORMATION BASE	
CONTROL OF TIME AND ITEMS SELECTED	**Central**	**Distributed**
Central	Allocution	Registration
Distributed	Consultation	Conversation

Figure 6.2 A model of network communication (Bordewijk and Kaam, 1986)

meta-communication has become pervasive with digital media, and because it often is not recognized *as* communication, it raises a special set of issues.

In each of the four cells, new as well as old aspects of the right to communicate – and to refrain from communicating – present themselves. Most of the classic dilemmas, as articulated in the age of mass media, can be identified along a diagonal axis stretching from allocution (mass communication) to conversation. Whereas freedom of speech and of access to information were key demands during the formation of the public sphere, and have been incorporated into the Universal Declaration of Human Rights[43] (www.un.org/Overview/rights.html#a19, accessed July 15, 2009), in practice mass media have served as the non-elected representatives of individual and institutional communicators. With everybody a potential broadcaster, new questions arise concerning appropriate (and simultaneously practicable) ways of coordinating and clearing common affairs through communication. From the perspective of the individual, digital media increase both the sheer mass of accessible information, the range and diversity of the other communicators on offer, and the varieties of turn-taking – generating a likely surplus of information. From the perspective of the collective, the shift from push to pull modes of communication (Negroponte, 1995: 170) reasserts the right of individuals to disregard information – spam emails, but also health information and topics promoting social inclusion and participation – arguably resulting in a deficit of information.[44]

Consultation, next, focuses attention on the exponentially increasing masses of information becoming available and being stored – and on the difficulties of accessing it. Digital media hold a significant potential for augmenting the cultural heritage[45] beyond the scientific articles, artworks, and public documents that fill most museums and libraries. Culture as a whole way of life[46]< (Williams, 1975/1958) includes the experiences and insights that arise from mundane communicative interactions. One quantitative issue is how, in practice, to structure the available information, so as to facilitate access, navigation, and use in later contexts of action. Future generations might be able to write a better, more differentiated, more applicable history of the present – their past – than what the present generations have written about *our* past. Some potentials and problems are suggested by projects such as the Internet Archive with its Wayback Machine (www.archive.org/index.php, accessed June 15, 2009) as well as national and international initiatives of digital archiving (e.g., World Digital Library, www.wdl.org/en/, accessed July 15, 2009). Another, qualitative issue is how to ensure that available information is not rendered culturally inaccessible – 'forgotten' for all practical purposes. While this is the classic difficulty of historical research, the specific programmability of digital media, combined with business practices of reprogramming and innovation, pose an unprecedented challenge to the cultural heritage. Imagine a situation in which extant knowledge about the Second World War was accessible only in systems resembling the contemporaneous 1946 ENIAC – the first

43 the Universal
   Declaration of
   Human Rights

44 information
   surplus and/or
   deficit

45 cultural heritage

46 > culture as a
   whole way of life,
   p. 107

general-purpose electronic computer – which was about the size of a family home, but had very little computing power by current standards (http://en.wikipedia.org/wiki/ENIAC, accessed July 15, 2009).

Registration, finally, presents perhaps the most controversial set of political and ethical issues. In a sense, you cannot receive without sending[47] in digital media, leaving some measure of meta-communicative trails for others to communicate about and act on. To an extent, audiences have long been both searchers and providers of information about their communicative practices, for instance, to market analysts on behalf of political and commercial interests. Cultural critics have also suggested that the preferred approach of modern intelligence operations is to document everything about everybody, only later to define the purpose of the information collected (DeLanda, 1991). However, given the quantities and qualities of information that digital media users routinely provide into self-documenting systems, it becomes relevant for individuals to ask whether and how they have "the right not to be identified" (Woo, 2006). As a matter of public debate and policy, it remains an open question who owns the information that media users contribute by searching the web and using social network sites:

47 **you cannot receive without sending**

> In short, Search 2.0 empowers search providers to capture the personal information flows inherent in Web 2.0 applications and link them to users' other search activities, resulting in the ability to amass detailed and comprehensive records of users' online activities.
> (Zimmer, 2008: n.p.)

The public interest in the issue was suggested when the social network site, Facebook, following protests and threats of legal action, "reversed changes to its contract with users that had appeared to give it perpetual ownership of their contributions to the service" (www.nytimes.com/ 2009/02/19/technology/internet/19facebook.html?_r=1, accessed July 15, 2009). From the individual's perspective, personal information can be a scarce resource.

Habeas signum

New information technologies have long generated concerns about privacy. In 1890, in the context of the control society[48]< (Beniger, 1986), Samuel D. Warren and Louis D. Brandeis commented in the *Harvard Law Review*:

48 > the control society, p. 114

> Recent inventions and business methods call attention to the next step which must be taken for the protection of the person, and for securing to the individual what Judge Cooley calls the right "to be let alone." Instantaneous photographs and newspaper enterprise have invaded the sacred precincts of private and domestic life; and numerous mechanical devices threaten to make good the prediction that "what is whispered in the closet shall be proclaimed from the house-tops."
> (Warren and Brandeis, 1890: n.p.)

Forty years ago, Alan F. Westin (1967: 3) had noted another "revolution in the techniques by which public and private authorities conduct scientific surveillance over the individual." A recent overview of information and privacy voiced similar concerns (Weitzner *et al.*, 2008: 84). The article pointed to three main policy challenges – personal information, copyright protection, and government surveillance[49] – which correspond to the three social spheres of private life, economic production, and state regulation. Elaborating on the work of Westin, this last article suggested that, in the context of an information or network society, privacy is not only a matter of personal information, but "the claim of individuals, groups, and institutions to determine for themselves when, how, and to what extent information about them is used lawfully and appropriately by others" (Weitzner *et al.*, 2008: 87). The overview, further, concluded that technological systems of encryption and access control will no longer serve this purpose in open information environments such as the internet. Instead, the authors, including Tim Berners-Lee, the initiator of the World Wide Web, outlined a socially defined system of information accountability whose purpose would be to place limits, not on the collection of or access to information, but on the uses to which specific items and types of information may be put. Some rights of communication must be reserved – for individuals, groups, and institutions – by social contract.

49 personal information, copyright protection, government surveillance

Communication establishes and maintains the most basic relations between the individual and the collective, agency and structure. Information is a general and strategic resource, not only in material and immaterial production, but in personal life and in the borderlands of private and public existence. Mass media studies have addressed the politics of information and communication,[50] broadly speaking, in two main ways. On the one hand, as explored particularly in critical research on the politics of representation within cultural studies (Grossberg *et al.*, 1992), postcolonial studies (Ashcroft *et al.*, 1995), and anthropology (Clifford and Marcus, 1986), media present contestable accounts of different groups and institutions in society. On the other hand, such accounts constitute resources of action, whether in support of or in opposition to a social status quo, as examined by both critical and administrative research (Lazarsfeld, 1941). Because information, refined and applied as knowledge, has historically been unevenly distributed within and between communities and nations, research has been commissioned to assess, remedy, and predict the social consequences of information and communication technologies. The examples range from attempts to foster social progress through communication in developing countries during the 1950–60s (Lerner, 1958; Schramm, 1964), through the debates on a New World Information and Communication Order (MacBride, 1980), to the World Summit on the Information Society (www.itu.int/wsis/index.html, accessed July 15, 2009). With digital media, the politics of representation and communication is extended into a politics of interactivity[51] (K. B. Jensen and Helles, 2005): who will be able to send and receive which kinds of information, in which sequences

50 the politics of information and communication

51 the politics of interactivity

and networks, and who will be able to do what, with – or to – whom, during and at the end of communication?

As individuals, we constantly delegate opportunities to communicate to each other; we take turns. As societies, we delegate such opportunities as rights that must be planned for, regulated, and supported by material infrastructures and institutional frameworks – physical networks and legal principles, but also literacy[52] skills regarding both text and image as cultivated formally and informally over a lifetime (Coiro *et al.*, 2008). Karl Marx had noted, in *The Eighteenth Brumaire of Louis Bonaparte* (1852), that "men make their own history, but they do not make it just as they please; they do not make it under circumstances chosen by themselves, but under circumstances directly encountered, given, and transmitted from the past" (Feuer, 1969: 360). As individuals as well as societies, we communicate under conditions that have been transmitted to us from the past, sometimes in order to change those conditions for the future.

52 multimedia literacy

The principle of *habeas corpus*,[53] dating from the English Magna Carta of 1215 and integral to modern jurisprudence around the world, was designed to guard against the unlawful imprisonment of individuals through the possibility of appeal. Courts were required to ascertain the whereabouts of a prisoner – his/her corporeal existence. A principle of *habeas signum*[54] would refocus attention on the manifestation of individuals in signs, as information, and on the rights of oneself and others to access and use such information. Neither *habeas corpus* nor *habeas signum* are absolute principles out of time; societies only allow and reserve certain rights for individuals to have, hold, and use their bodies and their information. However, compared with the classic freedoms of expression, information exchange, assembly, and political organization, digital media invite renewed research and debate – and a new agenda – concerning the right to communicate.

53 *habeas corpus*

54 *habeas signum*

In a recent discussion of the prospects of digital media and networked communication for the right to communicate and for the public sphere, Jürgen Habermas (2006: 423) was decidedly skeptical:

> computer-mediated communication in the web can claim unequivocal *democratic* merits only for a special context: It can undermine the censorship of authoritarian regimes that try to control and repress public opinion. In the context of liberal regimes, the rise of millions of fragmented chat rooms across the world tend instead to lead to the fragmentation of large but politically focused mass audiences into a huge number of isolated issue publics. Within established national public spheres, the online debates of web users only promote political communication, when news groups crystallize around the focal points of the quality press, for example, national newspapers and political magazines.

Compare this with Habermas' original, retrospective analysis of the formation of the public sphere. In it, he remarked that "the eighteenth century became the century of the letter" (Habermas, 1989/1962: 48). Not only did many more people begin writing letters and diaries, but these everyday cultural practices anticipated, in addition to the novel, public debate in a contemporary sense. In historical perspective, it seems far from clear that digital media and networked communication are destined to "fragment" or further refeudalize the public sphere. Nor, of course, is it a given that new networked forms of production and politics will necessarily "transform markets and freedom" (Benkler, 2006) for the better. In the last two chapters, I address the role of media and communication research in examining and assessing the emerging media environment.

part III

The double hermeneutics of media and communication research

Media of science

Doing communication research

7

Media of science

Doing communication research

Signs of science

It is a basic insight of communication studies since classical rhetoric that language and other signs and symbols lend shape to human knowledge. The form is (part of) the message of science, bearing witness to distinctive procedures and purposes of inquiry. The prototypical social-scientific journal article, for example, implies that research questions, their operationalization in empirical research designs, the resulting findings, and the subsequent interpretive discussion can and should be separated into stages of inquiry and sections of reporting. In comparison, the equivalent humanistic essay typically moves more freely across the various stages of collecting, analyzing, interpreting, and presenting evidence and arguments. The two publication formats can be seen to mimic two familiar communication models:[1]< social scientists 'transmit' their findings to the audience; humanistic scholars invite their readers into a 'ritual' of communal deliberation. The activity of research is itself a communicative practice[2] that is conducted and concluded through distinctive signs – verbal language, mathematical notations, graphical representations, and other meaningful units and processes. Also, scientific communication articulates purposes or knowledge interests[3]< (Habermas, 1971/1968), whether administrative or critical (Lazarsfeld, 1941). The signs of science bear witness to their social origins, contexts, and objectives.

Researchers process information about selected aspects of reality; they communicate among themselves about findings and insights; and they present the implications to larger communities – in government, business, civil society, and the public at large – who may make the conclusions real in their consequences. Research cannot *not* communicate and meta-communicate[4] – research institutions are constitutively related to the rest of society through communication and double hermeneutics[5]< (Giddens, 1979). At the intersection of arts and sciences, the field of media and communication research has had the mixed blessing of inheriting very different conceptions of information and interpretation. Its conflict of the faculties[6]< is especially noticeable when it comes to the choice of concrete analytical procedures. In this chapter, I argue that the diverse methodologies that constitute the field are different, but equal. While complementary, they are not reducible to each other, and they are to be unified, not in the first instance – at the level of minimal

1 > transmission and ritual models of communication, Chapter 3, p. 50

2 research as communicative practice

3 > knowledge interests, Chapter 8, p. 154

4 research cannot *not* communicate and meta-communicate

5 > double hermeneutics, Chapter 1, p. 11

6 > the conflict of the faculties, Chapter 3, p. 40

measurements – but in the final instance – in concluding the process of inquiry, in a context, and for a purpose.

I first review some of the main methods of empirical communication studies and their uses in research on media of the third degree. On the one hand, digital technologies present new opportunities and challenges, also as tools of analysis. On the other hand, new media, in many respects, invite old methods, as suggested by the interpersonal aspect of networked one-to-one as well as many-to-many communications. For illustration, I refer, in some instances, to classic studies of old media and genres. I, further, emphasize the distinction between methods – the concrete instruments for collecting and analyzing empirical data – and methodologies – the theoretically grounded research designs that motivate the selection of specific methods, and through which inferences can be made about the implications of a given set of findings. In the middle section, I return to the classic forms of inference – induction and deduction – and argue that a third form – abduction – though widely neglected in methods textbooks, has a special place in the research process. This is especially true for emerging phenomena such as the current media environment. In the last part of the chapter, I outline a realist position in the theory of science that accommodates multiple methodologies and forms of evidence. The signs of science are all partial and preliminary. As communicated within scientific and other communities, however, they enable individuals, institutions, and societies to deliberate before committing themselves to conclusions and acting accordingly.

New media, old methods

Methods and methodologies

Figure 7.1 lays out six basic kinds of evidence regarding media and communication, with examples from the internet in each cell. The various data types constitute vehicles of information about the contents, forms, and contexts of communication. First, verbal evidence is a mainstay of social-scientific and humanistic inquiry into society and culture. As noted common-sensically by Bower (1973: vi), "the best way to find out what the people think about something is to ask them" – although inferences from what people say, in either surveys or focus groups, to what they think, let alone what they may do, are fraught with methodological and epistemological difficulties. Second, human actions are meaningful, as recognized by social actors themselves and as interpreted by researchers observing them either in the field or the laboratory. Third, the records that individuals, organizations, and historical epochs leave behind, bear witness to what people once said, thought, and did. Historical sources, of course, amount to one-way communication. Luckily, several sources commonly lend themselves to comparison. Different media of research complement each other.

	Quantitative	**Qualitative**
Discourse / speech / writing	Survey interviewing (offline and online)	In-depth individual and focus-group interviewing (offline and online)
Behavior / action	Experiment (e.g., web usability studies)	Participating observation (e.g., digital ethnographies)
Texts / documents / artifacts	Content analysis (e.g., of political information resources and search engines as meta-information)	Discourse analysis; historical and aesthetic criticism (e.g., of 'netspeak' and digital artworks)

Figure 7.1 Basic methods in media and communication research

7 the 'how' of research depends on 'what' and 'why'

Methods handbooks, during recent decades, have underlined that the 'how' of research depends on the 'what' and the 'why':[7] the approach must fit the domain and the purpose of inquiry. This is in contrast to past calls for the application of a unitary "scientific method" (cited in Jankowski and Wester, 1991: 46). The difficulty remains how, specifically, to link theoretical conceptions of media and communication, and of the public issues they raise, with particular empirical instruments, data sets, and analytical procedures. Studies *about* networked communication do not entail a focus on samples or specimens *of* digital media and their uses in any simple technological, organizational, or demographic sense. In order to clarify some of the options and necessary choices in empirical research, Figure 7.2 lays out some basic levels of planning, conducting, documenting, and interpreting studies of (new) media (K. B. Jensen, 2002c: 258).

Each of the levels can be understood in terms of the discourses through which research is constituted as an intersubjective, communicative practice (illustrated, again, with reference to the internet):

● The *empirical objects of analysis* include discourses arising from or addressing the internet (from web sites and chat sequences, to policy documents and user test responses), but also discourses with different origins for comparative purposes. In order to understand what the internet is today, it is important to ask what it was once (thought to be), what it is not, and what it might become.

● *Data collection methods* – from content sampling frames to interview guides – delineate that small portion of reality from which inferences and interpretations must be made. I return below to the distinction between data that are 'found' (e.g., archives of internet debate fora), and those that are 'made' (e.g., interviews with their moderators), which has taken on new salience in digital media.

- *Data analysis methods* cover diverse operations of segmenting, categorizing, and interpreting evidence. In addition, empirical projects typically include forms of quality control:[8] meta-analytical components in the shape of statistical tests for significance and 'audit trails' (Lincoln and Guba, 1985) documenting the steps of qualitative inquiry.

- *Methodology* can be defined as a theoretically informed plan of action[9] in relation to a particular empirical domain. It is at this level that the status of the data that *methods* produce, and their relevance for interpreting or explaining 'the internet,' is explicated and justified. If methods are techniques, methodologies are technologies of research, mapping theories onto empirical domains.

- *Theoretical frameworks* lend meaning to a given configuration of empirical findings, linking a highly selective empirical microcosm with a conceptual macrocosm.[10] Theories can be thought of as frames,[11]< broadly speaking (Goffman, 1974; Lakoff and Johnson, 1980), which enable – afford[12]< (J. J. Gibson, 1979) – certain interpretations, while discouraging others. Is cyberspace (W. Gibson, 1984) (still) a helpful metaphor for grasping the nature of the internet?

- Whereas theoretical frameworks normally are concerned with particular substantive domains – nature, culture, society, the human psyche – such a partitioning of reality is supported by more general, meta-theoretical, or *epistemological* arguments and assumptions. In the practice of research, epistemology provides preliminary definitions and justifications of the 'what' and 'why' of empirical research, its object and purpose, so as to motivate the 'how.' In the perspective of contemporary communication theory, the internet is a medium.

8 meta-analytical quality control

9 methodology – a theoretically informed plan of action

10 empirical microcosm, theoretical macrocosm

11 >frames, Chapter 5, p. 95

12 >affordances, Chapter 4, pp. 74–77

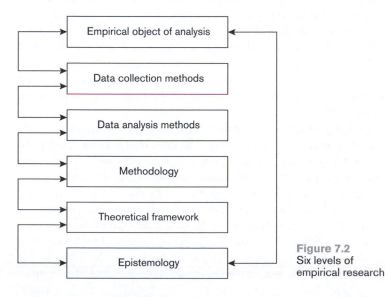

Figure 7.2
Six levels of empirical research

In this layered and comparative perspective, methods and methodologies are the two sides of the interface – Janus face – of research. Methods face our objects of analysis; methodologies spring from human subjectivity, which, far from being an eliminable source of noise, is a necessary condition and resource for scholarship, as disciplined through communication within research communities. Methods only yield insight in response to theoretically informed questions and plans to answer them. In order to discern appropriate methods and methodologies for digital media and communication studies, it is important to consider the new kinds of evidence that become available with meta-technologies.

Remediated methods

The issue of data regarding digital media highlights a common distinction between research evidence that is either 'found' or 'made.'[13] In one sense, all the evidence that is needed for internet studies is already there, documented in and of servers and clients, with a little help from network administrators, service providers, and user panels. In this sense, the system *is* the method. In another sense, hardly anything is documented in advance, given the radically dispersed and locally embedded nature of networked communications. Joining the two extremes of auto-generated and contextualized evidence poses one of the main methodological challenges for future media studies.

Returning to the six prototypical methods of Figure 7.1, the two lower cells – content analysis and discourse studies – have been coming back in style with the internet. A wealth of information lends itself to study as texts and documents, and additional meta-information or meta-data[14]< situates this information in relation to diverse contexts of communication: the origins of the information, its interrelations with other items, their interdependent trajectories, the users accessing the information and, perhaps, adding meta-information themselves, and so on. Not just the contents, but the forms and some of the contexts of communication, thus, become available and accessible for analysis, depending on formal conditions of access, ethical considerations, as well as the sociological imagination (Mills, 1959) of researchers anticipating information of interest to be auto-generated. Also for research, code is an enabling and constraining condition of what comes to be known and acted upon (Lessig, 2006).[15]

For other prototypical methods, as well, the line between what is made and what is found has been shifting. The most obvious case is digital or virtual ethnographies[16] (Hine, 2000), in which the archives of social network sites and virtual worlds present themselves as 'contents' and 'discourses' for analysis. In comparison with the written and, later, electronic records of anthropological fieldwork, such archives provide a measure of real-time details, still to be complemented by other sources of evidence. Digital media, further, give rise to natural experiments in organizations and subcultures,[17] akin to earlier studies of how, for instance, the introduction of television affected the lives of communities

13 data as found or made

14 > meta-data, Chapter 5, p. 93

15 code as a condition of research

16 digital ethnography

17 natural experiments

(Gunter, 2002: 226). For surveys as well as qualitative interviews (Mann and Stewart, 2000), digital media provide a research tool that complements, for instance, the (still common) telephone interview – and a sprawling repository of data on the public's lifestyle preferences and everyday activities. Amid legal and ethical concerns, data mining (Han and Kamber, 2006) has become another standard approach to examining what people say, think, and do in and around digital media.

The challenge of how to employ digitally remediated methods is matched, or trumped, by the challenge of how to document the interplay of online and offline interactions.[18] How do digital media users exercise their communicative agency in public as well as private contexts? In what ways do these practices serve to reproduce and readjust existing political, economic, and cultural institutions? And, to what extent do digital media either replace or complement other media as means of agency and instances of structure? Auto-generated evidence in computer systems is an instance of what Webb *et al.* (2000) had referred to, in 1966, as "unobtrusive measures," which avoid the direct elicitation of input from research subjects. Since then, the resurgence of qualitative approaches in social and cultural research (Denzin and Lincoln, 2005) has brought new attention to the relative merits of unobtrusive and naturalistic data. The everyday contexts of digital media use, evidently, lend themselves to both unobtrusive and naturalistic methods. The question is how to balance what evidence can be found, with what must be made, so as to make appropriate inferences about the place of new media in, mostly, old communicative practices.

18 online and offline interaction

Information and inference

The relationship between information, as articulated in signs and discourses, and inferences, as performed in human cognition and social interaction, has preoccupied classical logic, semiotics, cognitive theory, computer science, as well as communication theory. Standard accounts of the theory of science still tend to assume that research infers either from a general principle or law to individual instances (deduction), or from the examination of several instances to a law (induction). The relevance of each for the humanities and the social sciences as well as for interdisciplinary fields has been debated fiercely since the *Methodenstreit* of the late nineteenth century (for overview, see Pitt, 1988). A third form of inference – abduction – is rarely considered as an explicit model of scientific reasoning.[19] While Aristotle had identified abduction as a type (Blaikie, 1993; Hanson, 1958), it was reintroduced to modern philosophy by Charles Sanders Peirce in an 1878 article that related it to the other two types. His basic idea was that there are three components to an inference – a rule which, when applied to a single case, produces a conclusion or result. These components yield three possible combinations:

19 deduction, induction, abduction

DEDUCTION
Rule. All the beans from this bag are white.
Case. These beans are from this bag.
Result. These beans are white.

INDUCTION
Case. These beans are from this bag.
Result. These beans are white.
Rule. All the beans from this bag are white.

[ABDUCTION
Result. These beans are white.
Rule. All the beans from this bag are white.]
Case. These beans are from this bag.

(Peirce, 1986: 325–26)

Formally, only the deduction is a valid inference. Here, given the meaning of the constituent terms, the rule can be applied without any uncertainty to the case, so that the result follows as a matter of course. In the induction, the implication is that, if one examines a sufficient number of beans (cases), one may be willing to conclude that they are all white. Such reasoning appears commonsensical, and enters into both everyday life and research practice. The point of the abduction, finally, is that it introduces a rule that may explain why one encounters specific (more or less surprising) facts, such as white beans, in a particular context. The bean example is, of course, trivial. In other cases, the newly devised rule represents an exceptionally bright idea, as in Sherlock Holmes' solution of crime mysteries, which are feats of abduction (Sebeok and Umiker-Sebeok, 1983). Also, theory development depends crucially on abduction.

In practice, the three forms of inference are rarely found in any pure form in empirical studies. In fact, it can be argued that an aspect of each type is required to produce new understanding. Take the proto-typical social-scientific study of a particular attitude or behavior. Such studies depart from a relatively specific hypothesis that has been derived from more general premises of a sociological or psychological nature (deduction), and which can be tested against a large number of concrete instances – responses or observations (induction). The outcome of the data analysis is a pattern of findings that may be only partly in accordance with the hypothesis, likely giving rise to the formulation of a new rule (abduction) to be investigated in further research. The original premise of the study, equally, might have been the outcome of a (more or less) bright idea – abduction. One advantage of such a combinatorial under-standing of scientific inferences is that it leaves open the question of whether, or to what extent, research projects in fact conform to the received models of either logic or methods textbooks. Studies of scientific practice suggest that they do not (e.g., Hacking, 1983; Latour, 1987). Another advantage is that this understanding of inference invites an open-ended consideration of which combinations may best account for new domains and issues of research. All three forms of inference are part of the heritage of media and communication studies.

An inductive heritage

Induction is a heritage both of the history of science and of human evolution. The human capacity for abstracting and generalizing from single events has been a key factor in natural selection and social formations and, hence, an instrument of adaptation and survival (Megarry, 1995). The lay theories[20]< (Furnham, 1988) that guide us all through the day hold important ingredients of induction. In scholarship, induction has represented a central problem for philosophers and empirical researchers alike since the Enlightenment. Whereas David Hume had noted, in the mid-1700s, that an induction from 'some' to 'all' can never, strictly speaking, be logically valid (Hume, 2006/1748), the inductive approach remained attractive throughout the nineteenth century, as elaborated, for example, in John Stuart Mill's influential *A System of Logic* (Mill, 1973–74/1843). In the twentieth century, an inductive ideal of science rose to new prominence, and then fell definitively, in the shape of logical positivism.[21]

Taking its cue from Mill's contemporary, Auguste Comte, and his call for a 'positive philosophy' that would be non-speculative and applicable to real human concerns, logical positivism developed into an influential school of thought between the two world wars of the twentieth century. A key inspiration was the linguistic, formal turn of philosophy,[22]< assuming a correspondence between the structure of propositions and the structure of facts in reality. An additional premise of logical positivism was an absolute distinction not only between facts and values, but also between empirical observations and theoretical conceptions of reality. Any meaningful statement about the world would be either elementary in itself (reducible to sense impressions in a given space and time), or decomposable into such elementary propositions. Within such a reductionist understanding of human knowledge, most topics of social-scientific and humanistic research fell outside the realm of science.

As explicit epistemological programs, both positivism and inductivism generally are positions of the past. In the practice of research, however, induction still plays a central and frequently unacknowledged role, also within media and communication research. Most important, this applies to the mass of descriptive, applied, and administrative studies that inform and support the daily operation of the media sector – which is probably the majority of all studies in the area, published and unpublished. Among the main examples are continuous market research on digital, broadcast, and print audiences, and evaluation research (Patton, 1990) informing the financing of media and supporting government policy decisions. Whereas the aim normally is not to develop or test particular theories, the findings are commonly taken to offer solid accounts of the infrastructures and uses of media, and are widely reported and debated

20 > lay theories, Chapter 8, p. 150

21 logical positivism

22 > the linguistic turn, Chapter 2, pp. 35–37

as such in both specialized and mass media. Commercial companies and state agencies base significant investments and legislation on the resulting information, inferences, and recommendations. To specify the status of this kind of research, Wober (1981), for one, called for a distinction between audience 'research' with an explanatory or interpretive ambi-

23 research and/vs. measurement

tion, and audience 'measurement' that provides baseline figures.[23]

The current media environment is ripe with research reports on new computer and mobile applications, their attractions for users, and their relationship with other social and cultural trends. News items, feature articles, and lifestyle programs depend on such reports to cover who does (will do) what with which new devices and services, in a multistep flow of double hermeneutics; the reports anticipate actions by corporations, political decision-makers, as well as ordinary users. The introduction of the 'personal computer' during the 1970–80s according to a principle of 'one person, one computer' entailed a particular social construction of this new meta-medium (K. B. Jensen, 1993). The point here is neither deceptive advertising nor coopted research (although both exist), but rather that human knowledge – information, inferences, and their presentation to others in communication – is necessarily interested (Habermas, 1971/1968). One task of research is to make explicit the implicit theories of media that not only senders and receivers, but also researchers themselves hold.

A deductive mainstream

The quantitative mainstream of international communication research, as applied for half a century to different media, is normally described as

24 hypothetico-deductive research

'hypothetico-deductive.'[24] Studies propose to test hypotheses that have been deduced from some general 'law.' In a first step, deduction ensures that a hypothesis is neither logically inconsistent nor tautological – which would make it irrelevant for empirical inquiry. If, next, a hypothesis can be seen to contradict or, more likely, specify an accepted law, it calls for further inquiry. It is deduction (from 'all' to 'some') that serves to predict what a study will find under specified circumstances. If, finally, the findings correspond to the predictions, the hypothesis is confirmed, and may be admitted into a body of accepted and accumulated theories in the field.

Importantly, confirmation does not equal 'verification' in the stronger sense of logical positivism. The hypothetico-deductive position, as associated above all with Karl Popper (1972b/1934), instead assumes that scientists must seek to falsify their hypotheses. Only if falsification fails,

25 falsificationism

is one justified in still holding the hypothesis, and only preliminarily.[25] Further studies, by oneself or by the research community, may end up falsifying it after all (which, in effect, admits inductivism through the back door in a multistep process). What might appear as philosophical hair-splitting, nevertheless, has important consequences for what constitutes an accepted body of knowledge and for the research procedures supporting it. Most media and communication studies cannot unequivocally falsify or verify a given hypothesis. Instead, hypothetico-deductive research in this field is backed by measures of statistical probability:[26] the 'laws' in question are ascertained in a stochastic rather than a determinist sense (Hempel and Oppenheim, 1988/1948: 13–18).

26 probabilism

But, where do hypotheses come from? Popper (1963) suggested that they constitute bold conjectures, though he offered little systematic or historical specification of how they emerge. At least in the social sciences and humanities, hypotheses are, in part, a product of their times, of double hermeneutics. In a negative aspect, this may result in what Marshall McLuhan dubbed rearviewmirrorism: the tendency to define new media and communicative practices in terms of the old, thus cutting short their potentials and perspectives (McLuhan, 1964; Theall, 1971). In a positive aspect, focused comparisons of present, delimited issues, as practiced by hypothetico-deductive research, is one necessary ingredient of theory development for the future, as exemplified by one of the classics of audience research.

MEDIA AS AGENDA-SETTERS

One early insight of the field – that the media do not tell people *what* to think, but may nevertheless suggest to them what to think *about* (B. Cohen, 1963; Trenaman and McQuail, 1961) – was given conceptual and empirical substance by McCombs and Shaw (1972: 176) in a study of political communication: "although the evidence that mass media deeply change attitudes in a campaign is far from conclusive, the evidence is much stronger that voters learn from the immense quantity of information available during each campaign." The authors, first, deduced a conceptual distinction between 'attitudes' and 'agendas,' and, next, operationalized this distinction in a comparison of news contents and voter statements. Their hypothesis stated that, "the mass media set the agenda for each political campaign, influencing the salience of attitudes toward the political issues." To test this hypothesis, the study matched "what . . . voters *said* were key issues of the campaign with the *actual content* of the mass media used by them during the campaign" (p. 177). To specify the test conditions, only voters who were undecided on who to vote for in the 1968 US presidential campaign, and hence might be more open to campaign information, were recruited as interviewees. In addition, these respondents were sampled randomly from lists of registered voters in a particular local community in North Carolina so as to limit other sources of variation, for example, regional differences in media coverage. (Following a pretest, major national sources such as television network news, *The New York Times*, *Time*, and *Newsweek* were also included in the content sample.)

The concrete empirical evidence consisted in respondents' answers regarding "major problems as they saw them" (p. 178) and news as well as editorial comments during a specified period, overlapping with the interview period. Each of these data sets was coded into predefined categories concerning political issues and other aspects of an electoral campaign. In sum, the analytical categories amounted to a mapping of conceptually deduced distinctions onto instances of political information, as offered by media and taken by some voters, to some extent.

Two findings, in particular, illustrate the hypothetico-deductive logic. First, the design aimed to establish causality, and found that the media had "exerted a considerable impact" (p. 180) on the respondents' perceptions of the political issues presented by the media. The coding of content had distinguished between 'major' and 'minor' coverage of topics, and in both instances, the analysis found strong correlations between media emphases and voters' judgments (+.967 and +.979).

Second, in order to determine whether voters might be attending to, and reproducing, the agenda that their preferred candidates advanced in the media, a further analysis was made of those respondents who had a preference for one candidate (without being finally committed). Both for major and minor issues, the findings suggested that "the voters attend reasonably well to *all* the news, *regardless* of which candidate or party issue is stressed" (p. 182). The fact that "the judgments of voters seem to reflect the *composite* of the mass media coverage" (p. 181), again lent support to the hypothesis that agenda-setting may be a general consequence of media use, at least in the political domain.

In their discussion of findings, McCombs and Shaw (1972) were concerned, again, to qualify their conclusions regarding the original hypothesis, acknowledging that the correlations did not *prove* the hypothesis. However, "the evidence is in line with the conditions that must exist if agenda-setting by the mass media does occur" (p. 184). Put differently, their carefully deduced design failed to falsify the hypothesis. The agenda-setting hypothesis, then, presents itself as a more justified alternative than, for example, theories concerning selective perception (Festinger, 1957; Klapper, 1960), which would have been supported if voters had been found to attend especially to their preferred candidates.

A more general lesson is that the weighing of competing hypotheses takes place at the theoretical level (see Figure 7.2), not at the level of measurements, correlations, or other analytical procedures. Whereas the correlations between media coverage and voter judgments were indicative of interdependence or causality, the specific nature of this causation must be accounted for within a conceptual framework. Compared with the relatively familiar terrain of national political issues, and with the delimited set of print and broadcast media that McCombs and Shaw (1972) selected from, digital media complicate the question of how public agendas are to be defined and understood, and how they may be set. As suggested in Chapter 6, networked media contribute to shifting boundaries between political and cultural public issues;[27]< as noted in Chapter 4, networked media promote the multistep flow of communication across media.[28]< While digital media, thus, pose new issues of how to collect, analyze, and interpret empirical evidence, the main current challenge may be how to conceive the communicative practices that they enable. It is status and origin of different conceptions of communication that the third form of inference – abduction – brings to the fore.

27 > shifting boundaries of political and cultural public spheres, Chapter 6, pp. 114–117

28 > multi-step flow of communication, Chapter 4, pp. 71–74

An abductive substream

Abduction is at once a general aspect of theory development and a specific ingredient of qualitative research practice.[29] Since Peirce's original statement, the relevance of abduction has occasionally been considered in both philosophy and other disciplines, including mainstream sociology (Merton, 1968: 158). It was reintroduced to interdisciplinary theory of science by, among others, Hanson (1958) as part of the post-1945 questioning of inductive as well as hypothetico-deductive prototypes of research. In direct opposition to Hempel and Oppenheim's (1988/1948) "covering-law model," Dray (1957) specified how historical events cannot be examined as a variant of natural events (which may all be 'covered' by one law), but require various other types of "rational explanation." In another influential contribution, Danto (1965) suggested that narratives provide a model for understanding, and for empirically studying, historical events and human actions. Ginzburg (1989) identified an "evidential paradigm" in which, for example, Sigmund Freud and Sherlock Holmes were able to identify underlying or deep structures, in dreams and crimes respectively. More recently, abduction has been characterized in research methodology as an alternative to the inductivist self-understanding of grounded theory (Alvesson and Sköldberg, 2000), as a strategy of interpretive social science (Blaikie, 1993), and as one characteristic of qualitative media research (K. B. Jensen, 1995).

29 abduction – theory development and qualitative research

READING AS COMMUNICATIVE PRACTICE

Why do people use various media and genres in the first place? What, for instance, does it mean to read popular fiction, as far as the readers are concerned? And, how can the act of reading be conceptualized and studied? The distinction between the native's internal perspective and the analyst's external perspective, and the effort of research at bridging the two – what anthropology and communication studies have referred as a balance between 'emic' and 'etic' approaches to culture and communication[30] (Pike, 1967) – was illustrated in Janice Radway's (1984) classic study of women's romance reading.

30 emic and etic approaches to communication

Appearing at a time when popular culture was being revaluated in empirical reception studies for its real significance and use value,[31]< the study probed the motivations of readers or users. Through audience ethnography as well as in-depth textual analysis, it served, for instance, to differentiate a blanket term such as 'escape' into additional categories of relaxation and time for self-indulgence. Radway summed up one attraction of romance reading in her conclusion that "it creates a time or space within which a woman can be entirely on her own, preoccupied with her personal needs, desires, and pleasure" (p. 61). A central implication was a shift of emphasis, from romances as texts that offer a more or less escapist universe for the reader's identification and gratification, toward an understanding of the very activity of reading as a social practice[32] that enables readers to position themselves within, but also outside everyday life. The act of reading enables the reader to

31 > revaluation of popular culture, Chapter 6, p. 106

32 reading as social practice

33 > time-in and time-
     out culture,
     Chapter 6, p. 107

traverse time-in and time-out culture.[33]< Media discourses are not only representations of alternative possible worlds, but resources in an actual world of practice.

Radway's research strategy might be taken as induction: the categories emerged from – were 'found' – in the field. It is more appropriate, however, to describe them as the outcome of communication: an interactive sequence aligning the informants' and the researcher's perspectives. By introducing concepts or rules that would make the informants' statements meaningful, the researcher was able to account for their experience, not only of the romantic narratives, but also of the social practice of reading. Here, first, is Radway's recapitulation of this main finding:

> In summary, when the act of romance reading is viewed as it is by the readers themselves, from within a belief system that accepts as given the institutions of heterosexuality and monogamous marriage, it can be conceived as an activity of mild protest and longing for reform necessitated by those institutions' failure to satisfy the emotional needs of women. Reading therefore functions for them as an act of recognition and contestation whereby that failure is first admitted and then partially reversed. Hence, the Smithton readers' claim that romance reading is a "declaration of independence" and a way to say to others, "This is my time, my space. Now leave me alone."
>
> (Radway, 1984: 213)

Next, the central and somewhat surprising notion, that romance reading is a "declaration of independence," can be explicated in the form of an abduction:

- Romance reading is a declaration of independence.
- All uses of texts by readers to claim their own time are declarations of independence.
- Conclusion: Romance reading is a use of texts by readers for claiming their own time.

Whereas the first premise registers a puzzling fact from within the universe of romance readers (puzzling to the extent that the romance genre tends to represent women in dependent roles), the second premise introduces the conception or rule that texts are resources in the readers' everyday lives. At the same time, the second premise can be seen to sum up a research process that had gradually articulated – abduced – a conception of the romance genre and of the act of reading in an iterative process.

Radway's informants produced new insight, not only for research, but presumably also for themselves as they verbalized their conceptions, perhaps for the first time. Abduction (like induction, unlike deduction)

is a common aspect of both everyday and scientific reasoning.[34] Umberto
Eco (1984) has suggested a wider typology of abduction:

34 abduction in
everyday
reasoning

- *Overcoded* abduction is a basic form of comprehension that works semi-automatically. "When someone utters /man/, I must first assume that this utterance is the token of a type of English word" (Eco, 1984: 41). No complex inference is needed to establish the fact that people speak different languages, and that English is the appropriate choice in context.
- In performing an *undercoded* abduction, however, one must choose between several possible interpretations of a word or statement. In Eco's words, "when one utters /this is a man/, we have to decide whether one says that this is a rational animal, a mortal creature, or a good example of virility, and so on" (p. 42).
- *Creative* abduction, finally, occurs when the very rule of interpretation has to be invented for the specific purpose, for example, in the case of poetic language, as found in poetry, jokes, and advertising. In science, Darwin's interpretation of humans as one animal within the evolutionary chain was an (unusually) creative abduction.

By recognizing abduction as an innovative component of diverse traditions of inquiry, and by relating it to deduction and induction, research is in a better position to consider the potential combination of various forms of inference for different purposes of communication study. The hypotheses of quantitative projects can be understood as the outcome of undercoded abductions that articulate new configurations of explanatory concepts from earlier studies. Qualitative projects, in comparison, perform sequences or, perhaps, networks of undercoded abductions which, ideally, accumulate as a consolidated interpretive framework. In qualitative as well as quantitative methodologies, overcoded abduction enters into the administration of already familiar analytical categories and procedures. Creative abduction, last, is the kind of unusual event and scarce resource that all traditions may hope to produce at least once in a while: the operationalization of an innovative hypothesis (agenda-setting) and the explorative establishment of an unrecognized meaning of media use (reading the romance).

Media and communication research needs all the inferences it can devise in order to understand the present digital media environment. Inductive monitoring of technologies, institutions, and users by commercial as well as public agencies provides indispensable baseline information. Hypothetico-deductive studies contribute focused comparisons of established and emerging media. Abductive research probes definitions and delimitations of what constitutes new and old media, genres, communicative practices, and contexts of use, simultaneously from the perspective of native users and researchers. In each case, studies seek to arrive at conclusions that will be accepted – in some sense, by some audience, and for some purpose – as general.

Case study: generalizing about generalization

Different disciplines and research traditions will disagree, fundamentally and vehemently, about what constitutes general knowledge. How does one generalize about generalization?

As a point of departure, it is instructive to compare the various kinds of 'quality control' that research projects undertake to support their primary analytical operations. Quality control documents and assesses findings according to scientific community standards, and makes both findings and standards accessible for collegial, public scrutiny. The concepts of validity and reliability have given rise to the most elaborate measures and procedures within quantitative research (Gunter, 2002). (Qualitative researchers have proposed alternative terminologies that would recognize the processual and con-textual nature of qualitative inquiry, for instance, trustworthiness, credibility, dependability, transferability, and confirmability (Lincoln and Guba, 1985); the terminology of validity and reliability, however, mostly stands.) In brief, reliability[35] addresses the consistency of descriptions and interpretations over time, typically in the form of repeated measurements. In the example from agenda-setting research above (McCombs and Shaw, 1972), the inter-subjective agreement of coders was expressed in a measure of intercoder reliability. Validity, next, addresses the extent to which a research instrument measures what it was intended or is claimed to measure. A further distinction is made between internal validity (evaluating the consistency of the concepts and procedures being applied) and external validity (assessing whether the findings from one context generalize to other contexts or populations).[36] In the agenda-setting example, both the conception of 'agenda' and the relationship between the community studied and the wider electorate were considered.

Validity and reliability have traditionally been expressed as summary measures in mathematical notations. In comparison, qualitative research has called for a more continuous and contextual assessment of both the research process and its outcome – validation rather than, or in addition to, measures of validity[37] (e.g., Kvale, 1996). Figure 7.3 outlines a model in which to address this balance. Reliability, first of all, can be said to concern the inter-subjective component of research generally. Intersubjectivity is established not only by comparing minimal measurements in the early stages of a study, but also by examining emerging findings, forms of documentation, and issues of interpretation. To exemplify, whereas two independent coders categorizing the same data set is standard procedure in quantitative research, intercoder reliability can also be ensured by, for example, consensual coding (e.g., Neuman *et al.*, 1992). Moreover, informants contribute to reliability, through several waves of interviewing, and by 'member checks,'[38] as employed in Radway's (1984) study of romance reading. Also, after the conclusion of the research process proper, reliability remains an issue. The collegial discussion of findings, the reanalysis of data, and the social uses of both single studies and research programs all converge on very practical questions: 'how certain can we be? – in order to do what?'

35 reliability

36 validity – internal and external

37 validation and/vs. validity measures

38 member checks

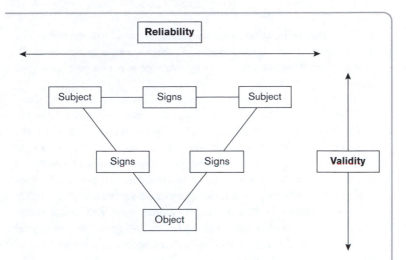

Figure 7.3 Dimensions of validity and reliability

Validity, equally, pertains to wider issues of the social uses of research. Compared with quantitative measures of validity, qualitative studies typically emphasize the internal validity of their categories in context, whereas an assessment of external validity must refer to additional cases, larger samples, or multimethod designs. These different notions of validity relate to two distinctive concepts of 'generalization' (e.g., Yin, 2003).[39] *Empirical* or statistical generalization refers to the capacity of quantitative methodologies to apply predefined (hypothetically deduced) categories to a representative set of empirical instances, thus supporting external validity. *Theoretical* or analytical generalization refers to the articulation (abduction) of new concepts or categories that conceive empirical instances in a more consistent or insightful manner, thus giving priority to internal validity.

The difficulty of distinguishing between, yet recognizing both aspects of generalization is illustrated by debates over the concept of probability. More or less probable claims can be considered more or less general. In a historical analysis, the philosopher, Ian Hacking (1975), concluded that 'probability' gradually acquired an ambiguous meaning in modern philosophy and empirical sciences. Two distinct meanings were conflated:[40]

- *Stochastic* probability has to do with stable relative frequencies, as established by statistical procedures. Here, the purpose is to rule out, beyond a reasonable doubt, that the particular configuration of empirical findings could have occurred by chance fluctuations or random error (the so-called null hypothesis).
- *Epistemological* probability, in comparison, concerns "the degree of belief warranted by evidence" (Hacking, 1975: 1). Here, the concept of probability refers to human knowledge of events and to underlying mechanisms to which the measures and frequencies bear witness.

39 empirical and/vs. theoretical generalization

40 stochastic and/vs. epistemological probability

The implication of the distinction is sometimes summed up in the dictum that 'correlation does not equal causation.' In other words, statistical measurements do not in themselves warrant conclusions about causality and other types of interdependence.

Relating Hacking's (1975) historical analysis to contemporary communication studies, Ritchie (1999) suggested that much empirical media research has failed on this crucial point. The slippage occurs when "the statistical probabilities associated with the null hypothesis are . . . used to support inferences about the epistemological probabilities of a preferred interpretation" (p. 7). Put differently, the fact that the null hypothesis,[41] which assumes random findings, is sufficiently improbable (statistically) is mistaken for evidence that a specific alternative hypothesis, namely, the one deduced at the outset of a study, is (more) probable (epistemologically). The logic of hypothesis testing, thus, may invite a confounding of two separate levels of scientific analysis and argument.

In sum, Figure 7.3 conceives research as a communicative practice that depends on 'signs' – research instruments, analytical procedures, means of documentation – which enable researchers as 'subjects' to engage their 'objects' of analysis according to specified procedures and explicated purposes. Signs make reality researchable and communicable.[42] In media and communication studies, the objects of analysis include subjects who contribute interpretations of themselves, their media, and their communicative practices. In George Herbert Mead's (1934) terms, researchers and their informants, at least for a moment, become 'significant others' for one another in communication.[43] As a social practice, research serves to recontextualize this communication as part of, and with a view to, other contexts and purposes. General findings constitute information that, once communicated about, individuals, institutions, and entire societies may be prepared to act upon. Empirically as well as theoretically general findings can be real in their consequences.

41 null hypothesis

42 signs make reality researchable and communicable

43 researchers and informants as significant others

Unification in the final instance

Realism has become an increasingly influential position in recent theory of science. Pavitt (1999), for one, suggested, not only that it is the dominant position across different fields of study, but also that it informs the practice of much current media and communication research. As noted in his overview, two prototypical positions of 'logical empiricism' (from logical positivism through Karl Popper) and constructivist 'perspectivism' (from Thomas Kuhn's (1970) account of conflicting paradigms, to poststructuralism and beyond) have sometimes been perceived as absolute opposites, or as the two horns of an unresolvable dilemma. Kuhn himself was less categorical about the incommensurability of paradigms than sometimes appears from textbooks; in his later work, he examined the potentials for translating between and 'learning' several 'languages' of research (Conant and Haugeland, 2000). Realism presents itself as a third framework[44]< accommodating multiple types of evidence and inference, interpretation and explanation, as suggested by several recent reference works in the media and communication field (Deacon *et al.*, 2007; K. B. Jensen, 2002e; Schrøder *et al.*, 2003). New, digital media comprise diverse domains and levels of reality that research must be equipped to match.

44 > a third way, Chapter 8, pp. 163–165

Whereas different variants of a contemporary realist position have appeared under headings of scientific, transcendental, or critical realism (see further Archer *et al.*, 1998), the implications for media and communication research can be laid out with reference especially to the early work of Roy Bhaskar (1979) (who later turned to metaphysical and political concerns). His critical realism[45] departs from three main premises:

45 critical realism

- *Ontological realism.* Rejecting skepticist and nominalist positions, which have held, variously, that no certain human knowledge of reality is possible, or that reality is nothing but the sum of our descriptions of it, realism reverses the burden of proof. Reiterating Peirce's point contra Descartes,[46]< namely, that doubts about any and all aspects of reality must be justified, realism approaches reality as a limit condition or regulatory ideal – what we must assume in order to account for the diverse natural and cultural phenomena that manifest themselves to the individual, and which we share in communication, in science as well as in everyday interaction. The proof of reality is in our interactions with and interventions into it (Hacking, 1983).

46 > Peirce vs. Descartes, Chapter 2, p. 32

- *Epistemological relativism.* From a moderately constructivist position, realism assumes that knowledge of nature, culture, as well as other minds depends on sequences of perceptions, cognitions, and inferences, all of which may be questioned, rejected, or revised – communicated about – for any number of reasons. Relativism does not entail that "anything goes" (Feyerabend, 1975), but rather that several things may go together in unexpected ways according to rational judgments.
- *Judgmental rationality.* Like other social practices, science depends on the exercise of rationality which, at some point, must end in (fallible) judgments and conclusions about what to do next. In the meantime, the business of individual scholars and scientific communities is to compare and contrast alternative accounts of reality with reference to as wide a range of means of representing, interpreting, and intervening into it as theoretically and practically possible.

Considering the classic issue of how human subjects relate to their objects of inquiry, Bhaskar questioned a certain persistent and presumptuous 'anthropocentrism' in philosophy and theory of science:

47 > the Copernican
turn, Chapter 2,
p. 25

48 > logical
positivism, p. 133

"Copernicus argued that the universe does not revolve around man. And yet in philosophy we still represent things as if it did"[47]< (cited in Archer *et al.*, 1998: 45). Logical positivism,[48]< for one, proposed to reduce reality, as legitimately studied by science, to what is immediately accessible to the human senses. Realism, instead, allows for a diversified reality of entities, events, and emergents – which may, or may not, prove accessible to humans through information and inference, immediately or by media still to be imagined or invented. With one of Bhaskar's key terms, reality is, in grammatical terms, 'intransitive': it does not take – does not need – an object (that is, paradoxically, a human subject). Material reality, such as optical fibers, does not communicate to or with us, but is made transitive by humans in and for communication. Reality, further, is 'transfactual': facts of several kinds exist – fiber optics, private email exchanges, and the internet as a global institution. And, reality is 'stratified': fibers, emails, and the internet are not reducible to each other, nor do they constitute separate realities.[49] A differentiated and distributed reality calls for an appropriately diversified set of methodologies.

49 intransitive,
transfactual, and
stratified reality

In methodological terms, critical realism involves a distinction between three domains of reality (Bhaskar, 1979) (Figure 7.4):

- The *empirical* domain is the source of concrete evidence – *experience* of the world. By describing and documenting, for example, the concrete verbal expressions and images by which Facebook users present themselves to family, friends, acquaintances, and anonymous visitors, media studies procure a necessary, though far from sufficient condition for interpreting and explaining many-to-many communications.
- The *actual* status of this information is matter of inference. It is by characterizing and conceptualizing empirical materials as evidence of particular *events* (e.g., formal birthday greetings or flirting via Facebook) that one may infer their status as instances of particular social practices.
- The domain of the *real* is more inclusive than either the empirical or the actual. Research seeks to establish, for example, psychological and sociological *mechanisms* of a 'general' nature – in some sense of the word[50]< – that may account for the events in question (e.g., cultural conventions, as compared with new technological potentials, as shapers of specific communicative practices on Facebook).

50 > generalization,
pp. 140–142

In sum, experiences, events, and mechanisms are all real. Experiences may seem to 'push' themselves upon researchers as evidence of events. One task of scholarship is to mount a countervailing 'pull' – to infer underlying mechanisms through a great deal of methodological and theoretical labor.

The three-domain framework is common to Peirce's pragmatism, to Popper's three worlds,[51]< and to Bhaskar's realism; their legacies and complementarities remain open to further theory development and debate (e.g., Archer, 2003; Bertilsson, 2004; Nellhaus, 1998). I take the

51 > Popper's three
worlds, Chapter 3,
p. 52

	The real	**The actual**	**The empirical**
Experiences	x	x	x
Events	x	x	
Mechanisms	x		

Figure 7.4 Three domains of reality, incorporating three types of phenomena

framework as a fertile ground on which to redevelop different traditions contributing to communication research at a time of transition in the real world of communicative practices. Articulated since Aristotle as a differentiated and distributed conception of what is,[52]< realism accommodates diverse levels at which media and communicative practices take shape. In Chapter 4, I introduced a premise of determination in the first instance.[53]< In an ontological sense,[54]< communication is enabled and constrained by several conditions – technological, discursive, and institutional – that determine what *cannot* be the case, but which, equally, cannot predict specifically what will be the case. In an epistemological sense, this chapter has outlined a principle of unification in the final instance:[55] different methodologies pose and answer different questions, sometimes for a common purpose.

Realism, like pragmatism, is an epistemology without guarantees. At the same time, both avoid the sort of skeptical perspectives on reality that are implied by the other two prototypical positions that Pavitt (1999) identified: logical empiricism and constructivist perspectivism. On the one hand, logical positivism depicted a reality which, tragically, is forever out of human reach. On the other hand, not least poststructuralist versions of constructivism have celebrated a comic view of the absence of any foundations of human knowledge (Baudrillard, 1988). What communication research in a realist and pragmatist vein can offer are explanatory concepts, analytical procedures, and preliminary conclusions as one basis of public deliberation about media, old and new. This chapter has addressed methodologies for the study of new, digital media as they currently exist. In the next and final chapter, I turn to some political agendas and normative issues for the future which, again, have invited both tragic and comic styles of reasoning.

52 > Aristotle's realism, Chapter 2, p. 23

53 > determination in the first instance, Chapter 4, p. 62

54 > ontology, Chapter 2, p. 25

55 unification in the final instance

The future of communication   8

Pragmatism between modernism and postmodernism

The future of communication

Pragmatism between modernism and postmodernism

"Nothing is as practical as a good theory"

This motto, offered by one of the founders of communication research in the United States, Kurt Lewin (1945: 129), suggests a classic conflict. On the one hand, researchers are frequently, and sometimes deservedly, perceived as detached from the world of practical affairs. On the other hand, policy makers, commercial entrepreneurs, and public interest groups will request answers to questions that have not yet been – and perhaps cannot be – stated in researchable terms. Communication theory might be expected to contribute to better communication in practice and, yet, the field is rarely in a position to simply resolve the normative issues that it helps to raise.

1 pragmatism – a good, practical theory

Pragmatism is a good, practical theory.[1] Like other theories, it does not translate directly into applied research projects on next-generation media. Nor does pragmatism provide a set of guidelines for better communication in either public or private settings. What pragmatism offers is a robust interdisciplinary framework for describing and debating both actual and potential forms of media and communication at a time of technological and social transition. The pragmatist tradition has made it its business to address the theory–practice divide as a communicative issue. As such, it presents a roadmap for media and communication studies, their potential social uses and implications. In the last chapter, I reviewed the forms of evidence, analysis, and inference that the field has to offer. In this final chapter, I take up some of the political and ethical questions that communication raises, and that joins media and communication research to other fields of theory and practice.

2 'theory' – the very idea

The first part of the chapter briefly unpacks the very idea of 'theory.'[2] Though mostly associated with general, abstract, and explicit frameworks of interpretation and explanation in science and scholarship, theories can be specific, concrete, and implicit ingredients of other social practices, as well. It is the origin of both scientific and other types of theory in human practice that philosophical pragmatism foregrounds. Taking stock, I devote the main portion of this chapter to two distinctive and influential variants of the pragmatist tradition, one modernist in orientation, the other postmodernist. I compare and contrast Jürgen Habermas' theory of communicative action (Habermas, 1984/1981;

1987b/1981) as an instance of modernist pragmatism with Richard Rorty's "postmodernist bourgeois liberalism" (Rorty, 1991b: 197). Critiquing and criticizing[3]< both, I note their equally un-pragmatist position regarding the end of communication – the differences that make a difference, the ideas that are real in their consequences, and the transformation of beliefs into actions. Communication ends; there is no lasting comfort in communication. As an illustration, I reexamine the 2006 cartoon controversy that brought into sharp focus the dilemmas of communication in a culturally diverse and increasingly networked world.

In conclusion, I characterize pragmatism as a third way for media studies – between modernism and postmodernism, and between deterministic and relativist conceptions of communication and community. If media are institutions-to-think-with,[4]< research is a second-order institution-to-think-with,[5] feeding findings and interpretations back to society – to media professionals, regulators, educators, as well as ordinary media users – in double hermeneutics. The field has a distinctive, if delimited role to play in the reproduction and reformation of contemporary society. Media research participates in brief moments of communication concerning the future.

3 > critique and/vs. criticism, Chapter 1, p. 13

4 > institutions-to-think-with, Chapter 6, p. 104

5 second-order institutions-to-think-with

Theories in practice

In his classic textbook, Denis McQuail (2005) listed five types of theory regarding media and communication:

- *Scientific* theory is the most common understanding of 'theory,' covering general explanatory concepts and models that apply to a variety of empirical instances, as associated particularly with (natural-scientific and) social-scientific research traditions, experimental and quantitative methodologies;
- *Cultural* theory is the legacy of arts and humanities, relying on textual, historical, and other qualitative approaches to account for human interpretations and social uses of different media and communicative practices;
- *Normative* theories address the legitimate ends and means of organizing the resources of communication as a social infrastructure, thus feeding into policy, planning, and public debate;
- *Operational* theory represents rules of thumb and tacit knowledge among media practitioners, including their professional and ethical standards and the audiences that they imagine for themselves;
- *Everyday* theory, finally, informs the common practice of communication – our interaction with media institutions and with each other as citizens, consumers, and sources of information in our own right.

Academic communication theories are neither necessary nor sufficient conditions of communication practice – even if they enable sustained reflection on the status of, and the interrelations between, everyday, operational, normative, and academic theories. The list is itself an illustration of the grounding of theories in practice. It emerged ad hoc, not as "a systematic, empirically grounded typology . . . It developed gradually as a way of describing what I was doing and accounting for different ways of thinking about mass media" (personal email communication, March 20, 2007). Of particular interest to the author in preparing the first edition (McQuail, 1983) was the inclusion of everyday or commonsense notions as a kind of theory. Lay theories[6] (Furnham, 1988) are indispensable resources of everyday life. The academic definition of what may count as (scientific) theories is itself contingent. In the latest, fifth edition of the textbook (McQuail, 2005), the original fourfold classification had become fivefold, acknowledging cultural theory alongside (social) scientific theory. While rooted in social science himself, McQuail now recognized the two "as having more or less equal weight. I suppose this does reflect an obvious development and greater integration of the 'field.'"

6 lay theories

The common denominator of the five types of theory is that they enable action – in media research, production, policy, education, public debate, and more. The exchange between the five types is of particular interest in a field which has developed, to a significant extent, as a practical discipline that sees itself as solving communication problems.[7]< As such, communication research has the opportunity to affect both journalism and other media production (operational theory) and education for media literacy in schools and among the public at large (lay theory). Normative conceptions of communication, however, occupy a special place at the juncture of theory and practice. Like academic theories, they are general. They pass judgment on the pros and cons of different ways of administering media institutions and communicative practices. Unlike academic theories, normative theories of media invite the involvement of the general public – anyone as someone.[8]< Whereas normative theories within communication study have traditionally addressed entire media systems (Nerone, 1995; Siebert *et al.*, 1956) – a commercial free press, a publicly funded broadcasting system, or an open-architecture internet – they, further, bring up the profoundly ideological and existential implications of communication: the meaning of communication, as in 'the meaning of life' (K. B. Jensen, 2008: 2803). Such questions break the scale from otherwise grand theories via middle-range theory (Merton, 1968: 39) to narrowly focused theories of empirical research. They are the questions concerning communication that most people care most deeply about. In shifting formulations, these are the sorts of questions that have preoccupied Jürgen Habermas for half a century.

7 > communication as a practical discipline, Chapter 1, p. 11

8 > anyone as someone, Chapter 2, p. 38

Modernist pragmatism

Habermas' arguments

In international media and communication research, Jürgen Habermas has been mostly, and justly, famous for his 1962 agenda-setting study of the historical development of the public sphere[9]< in Europe. Though translated into English only in 1989, the implications of the account were well known by then from other publications by Habermas in English, and his framework has been widely applied both to contemporary issues and to other cultural settings. A second phase of his thinking was consummated in the two-volume theory of communicative action (Habermas, 1984/1981; 1987b/1981), which proposed to deduce ideal forms of communication from imperfect historical practices. In the present context, it is the shift of focus from historical (1962) toward systematic and normative (1981) arguments that is of special interest. As indicated in Chapter 6, Habermas appears to have already concluded that the internet holds no significant promise as an arena of democratic communication and public participation. It is both remarkable and puzzling that a thinker who, in historical retrospective, identified the ambiguous potential of media of the second degree, should discount media of the third degree even as they emerge.

9   > the public sphere, Chapter 6, p. 112

Habermas' (1989/1962) account of the public sphere was at once a sociologist's analysis of the coming of modern mass media and a social philosopher's diagnosis of their contemporary decline. By 1981, the social philosopher had gained hegemony over the sociologist. Extending Kant's analysis of the transcendental conditions of human experience,[10]< Habermas outlined the transcendental conditions of an ideal communication situation. His theory of communication is premised on a fundamental distinction between lifeworld and system world[11] – the immediate, primordial, and authentic aspects of human experience and social interaction, as contrasted with their institutionalized, rationalized, and technologically mediated manifestations in contemporary society. Importantly, 'communicative action'[12] does not equal communication, understood as a kind of social action. It is, instead, a privileged or preferred kind of interaction that serves to produce genuine intersubjective understanding as the basis of coordinated action in the common interest. It occurs on lifeworld terms; for Habermas, it is not structured by the many practical purposes that derive from and drive the system world. As such, communicative action is contrasted with both *instrumental* action (which is typically oriented toward material outcomes and efficiency) and *strategic* action (oriented toward social outcomes and "the efficacy of influencing the decisions of a rational opponent" (Habermas, 1984/1981: 285)). Whereas other forms of action seek to master matter, human beings, or both, communicative action is presented as the master of nothing and nobody.

10 > transcendental categories, Chapter 2, p. 26

11 lifeworld and system world

12 communicative action

Under a rubric of concealed strategic action, Habermas is particularly concerned to avoid what he calls systematically distorted communication.[13] Such communication is described as a source of both personal

13 systematically distorted communication

14 > double binds,
Chapter 5, p. 94

and social pathologies, akin to Bateson's account of the double binds[14]< that follow from mixed messages. Compared with conscious deception or propaganda, it is the structural outcome of certain prevailing institutions and practices of interaction that take effect behind communicators' back. A primary example of systematically distorted communication is the output of commercial media systems and cultural industries, which, in Habermas' analysis, represent a public sphere in decline. The predominant media of mass and networked communication, thus, might be said to legitimate a dominant system world against the best interests of the lifeworld and the humans inhabiting it.

It should be noted that, as clarified by Habermas' English translator in a note, "the 'ideal speech situation' is *not* the image of a concrete form of life." Instead, it represents a counterfactual category[15]< that enables research "to identify empirically the actually existing possibilities for embodying rationality structures in concrete forms of life" (Thomas McCarthy in Habermas, 1984/1981: 405–6). Standard counterfactual arguments, however, specify what might be, or might have been, the case under different circumstances: if X rather than Y had happened, then Z rather than Q might have been the result. Habermas, in contrast, proposes to derive an 'ought' from an 'is' in this manner: because the form of communication that he identifies as ideal is possible in practice, it is desirable in general, even an ethical commandment. Here and elsewhere, Habermas construes communicative action as a universal maxim on the order of Immanuel Kant's (2004a/1785: n.p.) categorical imperative[16] of ethical conduct: "Act always on such a maxim as thou canst at the same time will to be a universal law," or in common parlance, 'do as you would be done by.' Everyone should always and anywhere treat anyone else as someone. Compared with Kant, and in accordance with the linguistic and communicative turns[17]< of twentieth-century philosophy, Habermas shifts the emphasis from the individual subject thinking and acting, to communication in communities coming to an agreement about what to do.

15 > counterfactual
arguments,
Chapter 2, p. 33

16 the categorical
imperative

17 > linguistic and
communicative
turns, Chapter 2,
pp. 35–38

Habermas is acutely aware that his argument will hold:

> only if it can be shown that the use of language with an orientation to reaching understanding is the *original mode* of language use, upon which indirect understanding, giving something to understand or letting something be understood, and the instrumental use of language in general are parasitic. In my view, Austin's distinction between illocutions and perlocutions accomplishes just that.
>
> (Habermas, 1984/1981: 288)

18 > speech-act
theory, Chapter 3,
p. 52

While the reference to J. L. Austin, the originator of speech-act theory,[18]< makes the argument slightly technical, Habermas' point is actually straightforward: humans both can and should communicate without ulterior purposes. The distinction referred to is one between "illocutionary acts (the act performed *in* saying something) and perlocutionary acts (the act performed *by* saying something)" (J. B.

Thompson, 1984: 295). The issue is whether it is possible to perform the first action (representing something for somebody else) without performing the second (achieving something for oneself). Habermas argues that this is not just possible, but essential: "I count as communicative action those linguistically mediated interactions in which all participants pursue illocutionary aims, and *only* illocutionary aims, with their mediating acts of communication" (Habermas, 1984/1981: 295). Austin might be thought to lend hard linguistic support to Habermas' normative agenda. In fact, Austin (1962) was quite clear, both that these are not separate types of actions, and that the effects of speech acts are quite diverse and frequently unrelated to any intentions, noble or not, that the speaker may have had:

> The perlocutionary act may be either the achievement of a perlocutionary object (convince, persuade) or the production of a perlocutionary sequel. Thus the act of warning may achieve its perlocutionary object of warning and also have the perlocutionary sequel of alarming, and an argument against a view may fail to achieve its object but have the perlocutionary sequel of convincing our opponent of its truth ('I only succeeded in convincing him'). What is the perlocutionary object of one illocution may be the sequel of another.
>
> (Austin, 1962: 118)

Habermas goes on, by his own account, to improve on Austin, who:

> did not keep these two cases separate as different types of interaction, because he was inclined to identify acts of communication, that is, acts of reaching understanding, with the interactions coordinated by speech acts. He didn't see that acts of communication or speech acts function as a coordinating mechanism for *other* actions.
>
> (Habermas, 1984/1981: 295)

What "Austin's distinction" accomplishes for Habermas is different in kind from what it accomplished for Austin. What Austin failed to "see" was something decisive, at least to Habermas, namely, "the original mode of language use." The immediate irony is that, in order to assert his version of communicative action as a transcendental ideal, Habermas performs a strategic interpretation of Austin. Habermas' appropriation of the wider pragmatist tradition has been not just strategic, but a case of systematically distorted communication.

Has Habermas understood Peirce?

In the voluminous literature on Habermas, it is generally recognized that pragmatism has been an important inspiration in his writings. At the same time, commentators have noted, both that Habermas has had an ambiguous relationship to central tenets of the tradition (Aboulafia *et al.*, 2002), and that his explicit references to pragmatism are surprisingly few

(Joas, 1993: 9, 90). In the theory of communicative action (Habermas, 1984/1981; 1987b/1981), the only substantial presence in a pragmatist lineage is George Herbert Mead (1934); the rest of the two volumes presents a synthesis of classic and modern social theory with a critical inflection. The ambiguity of Habermas' pragmatism has been especially apparent in his accounts of the founder of pragmatism, Charles Sanders Peirce. The most elaborate assessment of Peirce's thinking by Habermas is still an early volume that was originally published in German in the year 1968, even if he has modified his criticism of Peirce in later work (Habermas, 1992).

As a contribution to the theory of science, *Knowledge and Human Interests* (Habermas, 1971/1968) identified three knowledge interests[19] that bear witness to different social purposes and distinctive ways of organizing the activity of research: the technical interest of the empirical-analytic, especially natural sciences; the contemplative interest of the historical-hermeneutic sciences; and the critical or emancipatory interest of the social sciences. A key point of Habermas' argument here was that social sciences, like natural sciences, can produce law-like knowledge, but with the important modification that social sciences help to change some of the laws or regularities which they identify in social reality (recalling the longer genealogy of double hermeneutics[20]< (Giddens, 1979)):

19 knowledge interests

20 > double hermeneutics, Chapter 1, p. 11

> the *critique of ideology*, as well, moreover, as *psychoanalysis*, take into account that information about lawlike connections sets off a process of reflection in the consciousness of those whom the laws are about. Thus the level of unreflected consciousness, which is one of the initial conditions of such laws, can be transformed.
>
> (Habermas, 1971/1968: 310)

It is on this point, in particular, that Habermas faults Peirce's pragmatism, suggesting that it succumbs to a general "logic of scientific progress" (p. 94) across different domains of reality. Casting Peirce as an objectivistic or scientistic thinker, Habermas concluded that "a hidden but unyielding positivism finally prevails" (p. 135). This is in spite of their agreement, in principle, on the twin principles of communalism and fallibilism:[21]< the community of inquirers is the only possible source of knowledge, which will remain preliminary. As it turns out, Habermas' sense of community is rather different from Peirce's. To Habermas, it is:[22]

21 > communalism and fallibilism, Chapter 2, p. 28

22 transcendental communities

> a community that constitutes the world from transcendental perspectives. This would be the subject of the process of learning and inquiry that is itself involved in a self-formative process until the point in time at which a definitive and complete knowledge of reality is attained. But it is this very subject that Peirce cannot conceive.
>
> (Habermas, 1971/1968: 135)

Moreover, Habermas finds that it is Peirce who engages in idealism in his reasoning:

> the identity of concept and object (*Sache*), which Peirce had first derived from a methodological conception of truth and thus understood as an *interpretation of the fact of scientific progress*, can only be justified in terms of an idealism that is not unlike Hegel's.
>
> (p. 111)

"Not unlike Hegel's": Peirce ends up an heir not just to ahistorical positivism, but also to historical idealism, both of which he explicitly denounced in his writings.

Part of an explanation as to why Habermas and Peirce might be failing to communicate is found in Habermas' understanding of Peirce's approach to language. In the early account, Habermas (1971/1968: 102), surprisingly, asserted that Peirce had based his epistemology on "his linguistic concept of reality," so that "reality is defined by the totality of possible true statements" and that "these statements are symbolic representations" – which is plainly incorrect. In the later account, Habermas (1992) recognized "the great achievement of Peircean semiotics in its consistent expansion of the world of symbolic forms beyond the borders of linguistic forms of expression" (p. 107). And yet, Habermas remained focused on "the structure of the simple predicative sentence, which is the semiotic form of perceptual judgments" (p. 98). What appears unacceptable, or incomprehensible, to Habermas is Peirce's starting-point: signs are of multiple kinds, and they do not necessarily translate into predicative sentences that enter into ideal sequences of turn-taking.[23]< Also, regarding the uses of signs by interpretive communities, Habermas continues to insist on a dichotomy: for Peirce, "communication is not for the sake of reaching mutual understanding between ego and alter about something in the world; rather, interpretation only exists for the sake of the representation and the ever more comprehensive representation of reality" (p. 109). Either one or the other; not both, or a third position.

23 > Peirce's semiotics, Chapter 2, pp. 28–30

Habermas' readings amount to a projection onto Peirce of traditional epistemological dilemmas. The dualism is in the eye of the beholder, the mind of the transcendentalist. Peirce's outline of a triadic model of human cognition and communication either is not recognized or it is not respected by Habermas. In the early reading (1968), the options were idealism (Hegel) and positivism (Comte); Peirce was found guilty as charged on both counts. In the later reading (1992), Habermas assumes that communication must serve the cause of either representation or mutual understanding; it cannot serve two masters. Because Peirce does not subscribe to Habermas' version of the ideal community of mutual understanding, his conception of the individual is labeled as "something merely subjective and egoistic" (Habermas, 1992: 108).

In response to the question that makes up the heading of this subsection – originally the title of a journal article (Tejera, 1996) – one must

24 > the principle of
charity, Chapter 2,
p. 22

agree with its author: no, Habermas has not understood Peirce, certainly not according to a principle of charity,[24]< let alone as part of an ideal communication situation. The question is: Why does Habermas not understand Peirce or, more charitably, what could explain his line of argument?

Whereas one might label Habermas the perpetrator of mis-communication about pragmatism for decades, it is more appropriate to interpret him as an unwitting accomplice, even a victim. Systematically distorted communication, if that is an appropriate vocabulary, comes in many shapes and forms, not just from media and cultural industries, but from institutions and traditions of learning, as well. Old dualisms die hard. Scholarly communities will not stop claiming transcendental status for their theories. Habermas' strategy is best understood as a last-ditch attempt to reaffirm and rescue the linguistic turn[25]< of philosophy. The early Wittgenstein (1972/1921) had approached the structure of language as a guide to the structure of reality; the later Wittgenstein (1953) shifted attention toward the uses of language in socially situated and contingent communications. Habermas' original mode of language use would remove the contingency. Communicators might, at last, grasp the human condition and their common interest in coordinating their affairs all the way through to mutual understanding. In the 1962 volume, such communicative democracy was examined as an ideal-type with reference to specific historical contexts. By 1981, it was construed as a transcendental foundation of politics and culture in a universal sense and on a global scale.

25 > the linguistic
turn, Chapter 2,
pp. 35–37

The irony of Habermas' strategic interpretations and systematically distorted communications is an implicit and tragic one. Pragmatism stands as the road not taken in practice by Habermas. Richard Rorty, in comparison, pursued an explicit strategy of comic irony in his engagement with pragmatism.

Postmodernist pragmatism

Rorty's narratives

Richard Rorty is best known for his contributions to neo-pragmatism – the revival of interest in philosophical pragmatism over recent decades in a variety of disciplines and fields (for overview, see Dickstein, 1998). Like Habermas' work, Rorty's publications can be grouped into periods. Unlike Habermas, Rorty emphatically changed his mind – from an early edited volume on analytic philosophy that served to name *The Linguistic Turn* (Rorty, 1967); via a historical monograph, *Philosophy and the Mirror of Nature* (Rorty, 1979), that fundamentally challenged the self-conception of contemporary philosophy as the discipline providing the foundation for all other sciences; to later writings of a more directly political and polemical character (Rorty, 1991a, 1991b, 1998, 2007).

Over time, Rorty came to assign quite a modest role to philosophy. Underlining "the priority of democracy to philosophy" (Rorty, 1991b:

175), he suggested that the brief of philosophy is to promote as well as contribute to the general conversation of mankind. Accordingly, the emphasis would shift from the nature of different aspects of reality to the different purposes of knowing about them:

> from a methodologico-ontological key into an ethico-political key. For now one is debating what purposes are worth bothering to fulfill, which are more worthwhile than others, rather than which purposes the nature of humanity or of reality obliges us to have.
>
> (p. 110)

The way to explore such purposes, for Rorty, was to tell ever more stories.[26]

Rorty (1979), initially, conceived story-telling in comparatively traditional terms as a possible source of edification. Narratives and conversations enable people to articulate, justify, and modify their understanding of reality. Increasingly, he radicalized his position to suggest that story-telling is not just a necessary, but a sufficient condition of mutual understanding and social coordination in the common interest. Both individual and cultural differences concerning people's vocabularies as well as their values "can get resolved by hashing thing out" (Rorty, 1991b: 218). Pragmatism might be, above all, practical. Rorty's turn from linguistic philosophy toward postmodern narratives was so emphatic that he even denounced "the tone of urgency" in poststructuralism,[27] for example, in Jacques Derrida's writings: "there is not an urgent task called 'deconstructing metaphysics' which needs to be performed before we can get to work on the rest of culture" (Rorty, 1991a: 104–5). Rorty had remarkably little advice to offer on other classic concerns of pragmatism, such as democracy and action. All stories are told by someone; all stories end.

Rorty's hero from classic pragmatism is John Dewey, who had called for a redefinition of philosophy: "pragmatism not as grounding, but as clearing the ground for, democratic politics . . . a democratic, progressive, pluralist community of the sort of which Dewey dreamt" (Rorty, 1991b: 13). Such a community, to Rorty, is more than a means to various social ends; it is an end in itself – all that is needed in pursuit of the good, the beautiful, and the true:

> Is the sort of community which is exemplified by groups of scientific inquirers and by democratic political institutions a means to an end, or is the formation of such communities the only goal we need? Dewey thought that it was the only goal we needed, and I think he was right.
>
> (Rorty, 1991b: 43)

Moreover, Rorty attributed special significance to other genres than conventional scientific analysis and political argument, describing literature, poetry, and journalism as more important sources of modernity and

26 **philosophy as story-telling**

27 > poststructuralism, Chapter 3, p. 45

moral progress than philosophy (Rorty, 1989: 192). In short, self-organizing communities should be left to define themselves and their stories, and to communicate among themselves about their ends and means.

Putting his own position to a severe test, Rorty repeatedly addressed the issue of universal human rights.[28] The only feature that we initially "share with all other humans is the same thing we share with all other animals – the ability to feel pain." However:

28 human rights

> human beings who have been socialized – socialized in any language, any culture – do share a capacity which other animals lack. They can all be given a special kind of pain: They can all be humiliated by the forcible tearing down of the particular structures of language and belief in which they were socialized (or which they pride themselves on having formed for themselves).
>
> (Rorty, 1989: 177)

The challenge is to decide what may be the best way of avoiding, or minimizing, pain and humiliation. At this point of his argument, Rorty characteristically shifted his attention, not to a possible consensus of different social and cultural formations, to actual institutions of inter-national politics, or to concrete practices of intercultural communica-tion, but to the general principles on which he – on behalf of "we heirs of the Enlightenment" (Rorty, 1991b: 187) – is unwilling to compromise. The summary of his position is 'anti-anti-ethnocentrism':[29] whereas ethnocentrism may be an inescapable outcome of socialization and acculturation, Rorty dismisses the relativism that he finds to be entailed by anti-ethnocentrism. Certain ideals – representative democracy, privacy rights, and procedural justice – "may be local and culture-bound, and nevertheless be the best hope of the species" (p. 208). To Rorty, "there is such a thing as moral progress" (Rorty, 1989: 192). As far as "we heirs of the Enlightenment" are concerned, opponents of liberal democracy as we know it "are crazy because the limits of sanity are set by what *we* can take seriously" (Rorty, 1991b: 187–88). Regarding the resolution of inevitable conflicts over the definition of social ends and means, he, again, has considerably less to say: "if we take care of political freedom, truth and goodness will take care of themselves" (Rorty, 1989: 84).

29 anti-anti-ethnocentrism

Rorty's model citizen is an ironist,[30] someone having continuous and radical doubts about any final vocabulary for describing reality and interacting with other people. It is on this point, in particular, that he parts company with Habermas, even if, to Rorty, they were joined in the pragmatist tradition by a narrative advocating "as much domination-free communication as possible" (Rorty, 1989: 68). (Their mutual respect and friendship were evident in Habermas' (2007) obituary when Rorty passed away.) For Rorty (1991a: 167), "the trouble with Habermas is not so much that he provides a metanarrative of emancipation as that he feels the need to legitimize, that he is not content to let the narratives which

30 the ironist as model citizen

hold our culture together do their stuff." Like Habermas, Rorty makes strategic use of pragmatism to tell his stories.

The Rorty factor

Rorty's version of pragmatism is an instructive example that signs are never safe[31]< – subject to continuous reinterpretation and recontextualization. While crediting Peirce with naming pragmatism, in addition to inspiring John Dewey, William James, and later thinkers, Rorty denounced Peirce's philosophy as objectivist and foundationalist, along similar lines as Habermas (for a detailed criticism of Rorty in this regard, see Haack, 1993). More important, Rorty's postmodernist framing of Dewey is at odds with Dewey's undoubted role as an activist philosopher, dedicated to the advancement of educational reform and participatory democracy (Bernstein, 1966; West, 1989: 69–111). Dewey's style of philosophical analysis helps to explain how Rorty's kidnap of his ideas might have been possible in the first place. As recognized by Rorty (1982: 35), Dewey still relied on the sort of abstract conceptual analyses that had been characteristic of nineteenth-century philosophy of consciousness, and which the linguistic turn had sought to replace with a more concrete and precise philosophy of language. "In contrast to Wittgenstein who, although he was the paradigmatic twentieth-century *philosopher* was in many ways a nineteenth-century *man*, John Dewey was a twentieth-century man although he was in certain ways a nineteenth-century philosopher" (Murphy, 1990: 79).

Rorty engaged in unusual practices of communication, also in relation to his contemporaries. When he enlisted a fellow philosopher, Donald Davidson, as an ally regarding his own conception of truth. Davidson explicitly questioned the move. That, however, did not phase Rorty: "Davidson cannot be held responsible for the interpretation I am putting on his views, nor for the further views I extrapolate from his" (Rorty, 1989: 10). By this standard, story-telling amounts to "two people taking turns broadcasting at each other" (Peters, 1999: 264). Turning Rorty's irony on himself, another fellow philosopher, Daniel Dennett (1982), proposed introducing a "Rorty Factor," specified as 0.742, to indicate the extent to which Rorty misstates the position of other philosophers. My point is not that Rorty ought not to communicate in this way – for either scholarly, ethical, or political reasons, as Habermas' ideal speech situation suggests. The practical issue is why anyone would want to communicate in this manner – what difference could it make?

In Rorty's own words, we might consider him "crazy" (Rorty, 1991b: 188), gone beyond the limits of what we heirs of pragmatism find reasonable and practicable. For every story, there are multiple readings and additional stories to be told. Digital media are the most recent source of an exponentially increasing number of stories. Narratives and interpretations – discursive and interpretive differences – may seem to be without end, but they end in actions – performative differences.[32]< Nor do either narratives or arguments, in practice, obey the ideal

31 > signs are never safe, Chapter 2, p. 45

32 > differences – discursive, interpretive, performative, Chapter 3, pp. 44–47

conditions that Habermas has set up. There is no comfort in either first premises or never-ending narratives of communication.

Modernism and postmodernism, as typified for communication theory by Habermas and Rorty, are representative positions in current academic as well as public debate. Modernism is an unfinished project of more than two centuries (as reviewed by Habermas, 1987a/1985). Postmodernism, while debated as epoch, theory, and style, has been an influential position at least since the naming of *The Postmodern Condition* by Jean-Francois Lyotard (1984/1979). More recently, the two have been joined on the agenda of international politics by a third position, namely, anti-modernism, as manifested in religious fundamentalism.[33] On a global scale, "three basic options . . . vie for intellectual and moral allegiance: enlightenment doubt, cultural pluralism, and fundamentalism" (Peters, 2005: 2). Whereas postmodernism has questioned the promise of modernism regarding a better future, antimodernism holds out the promise of an eternal future. Debates between modernists and post-modernists have, for most practical purposes, been an academic matter, centering on different conceptions of modernity. With antimodernism in action, the question is whether and how communication between the camps might still be possible. The much publicized cartoon controversy reached most corners of the world through mass, network, as well as interpersonal communication.

33 modernism, postmodernism, antimodernism

Case study: cartoon communications

34 the *Jyllands-Posten* Muhammad cartoons controversy

35 > Wikipedia vs. *Encyclopedia Britannica*, Chapter 6, p. 107

What is known in Wikipedia as the "*Jyllands-Posten* Muhammad cartoons controversy"[34] (accessed July 15, 2009) refers to a complex sequence of events that began on September 30, 2005, but which had been anticipated in much previous communication. (The high quality of this entry might be taken as testimony to Wikipedia's viability also in highly contested matters.)[35] < On this date, the Danish daily morning newspaper, *Morgenavisen Jyllands-Posten*, published twelve editorial cartoons, most of which depicted the Islamic prophet, Muhammad. In an explanatory text, the culture editor of the newspaper, Flemming Rose, described them as a manifestation for free speech, against self-censorship, at a time when, according to Rose, some Muslims were insisting on special consideration for their religious feelings in the public sphere. In the sender's perspective, the publication had two interrelated purposes: practicing the right to critique anyone and anything in general, and directing a particular criticism at antimodernist positions within Islam, specifically, religiously motivated limitations on freedom of expression. As received, the cartoons spawned death threats against the cartoonists, diplomatic protests to the Danish government, economic boycotts against Danish goods and services, torching of Danish embassies, burning of Danish and other European flags, and violent incidents in the Muslim world that resulted in more than 100 deaths.

The cartoons crystallized a number of cultural issues in the post-9/11 world.[36] For one thing, they appeared in a country participating in military operations in both Iraq and Afghanistan. The Danish prime minister at the time, Anders Fogh Rasmussen, noted that the events constituted Denmark's worst international crisis after the Second World War. For another thing, the cartoons have remained a symbol with real consequences for individuals as well as institutions, cartoonists and politicians. They reappeared high on an international political agenda when Rasmussen was appointed general secretary of NATO in the spring of 2009 – a decision that was contested by Turkey with reference, in part, to his handling of the cartoon incident.

36 9/11

As an instance of communication, the cartoon controversy calls for an amendment of Lasswell's (1948) standard communication model. Not only did the cartoons feed into a multistep flow of communication; they also recalled, and fed on, many preceding communicative events. Like other media discourses, the cartoons were both contextual and intertextual.[37]< They also inevitably involved meta-communication[38]< on who was communicating with, or to, whom, and why.

37 > intertextuality, Chapter 5, pp. 88–92

38 > meta-communication, Chapter 5, pp. 94–100

- *Who*. The sender of the cartoons was construed, by different interpretive communities,[39]< as the cartoonists, the newspaper, the Danish state, the center-right government with its xenophobic support party (the Danish People's Party), and "the west against the rest" (Huntington, 1993) as part of a wider cultural confrontation.

39 > interpretive communities, Chapter 2, pp. 32–34

- *Says*. Cartoons, like other images and texts in general, commonly articulate meanings that are ambiguous (Messaris, 1994), to be disambiguated with reference to a context of interaction – which, in this case, were many widely dispersed contexts. A conventional purpose of cartoons is to misrepresent something so as to represent it more accurately to an audience that is in the know.

- *What*. The message of the cartoons was, at once, their form and their content. While identifying the prophet, Muhammad, the use of images was a deliberate challenge to aniconism:[40] the belief of (some) Muslims (and other faiths) that graphic representations of deities (and sometimes humans and animals) should be avoided. The content of some of the drawings, including a bomb lodged in a Muhammad figure's turban, was particularly controversial in a post-9/11 context.

40 aniconism

- *In which channel*. While the immediate channel was a national newspaper, published in a language spoken by only five million people, the publication initiated a multistep chain of communication. On the one hand, national newspapers are part of an internationally integrated press system. On the other hand, local publics, including diasporic communities, enter into networks of communication that rely on the internet as well as satellite television.

- *In which code*. As brought home by Roman Jakobson's (1960) communication model,[41]< communication depends on both channels and codes – matter as well as modality. Not least in communications that

41 > Jakobson's communication model, Chapter 5, p. 96

are cross-cultural as well as multimodal, the nature of the code is subject to negotiation – if there is time[42]< and a willingness to negotiate it.

42 > time in
communication,
Chapter 6, p. 104

- *To whom.* Appearing in a Danish newspaper, the cartoons, first of all, addressed a divided national public opinion. Before, during, and after 2005, the topics of refugees, immigrants, integration, and international terrorism – and their possible interrelations – have made up a constant and key agenda of Danish national politics.

- *In which steps.* Next, the cartoons were both reproduced and reported on in media around the world; the internet served as an additional forum for the exchange of information and viewpoints. Analog newspapers, digital networks, and interpersonal interaction, thus, constituted a three-step flow[43]< of communication in diverse cultural contexts.

43 > three-step flow,
Chapter 4,
pp. 71–74

- *In which contexts.* Interpersonal communication played a specific and controversial role in the dissemination of the controversy in the Muslim world. On a tour of the Middle East in late 2005, two Danish imams solicited international support from a number of religious and political leaders, bringing with them a long document in texts and images that, arguably like the original cartoons, pitted a Christian west against a Muslim rest. The controversy flared up in places when the cartoons were republished by several Danish newspapers in 2008, following the arrest of three men accused of planning to assassinate Kurt Westergaard, the cartoonist behind the bomb-in-the-turban drawing.

- *With what effects.* The effects of the original publication of the cartoons, and of the ensuing communications, are open-ended – real when acted upon. Like most media in most cases, the cartoons did not in themselves create conflicts between individuals, nations, or cultures. They stand as a symbol and a reference point with an afterlife in both formal and informal international and intercultural communication.

The cartoons, while unusual in their consequences, were standard fare in diverse media, genres, and contexts of communication. They presented already available information: existing conceptions, representations, and interpretations of the prophet, Muhammed. They made this information accessible to a variety of audiences, in sequences and networks, who themselves became senders of similar, alternative, or opposing conceptions, representations, and interpretations. And, as always, the information and interpretations oriented social action[44]< – material as well as immaterial, peaceful as well as violent. Communications serve as means to ends, both of which may entail disagreements, some of which are irreconcilable. In a good percentage of cases, we do not agree in the end.

44 > availability,
accessibility, and
performativity of
information,
Chapter 1, p. 7

Both the cartoons themselves and the subsequent controversies meta-communicated – about the content and form of the message and about the relationship between the many potential partners to the communication. In each case, double binds[45]< might follow, or continued communication might prove impossible. The opening turn by *Jyllands-Posten* mixed two messages: asserting the sender's right to communicate about anything, to anyone,

45 > double binds,
Chapter 5, p. 94

and placing in doubt the 'we' of communication. The imams, and others, responded in kind, mixing vocabularies of universal human rights and religious fundamentalism. Whereas both of the self-defined main sides to the controversy went through the motions of communication, they also seemed to take Rorty's terminology to heart: the others were "crazy."

Habermas (2008: 18) has referred to the cartoon incident, in general terms, as part of his involvement in debates concerning secularism and religiosity; Rorty, to my knowledge, did not address the events in writing. In Rorty's (1991b: 188) perspective, presumably, the story-telling should go on – but only up to a point that "*we* can take seriously." Habermas recognizes that his claim to transcendentalism and universalism is "the most difficult aspect of his philosophy to defend," and "when I then asked why he thought that he had to defend it – not an unusual question from a pragmatist vantage point – his answer was straightforward: the Holocaust" (Aboulafia, 2002: 4). One of Habermas' teachers, Theodor W. Adorno (1990/1966: 361), similarly, suggested that, "after Auschwitz," human reason finds itself in a new condition. Abominable as the Holocaust was and is, historical events cannot justify transhistorical ideals of either scientific inquiry or public communication. The practical question is how societies and cultures may organize, conduct, and conclude their communications so as to avoid anything resembling the Holocaust – or Rwanda, or deaths as a chain effect of humiliation by cartoon.

A third way

Pragmatism's only claim to grandeur is a lot of hard discursive and communal work with a view to the future. In Peirce's semiotics, Objects orient to the past (what is, and how it came about), as manifested in present Signs, whereas Interpretants orient to the future (what could be) (Fisch, 1984: xxviii).[46]< Cybernetics, in turn, described communication as a mediator between past and present: "Whatever communication we consider . . . the message is a statement or report about events at a previous moment, and on the other hand it is a command – a cause or stimulus for events at a later moment" (Ruesch and Bateson, 1987/1951: 179). Peirce offered vivid images of what the future might hold: "Give science only a hundred more centuries of increase in geometrical progression, and she may be expected to find that the sound waves of Aristotle's voice have somehow recorded themselves" (Peirce, 1931–58: 5.542) (cited in Peters, 1999: 162). Whereas Peirce's expectation is unlikely to be met, the historical record indicates that new media and communicative affordances will, indeed, be discovered and developed. Another degree of media is in the making.[47]<

46 > Signs, Objects, Interpretants, Chapter 2, pp. 28–30

47 > media of the fourth degree, Chapter 4, pp. 80–82

Pragmatism has charted a third way – between first premises and final certainties; between received theoretical, methodological, and epistemo-logical dichotomies; and between modernism and postmodernism. Like

48 > modernity and
modernization,
Chapter 6, p. 111

49 > sensitizing
concepts,
Chapter 2, p. 25

modernity as epoch and mindset,[48]< the pragmatist tradition is an unfinished project. Like modernity, it provides uniquely sensitizing[49]< perspectives on the political, economic, and cultural potentials of human practice. In science and scholarship, it holds perspectives for an interdisciplinary third culture (Brockman, 1995) that might bridge the still separate cultures of arts and sciences (Snow, 1964).

As a third way, pragmatism is encapsulated in a simple figure of thought and analysis, as expressed in Peirce's triadic model of human consciousness and communication. The interrelation between subject and object, and between subjects with reference to their common objects of interest and concern, is necessarily mediated. We cannot *not* relate to the world(s) in our bandwidth, and we cannot *not* communicate with others about them. Tools, technologies, and meta-technologies[50]< have extended human agency and social structures across time and space. Media of three degrees and three-step flows of communication enable more distributed and differentiated forms of interaction than ever before in human history, still without guarantees of understanding other people, let alone agreeing with them about what to do. Regardless, we must act – as individuals, groups, institutions, societies, and species – in the face of natural and cultural circumstances. Communication may want to go on, but we do not, because we cannot.

50 > tools,
technologies, and
meta-technologies,
Chapter 4, p. 65

In summary, I have retraced the idea of communication in the history of ideas and into digital media studies in order to suggest some of the opportunities for the present field of study. Kant had placed the enlightened, self-reliant, but solitary individual at the center of the modern universe; Peirce and pragmatism signaled a communicative turn that would recontextualize individuals within communities, so that they might deliberate on the ends and means of their coexistence through the media at their disposal. Twentieth-century communication theories represented so many attempts to specify this process – its upper and lower limits and the degrees of freedom that have been associated with changing material, institutional, and discursive conditions of communication.

Media of the third degree bring back the big questions of determination, meta-communication, and social structuration – what media do to people, cultures, and societies, and vice versa. I have argued that media technologies determine communication, but only in the first instance[51]< – in the negative sense of deciding which communicative practices are impossible or improbable, and in the positive sense of presenting affordances[52]< that constitute new windows of opportunity. Affordances are only actualized in steps and stages of social innovation and collaboration. Each instance of communication, further, takes place in social contexts of meta-communication that raise questions of who we are, and why we seek to communicate. Meta-communication has become a more manifest, pervasive aspect of digital media and network communication, for better or worse. Search and surveillance are integral to the ongoing structuration of contemporary society.

51 > determination in
the first instance,
Chapter 4, p. 62

52 > affordances,
Chapter 4,
pp. 74–77

Media and communication research has a contribution to make, mostly through double hermeneutics. The field could and should become

more unified in its attempts to describe, interpret, and explain communication, its problems as well as its potentials – but only in the final
instance.[53]< By refocusing attention on the end of communication as the
beginning of other social interaction, the field may become more
coherent; it may also make itself more relevant and useful to other fields
of theory and practice. Communication is neither a dream nor a night-
mare, but a practice in the real world – a unique resource for producing
and contesting human knowledge, before translating it into social action.

In early critical communication research in Europe, it was common
to insist that the center of media studies lies outside the media (Negt,
1973: iv). In this book, I have advocated a shift of focus from media to
communicative practices. An important center of future research lies
outside communication – at the end of communication and in its inter-
sections with other political, economic, and cultural practices. Now is a
good time to consider how media and communication studies might be
different.

53 > unification in
the final instance,
Chapter 7,
pp. 142–145

References

Aarseth, E. J. (1997). *Cybertext: Perspectives on Ergodic Literature*. Baltimore, MD: Johns Hopkins University Press.

—— (2003). We All Want to Change the World: The Ideology of Innovation in Digital Media. In G. Liestøl, A. Morrison and T. Rasmussen (Eds.), *Digital Media Revisited*. Cambridge, MA: MIT Press.

Abbate, J. (1999). *Inventing the Internet*. Cambridge, MA: MIT Press.

Aboulafia, M. (2002). Introduction. In M. Aboulafia, M. Bookman and C. Kemp (Eds.), *Habermas and Pragmatism*. London: Routledge.

Aboulafia, M., Bookman, M., and Kemp, C. (Eds.). (2002). *Habermas and Pragmatism*. London: Routledge.

Adorno, T. W. (1990). *Negative Dialectics*. London: Routledge. (Orig. publ. 1966.)

Althusser, L. (1977). *For Marx*. London: Verso. (Orig. publ. 1965.)

Altman, R. (2004). *Silent Film Sound*. New York: Columbia University Press.

Alvesson, M., and Sköldberg, K. (2000). *Reflexive Methodology: New Vistas for Qualitative Research*. London: Sage.

Anderson, B. (1991). *Imagined Communities: Reflections on the Origin and Spread of Nationalism* (2nd ed.). London: Verso.

Apel, K.-O. (1972). From Kant to Peirce: The Semiotical Transformation of Transcendental Logic. In L. W. Beck (Ed.), *Proceedings of the Third International Kant Congress*. Dordrecht, The Netherlands: D. Reidel Publishing Company.

Appadurai, A. (1996). *Modernity at Large: Cultural Dimensions of Globalization*. Minneapolis: University of Minnesota Press.

Archer, M. (2003). *Structure, Agency, and the Internal Conversation*. Cambridge: Cambridge University Press.

Archer, M., Bhaskar, R., Collier, A., Lawson, T., and Norrie, A. (Eds.). (1998). *Critical Realism: Essential Readings*. London: Routledge.

Aristotle (2007a). *Metaphysics*. Retrieved January 8, 2008, from http://etext.library.adelaide.edu.au/a/aristotle/metaphysics/complete.html

—— (2007b). *On Interpretation*. Retrieved August 15, 2007, from http://etext.library.adelaide.edu.au/a/aristotle/interpretation/complete.html

Arnold, M. (2003). *Culture and Anarchy*. Retrieved March 15, 2009, from www.gutenberg.org/etext/4212 (Orig. publ. 1869.)

Ashcroft, B., Griffiths, G., and Tiffin, H. (Eds.). (1995). *The Post-Colonial Studies Reader*. London: Routledge.

Austin, J. L. (1962). *How to Do Things with Words*. Oxford: Oxford University Press.

Bakhtin, M. M. (1981). *The Dialogic Imagination*. Austin: University of Texas Press.

Barnes, S. H. (1988). *Muzak. The Hidden Messages in Music: A Social Psychology of Culture*. Lewiston, NY: The Edwin Mellen Press.

Baron, N. S. (2008). *Always On: Language in an Online and Mobile World*. New York: Oxford University Press.

Barthes, R. (1970). *S/Z*. Paris: Seuil.

—— (1973). *Mythologies*. London: Paladin. (Orig. publ. 1957.)

Bateson, G. (1972). *Steps to an Ecology of Mind*. London: Granada.

—— (1979). *Mind and Nature: A Necessary Unity*. New York: E.P. Dutton.

Bateson, G., and Bateson, M. C. (1988). *Angels Fear: Towards an Epistemology of the Sacred*. Toronto: Bantam.

Baudrillard, J. (1988). *Selected Writings*. Cambridge: Polity Press.

Bawarshi, A. (2000). The Genre Function. *College English*, *62*(3), 335–56.

Bell, D. (1973). *The Coming of Post-Industrial Society*. New York: Basic Books.

Bell, D., and Kennedy, B. M. (Eds.). (2000). *The Cybercultures Reader*. London: Routledge.

Benedikt, M. (Ed.). (1991). *Cyberspace: First Steps*. Cambridge, MA: MIT Press.

Beniger, J. (1986). *The Control Revolution*. Cambridge, MA: Harvard University Press.

Benjamin, W. (1977). The Work of Art in the Age of Mechanical Reproduction. In J. Curran, M. Gurevitch and J. Woollacott (Eds.), *Mass Communication and Society*. London: Edward Arnold. (Orig. publ. 1936.)

Benkler, Y. (2006). *The Wealth of Networks: How Social Production Transforms Markets and Freedom*. New Haven, CT: Yale University Press.

Bennett, T., and Woollacott, J. (1987). *Bond and Beyond*. London: Methuen.

Benveniste, É. (1985). The Semiology of Language. In R. E. Innis (Ed.), *Semiotics: An Introductory Anthology*. Bloomington: Indiana University Press. (Orig. publ. 1969.)

Berelson, B. (1952). *Content Analysis in Communication Research*. Glencoe, IL: The Free Press.

Bergman, M. (2004). *Fields of Signification: Explorations in Charles S. Peirce's Theory of Signs*. Helsinki, Finland: University of Helsinki.

—— (2008). The New Wave of Pragmatism in Communication Studies. *Nordicom Review*, *29*(2), 135–53.

Bergson, H. (2005). *Creative Evolution*. New York: Barnes & Noble Books. (Orig. publ. 1907.)

Bernstein, R. (1966). *John Dewey*. Atascadero, CA: Ridgeview.

Bertilsson, T. M. (2004). The Elementary Forms of Pragmatism: On Different Types of Abduction. *European Journal of Social Theory*, *7*(3), 371–89.

Bhaskar, R. (1979). *The Possibility of Naturalism*. Brighton, UK: Harvester Press.

Biagioli, M. (Ed.). (1999). *The Science Studies Reader*. New York: Routledge.

Biocca, F., Harms, C., and Burgoon, J. K. (2003). Toward a More Robust Theory and Measure of Social Presence: Review and Suggested Criteria. *Presence, 12*(5), 456–80.

Blaikie, N. (1993). *Approaches to Social Enquiry*. Cambridge: Polity Press.

Blondheim, M. (2008). Innis, Harold. In W. Donsbach (Ed.), *International Encyclopedia of Communication* (Vol. 5, pp. 2286–88). Malden, MA: Blackwell.

Blumer, H. (1954). What Is Wrong with Social Theory? *American Sociological Review, 19*, 3–10.

Boden, M. (Ed.). (1996). *Artificial Intelligence*. San Diego, CA: Academic Press.

Bohr, N. (1958). *Atomic Physics and Human Knowledge*. New York: Wiley.

Bolter, J. D. (1991). *Writing Space: The Computer, Hypertext, and the History of Writing*. Hillsdale, NJ: Lawrence Erlbaum.

Bolter, J. D., and Grusin, R. (1999). *Remediation: Understanding New Media*. Cambridge, MA: MIT Press.

Bordewijk, J., and Kaam, B. (1986). Towards a New Classification of Tele-Information Services. *Intermedia, 14*(1), 16–21.

Bourdieu, P. (1984). *Distinction*. Cambridge, MA: Harvard University Press. (Orig. publ. 1979.)

Bower, R. T. (1973). *Television and the Public*. New York: Holt, Rinehart & Winston.

Bowrey, K., and Rimmer, M. (2002). *Rip, Mix, Burn: The Politics of Peer to Peer and Copyright Law*. Retrieved July 25, 2007 from www.first monday.org/issues/issue7_8/bowrey/

Boyarin, J. (Ed.). (1992). *The Ethnography of Reading*. Berkeley: University of California Press.

Boyd, D. M., and Ellison, N. B. (2007). Social Network Sites: Definition, History, and Scholarship. *Journal of Computer-Mediated Communication, 13*(1).

Braman, S. (2006). *Change of State: Information, Policy, and Power*. Cambridge, MA: MIT Press.

Briggs, A., and Burke, P. (2005). *A Social History of the Media: From Gutenberg to the Internet* (2nd ed.). Cambridge: Polity.

Brockman, J. (Ed.). (1995). *The Third Culture*. New York: Simon & Schuster.

Bull, M. (2000). *Sounding Out the City: Personal Stereos and the Management of Everyday Life*. Oxford: Berg.

Bull, M., and Back, L. (Eds.). (2003). *The Auditory Culture Reader*. Oxford: Berg.

Calhoun, C. (Ed.). (1992). *Habermas and the Public Sphere*. Cambridge, MA: MIT Press.

Capella, J. N. (Ed.) (1996). Symposium: Biology and Communication. *Journal of Communication, 46*(3), 4–84.

Carey, J. W. (1989a). *Communication as Culture*. Boston, MA: Unwin Hyman.

—— (1989b). A Cultural Approach to Communication. *Communication as Culture* (pp. 13–36). Boston, MA: Unwin Hyman. (Orig. publ. 1975.)

Carroll, N. (1988). *Mystifying Movies: Fads and Fallacies in Contemporary Film Theory*. New York: Columbia University Press.

Castells, M. (1996). *The Rise of the Network Society*. Oxford: Blackwell.

—— (1999). *End of Millennium* (Revised ed.). Oxford: Blackwell.

—— (2001). *The Internet Galaxy*. Oxford: Oxford University Press.

Castells, M., Fernández-Ardèval, M., Qui, J. L., and Sey, A. (2007). *Mobile Communication and Society*. Cambridge, MA: MIT Press.

Cater, D. (1959). *The Fourth Branch of Government*. Boston, MA: Houghton-Mifflin.

Chauviré, C. (2005). Peirce, Popper, Abduction, and the Idea of Logic of Discovery. *Semiotica*, *153*(1/4), 209–21.

Chomsky, N. (1965). *Aspects of the Theory of Syntax*. Cambridge, MA: MIT Press.

Clarke, B. (1979). Eccentrically Contested Concepts. *British Journal of Political Science*, *9*(1), 122–26.

Clarke, D. S. (1990). *Sources of Semiotic*. Carbondale, IL: Southern Illinois University Press.

Clarke, R. (2001). *Information Wants To Be Free*. . .Retrieved July 10, 2009, from www.anu.edu.au/people/Roger.Clarke/II/IWtbF.html

Clifford, J., and Marcus, G. E. (Eds.). (1986). *Writing Culture: The Poetics and Politics of Ethnography*. Berkeley: University of California Press.

Cohen, B. (1963). *The Press and Foreign Policy*. Princeton, NJ: Princeton University Press.

Cohen, E. L., and Willis, C. (2004). One Nation under Radio: Digital and Public Memory after September 11. *New Media & Society*, *6*(5), 591–610.

Coiro, J., Knobel, M., Lankshear, C., and Leu, D. J. (Eds.). (2008). *Handbook of Research on New Literacies*. New York: Lawrence Erlbaum.

Colapietro, V. (1989). *Peirce's Approach to the Self*. Albany: State University of New York Press.

Collins, S. L., and Hoopes, J. (1995). Anthony Giddens and Charles Sanders Peirce: History, Theory, and a Way Out of the Linguistic Cul-de-Sac. *Journal of the History of Ideas*, *56*(3), 625–50.

Conant, J., and Haugeland, J. (Eds.). (2000). *Thomas S. Kuhn: The Road since Structure*. New York: Basic Books.

Coward, R., and Ellis, J. (1977). *Language and Materialism*. London: Routledge & Kegan Paul.

Craig, R. T. (1999). Communication Theory as a Field. *Communication Theory*, *9*(2), 119–61.

—— (2007). Pragmatism in the Field of Communication Theory. *Communication Theory*, *17*(2), 125–45.

Craig, R. T., and Muller, H. L. (Eds.). (2007). *Theorizing Communication: Readings Across Traditions*. Los Angeles, CA: Sage.

Culler, J. (1975). *Structuralist Poetics*. London: Routledge & Kegan Paul.

Danto, A. C. (1965). *Analytical Philosophy of History*. Cambridge: Cambridge University Press.

Davidson, D. (1973–74). On the Very Idea of a Conceptual Scheme. *Proceedings and Addresses of the American Philosophical Association, 47,* 5–20.

Dawkins, R. (1989). *The Selfish Gene* (New ed.). New York: Oxford University Press.

Deacon, D., Pickering, M., Golding, P., and Murdock, G. (2007). *Researching Communications: A Practical Guide to Methods in Media and Cultural Analysis* (2nd ed.). London: Hodder Arnold.

DeLanda, M. (1991). *War in the Age of Intelligent Machines*. New York: Zone Books.

Dennett, D. (1982). Comments on Rorty. *Synthèse, 53,* 349–56.

Denzin, N. K., and Lincoln, Y. S. (Eds.). (2005). *The Sage Handbook of Qualitative Research* (3rd ed.). Thousand Oaks, CA: Sage.

Derrida, J. (1973). *Speech and Phenomena. And Other Essays on Husserl's Theory of Signs*. Evanston, IL: Northwestern University Press. (Orig. publ. 1967.)

—— (1976). *Of Grammatology*. Baltimore, MD: Johns Hopkins University Press. (Orig. publ. 1967.)

Dickstein, M. (Ed.). (1998). *The Revival of Pragmatism*. Durham, NC: Duke University Press.

Divers, J. (2002). *Possible Worlds*. London: Routledge.

Douglas, M. (1987). *How Institutions Think*. London: Routledge & Kegan Paul.

Dray, W. (1957). *Laws and Explanation in History*. London: Oxford University Press.

Eco, U. (1976). *A Theory of Semiotics*. Bloomington: Indiana University Press.

—— (1984). *Semiotics and the Philosophy of Language*. London: Macmillan.

—— (1999). *Kant and the Platypus: Essays on Language and Cognition*. London: Vintage.

Edwards, M. (2004). *Civil Society*. Cambridge: Polity.

Ehrenberg, R. E. (Ed.). (2006). *Mapping the World: An Illustrated History of Cartography*. Washington, DC: National Geographic Society.

Eisenstein, E. L. (1979). *The Printing Press as an Agent of Change: Communication and Cultural Transformation in Early-Modern Europe*. Cambridge: Cambridge University Press.

Emmeche, C., Køppe, S., and Stjernfelt, F. (2000). Levels, Emergence, and Three Versions of Downward Causation. In P. B. Andersen, C. Emmeche, N. O. Finnemann and P. V. Christiansen (Eds.), *Downward Causation: Minds, Bodies, and Matter*. Aarhus, Denmark: Aarhus University Press.

Ericson, R. V., Baranak, P. M., and Chan, J. B. L. (1987). *Visualizing Deviance: A Study of News Organization*. Toronto: University of Toronto Press.

Erlich, V. (1955). *Russian Formalism: History, Doctrine*. The Hague: Mouton.

Fagan, B. (2000). *The Little Ice Age: How Climate Made History 1300–1850*. New York: Basic Books.

Fallon, D. (1980). *The German University: A Heroic Ideal in Conflict with the Modern World*. Boulder: Colorado Associated University Press.

Feldman, L. (2007). The News about Comedy: Young Audiences, The Daily Show, and Evolving Notions of Journalism. *Journalism: Theory, Practice & Criticism, 8*(4), 406–27.

Festinger, L. (1957). *A Theory of Cognitive Dissonance*. Evanston, IL: Row.

Feuer, L. S. (Ed.). (1969). *Marx and Engels: Basic Writings on Politics and Philosophy*. London: Fontana.

Feyerabend, P. (1975). *Against Method: Outline of an Anarchistic Theory of Knowledge*. London: New Left Books.

Finnemann, N. O. (2005). The Cultural Grammar of the Internet. In K. B. Jensen (Ed.), *Interface://Culture – The World Wide Web as Political Resource and Aesthetic Form*. Copenhagen, Denmark: Samfundslitteratur / Nordicom.

—— (2008). *The Internet and the Emergence of a New Matrix of Media: Mediatization and the Coevolution of Old and New Media*. Paper presented at the Internet Research 9.0 Conference, Copenhagen, Denmark.

Fisch, M. H. (1954). Alexander Bain and the Genealogy of Pragmatism. *Journal of the History of Ideas, 15*(3), 413–44.

—— (1984). Introduction. In C. S. Peirce, *Writings of Charles S. Peirce* (Vol. 2). Bloomington: Indiana University Press.

Fish, S. (1979). *Is There a Text in This Class? The Authority of Interpretive Communities*. Cambridge, MA: Harvard University Press.

Fiske, J. (1987). *Television Culture*. London: Methuen.

Foucault, M. (1972). *The Archaeology of Knowledge*. London: Tavistock. (Orig. publ. 1969.)

Fox, J. R., Koloen, G., and Sahin, V. (2007). No Joke: A Comparison of Substance in The Daily Show with Jon Stewart and Broadcast Network Television Coverage of the 2004 Presidential Election Campaign. *Journal of Broadcasting and Electronic Media, 51*(2), 213–27.

Fraser, N. (1992). Rethinking the Public Sphere: A Contribution to the Critique of Actually Existing Democracy. In C. Calhoun (Ed.), *Habermas and the Public Sphere*. Cambridge, MA: MIT Press.

—— (2007). Transnationalizing the Public Sphere: On the Legitimacy and Efficacy of Public Opinion in a Post-Westphalian World. *Theory, Culture, & Society, 24*(4), 7–30.

Freud, S. (1911). *The Interpretation of Dreams*. Retrieved July 15, 2009, from www.psywww.com/books/interp/toc.htm (Orig. publ. 1900.)

Furnham, A. F. (1988). *Lay Theories: Everyday Understanding of Problems in the Social Sciences*. Oxford: Pergamon Press.

Gallie, W. B. (1956). Essentially Contested Concepts. *Proceedings of the Aristotelian Society, 56*, 167–98.

Garfinkel, H. (1967). *Studies in Ethnomethodology*. Englewood Cliffs, NJ: Prentice-Hall.

Gay, P. D., Hall, S., Janes, L., Mackay, H., and Negus, K. (1997). *Doing Cultural Studies: The Story of the Sony Walkman*. London: Sage.

Geertz, C. (1983). *Local Knowledge*. New York: Basic Books.

Gena, P., and Strom, C. (2001). *A Physiological Approach to DNA Music*. Paper presented at the 4th Computers in Art and Design Education Conference, Glasgow.

Genette, G. (1997). *Palimpsests: Literature in the Second Degree*. Lincoln: University of Nebraska Press. (Orig. publ. 1982.)

Gibson, J. J. (1979). *The Ecological Approach to Visual Perception*. Boston, MA: Houghton-Mifflin.

Gibson, W. (1984). *Neuromancer*. New York: Ace.

Giddens, A. (1979). *Central Problems in Social Theory*. London: Macmillan.

—— (1984). *The Constitution of Society*. Berkeley: University of California Press.

Giles, J. (2005). Internet Encyclopaedias Go Head to Head. *Nature, 438*, 900–901.

Ginzburg, C. (1989). Clues: Roots for an Evidential Paradigm. In *Clues, Myths, and the Historical Method*. Baltimore, MD: Johns Hopkins University Press.

Gitlin, T. (1980). *The Whole World Is Watching*. Berkeley: University of California Press.

Gleick, J. (1987). *Chaos: Making a New Science*. London: Penguin.

Goffman, E. (1971). The Territories of the Self. *Relations in Public: Microstudies of the Public Order* (pp. 51–87). Harmondsworth: Penguin.

—— (1974). *Frame Analysis*. Cambridge, MA: Harvard University Press.

—— (1983). Felicity's Condition. *American Journal of Sociology, 89*(1), 1–53.

Goggin, G. (2006). *Cell Phone Culture: Mobile Technology in Everyday Life*. London: Routledge.

Gomm, R., Hammersley, M., and Foster, P. (Eds.). (2000). *Case Study Method: Key Issues, Key Texts*. London: Sage.

Goody, J., and Watt, I. (1963). The Consequences of Literacy. *Comparative Studies in Society and History, 5*, 304–45.

Gow, G. A., and Smith, R. K. (2006). *Mobile and Wireless Communications: An Introduction*. Maidenhead, UK: Open University Press.

Gramsci, A. (1971). *Selections from the Prison Notebooks*. New York: International Publishers.

Greenfield, A. (2006). *Everyware: The Dawning Age of Ubiquitous Computing*. Indianapolis, IN: New Riders.

Grossberg, L., Nelson, C., and Treichler, P. (Eds.). (1992). *Cultural Studies*. London: Routledge.

Gunter, B. (2002). The Quantitative Research Process. In K. B. Jensen (Ed.), *A Handbook of Media and Communication Research: Qualitative and Quantitative Methodologies*. London: Routledge.

Haack, S. (1993). Philosophy/Philosophy: An Untenable Dualism. *Transactions of the Charles S. Peirce Society, 29*(3), 411–26.

Habermas, J. (1971). *Knowledge and Human Interests*. Boston, MA: Beacon Press. (Orig. publ. 1968.)

—— (1984). *The Theory of Communicative Action* (Vol. 1). Boston, MA: Beacon Press. (Orig. publ. 1981.)

—— (1987a). *The Philosophical Discourse of Modernity*. Cambridge: Polity.

—— (1987b). *The Theory of Communicative Action* (Vol. 2). Cambridge: Polity Press. (Orig. publ. 1981.)

—— (1989). *The Structural Transformation of the Public Sphere*. Cambridge, MA: MIT Press. (Orig. publ. 1962.)

—— (1992). Peirce and Communication. *Postmetaphysical Thinking* (pp. 88–112). Cambridge, MA: MIT Press.

—— (2006). Political Communication in Media Society: Does Democracy Still Enjoy an Epistemic Dimension? The Impact of Normative Theory on Empirical Research. *Communication Theory*, *16*(4), 411–26.

—— (2007). *Philosopher, Poet, and Friend.* Retrieved May 3, 2009, from www.signandsight.com/features/1386.html

—— (2008). Notes on Post-Secular Society. *New Perspectives Quarterly*, *25*(4), 17–29.

Hacking, I. (1975). *The Emergence of Probability*. London: Cambridge University Press.

—— (1983). *Representing and Intervening: Introductory Topics in the Philosophy of Natural Science*. Cambridge: Cambridge University Press.

—— (1992). 'Style' for Historians and Philosophers. *Studies in the History and Philosophy of Science*, *23*(1), 1–20.

—— (1999). *The Social Construction of What?* Cambridge, MA: Harvard University Press.

Haddon, L. (2004). *Information and Communication Technologies: A Concise Introduction and Research Guide*. Oxford: Berg.

Halavais, A. (2009). *Search Engine Society*. Cambridge: Polity.

Hall, E. T. (1959). *The Silent Language*. New York: Doubleday.

Hall, S. (1973). *Encoding and Decoding in the Television Discourse* (Stencilled Occasional Paper No. 7). Birmingham, UK: Centre for Contemporary Cultural Studies.

—— (1980). Cultural Studies: Two Paradigms. *Media, Culture & Society*, *2*, 57–72.

—— (1983). The Problem of Ideology – Marxism without Guarantees. In B. Matthews (Ed.), *Marx: A Hundred Years On*. London: Lawrence & Wishart.

Halliday, M. A. K., Teuberg, W., Yallop, C., and Cermakova, A. (2004). *Lexicology and Corpus Linguistics: An Introduction*. London: Continuum.

Han, J., and Kamber, M. (2006). *Data Mining: Concepts and Techniques* (2nd ed.). Boston, MA: Elsevier.

Hanson, N. R. (1958). *Patterns of Discovery: An Inquiry into the Conceptual Foundations of Science*. Cambridge: Cambridge University Press.

Haraway, D. J. (1991). *Simians, Cyborgs, and Women: The Reinvention of Nature*. New York: Routledge.

Hargittai, E. (Ed.) (2007). Special Theme I: The Social, Political, Economic, and Cultural Dimensions of Search Engines. *Journal of Computer-Mediated Communicaiton*, *12*(3).

Hartley, J. (1982). *Understanding News*. London: Routledge.

Hartnack, J. (1965). *Wittgenstein and Modern Philosophy*. New York: New York University Press.

Hartson, H. R. (2003). Cognitive, physical, sensory, and functional affordances in interaction design. *Behaviour & Information Technology*, 22(5), 315–38.

Harvey, D. (1989). *The Condition of Postmodernity*. Oxford: Blackwell.

Hawthorn, G. (1991). *Plausible Worlds: Possibility and Understanding in History and the Social Sciences*. Cambridge: Cambridge University Press.

Hayles, N. K. (1999). *How We Became Posthuman: Virtual Bodies in Cybernetics, Literature, and Informatics*. Chicago, IL: University of Chicago Press.

Heims, S. J. (1991). *The Cybernetics Group*. Cambridge, MA: MIT Press.

Heisenberg, W. (1971). Quantum Mechanics and Kantian Philosophy (1930–34). *Physics and Beyond: Encounters and Conversations* (pp. 117–24). New York: Harper and Row.

Helle-Valle, J., and Slettemeås, D. (2008). ICTs, Domestication, and Language-Games: A Wittgensteinian Approach to Media Uses. *New Media & Society*, 10(1), 45–66.

Hempel, C. G., and Oppenheim, P. (1988). Studies in the Logic of Explanation. In J. Pitt (Ed.), *Theories of Explanation*. New York: Oxford University Press. (Orig. publ 1948.)

Herring, S. (2004). Slouching toward the Ordinary: Current Trends in Computer-Mediated Communication. *New Media & Society*, 6(1), 26–36.

Higgins, D. (2001). Intermedia. *Leonardo*, 34(1), 49–54. (Orig. publ. 1965.)

Hine, C. (2000). *Virtual Ethnography*. London: Sage.

Hjelmslev, L. (1963). *Prolegomena to a Theory of Language*. Madison: University of Wisconsin Press. (Orig. publ. 1943.)

Hobsbawm, E. (1995). *The Age of Extremes: A History of the World, 1914–1991*. New York: Random House.

Holub, R. C. (1984). *Reception Theory: A Critical Introduction*. London: Methuen.

Hughes, T. P. (1983). *Networks of Power: Electrification in Western Society 1880–1930*. Baltimore, MD: Johns Hopkins University Press.

—— (1994). Technological Momentum. In M. R. Smith and L. Marx (Eds.), *Does Technology Drive History? The Dilemma of Technological Determinism*. Cambridge, MA: MIT Press.

Hume, D. (2006). *An Enquiry Concerning Human Understanding*. Retrieved April 7, 2009, from www.gutenberg.org/etext/9662 (Orig. publ. 1748.)

Humphreys, L. (2005). Cellphones in Public: Social Interactions in a Wireless Era. *New Media & Society*, 7(6), 810–33.

Huntington, S. (1993, June 6). The Coming Clash of Civilizations, Or, the West Against the Rest. *The New York Times*, E19.

Hutchby, I. (2001). *Conversation and Technology: From the Telephone to the Internet*. Cambridge: Polity.

Hutchins, E. (1995). *Cognition in the Wild*. Cambridge, MA: MIT Press.

Huyssen, A. (1986). *After the Great Divide: Modernism, Mass Culture, and Postmodernism*. London: Macmillan.

Innis, H. A. (1951). *The Bias of Communication*. Toronto: University of Toronto Press.

—— (1972). *Empire and Communications*. Toronto: University of Toronto Press. (Orig. publ. 1950.)

Introna, L. D., and Nissenbaum, H. (2000). Shaping the Web: Why the Politics of Search Engines Matters. *The Information Society, 16*(3), 169–85.

Ito, M., Okabe, D., and Matsuda, M. (Eds.). (2005). *Personal, Portable, Pedestrian: Mobile Phones in Japanese Life*. Cambridge, MA: MIT Press.

ITU (2005). *The Internet of Things: Executive Summary*. Retrieved March 28, 2008, from www.itu.int/dms_pub/itu-s/opb/pol/S-POL-IR.IT-2005-SUM-PDF-E.pdf

Jackson, H.-J. (2001). *Marginalia: Readers Writing in Books*. New Haven, CT: Yale University Press.

Jakobson, R. (1960). Closing Statement: Linguistics and Poetics. In T. A. Sebeok (Ed.), *Style in Language*. Cambridge, MA: MIT Press.

James, J. (1995). *The Music of the Spheres: Music, Science, and the Natural Order of the Universe*. London: Abacus.

James, W. (1981). *The Principles of Psychology* (Vol. 1). Cambridge, MA: Harvard University Press. (Orig. publ. 1890.)

Jankowski, N. W., and Wester, F. (1991). The Qualitative Tradition in Social Science Inquiry: Contributions to Mass Communication Research. In K. B. Jensen and N. W. Jankowski (Eds.), *A Handbook of Qualitative Methodologies for Mass Communication Research*. London: Routledge.

Jensen, J. F. (1999). Interactivity: Tracking a New Concept in Media and Communication Studies. In P. A. Mayer (Ed.), *Computer Media and Communication: A Reader*. Oxford: Oxford University Press.

Jensen, K. B. (1987). Qualitative Audience Research: Toward an Integrative Approach to Reception. *Critical Studies in Mass Communication, 4*(1), 21–36.

—— (1991). When Is Meaning? Communicaton Theory, Pragmatism, and Mass Media Reception. In J. Anderson (Ed.), *Communication Yearbook* (Vol. 14). Newbury Park, CA: Sage.

—— (1993). One Person, One Computer: The Social Construction of the Personal Computer. In P. B. Andersen, B. Holmqvist and J. F. Jensen (Eds.), *The Computer as Medium*. Cambridge: Cambridge University Press.

—— (1994). Reception as Flow: The "New Television Viewer" Revisited. *Cultural Studies, 8*(2), 293–305.

—— (1995). *The Social Semiotics of Mass Communication*. London: Sage.

—— (2000). *We Have Always Been Virtual*. Paper presented at the Internet Research 1.0 Conference, Kansas City.

—— (2002a). Media Effects: Quantitative Traditions. In K. B. Jensen (Ed.), *A Handbook of Media and Communication Research: Qualitative and Quantitative Methodologies*. London: Routledge.

—— (2002b). Media Reception: Qualitative Traditions. In K. B. Jensen (Ed.), *A Handbook of Media and Communication Research: Qualitative and Quantitative Methodologies*. London: Routledge.

—— (2002c). The Complementarity of Qualitative and Quantitative Methodologies in Media and Communication Research. In K. B. Jensen (Ed.), *A Handbook of Media and Communication Research: Qualitative and Quantitative Methodologies*. London: Routledge.

—— (2002d). The Social Origins and Uses of Media and Communication Research. In K. B. Jensen (Ed.), *A Handbook of Media and Communication Research: Qualitative and Quantitative Methodologies*. London: Routledge.

—— (Ed.) (2002e). *A Handbook of Media and Communication Research: Qualitative and Quantitative Methodologies*. London: Routledge.

—— (2006). Sounding the Media: An Interdisciplinary Review and a Research Agenda for Digital Sound Studies. *Nordicom Review, 27*(2), 7–33.

—— (2007). Mixed Media: From Digital Aesthetics towards General Communication Theory. In A. Fetveit and G. Stald (Eds.), *Digital Aesthetics and Communication: Northern Lights – Film and Media Studies Yearbook 2006*. Brighton, UK: Intellect.

—— (2008). Meaning. In W. Donsbach (Ed.), *International Encyclopedia of Communication* (Vol. 6, pp. 2803–7). Malden, MA: Blackwell.

—— (in press). New Media, Old Methods: Internet Methodologies and the Online/Offline Divide. In R. Burnett, M. Consalvo and C. Ess (Eds.), *The Blackwell Companion to Internet Studies*. Malden, MA: Wiley-Blackwell.

Jensen, K. B., and Helles, R. (2005). Who Do You Think We Are? – A Content Analysis of Websites as Participatory Resources for Politics, Business, and Civil Society. In K. B. Jensen (Ed.), *Interface://Culture – The World Wide Web as Political Resource and Aesthetic Form*. Copenhagen: Samfundslitteratur / Nordicom.

—— (2009). *The Internet as a Cultural Forum: Implications for Research*. Paper presented at the "The Future Is Prologue" preconference, 59th Annual Conference of the International Communication Association.

Joas, H. (1993). *Pragmatism and Social Theory*. Chicago, IL: University of Chicago Press.

Johansen, J. D. (1985). Prolegomena to a Semiotic Theory of Text Interpretation. *Semiotica, 57*(3–4), 225–88.

—— (1993). *Dialogic Semiosis*. Bloomington: Indiana University Press.

Johnson, J. H. (1995). *Listening in Paris: A Cultural History*. Berkeley: University of California Press.

Johnson, M. (1987). *The Body in the Mind*. Chicago, IL: University of Chicago Press.

Jones, S. G. (Ed.). (1998). *Cybersociety 2.0*. Thousand Oaks, CA: Sage.

Jørgensen, K. (2007). *What are those grunts and growls over there? Computer game audio and player action*. PhD dissertation. University of Copenhagen.

Joseph, J. E. (2007, November 16). He was an Englishman. *Times Literary Supplement*, 14–15.

Kakihara, M., and Sørensen, C. (2002). *Mobility: An Extended Perspective*. Paper presented at the Hawai'i International Conference on System Sciences, Big Island, Hawai'i.

Kant, I. (1970). An Answer to the Question: 'What Is Enlightenment?'. In H. Reiss (Ed.), *Kant's Political Writings*. Cambridge: Cambridge University Press. (Orig. publ. 1784.)

—— (1992). *The Conflict of the Faculties* (M. J. Gregor, Trans.). Lincoln: University of Nebraska Press. (Orig. publ. 1798.)

—— (1998). *The Critique of Pure Reason* (2nd ed). Retrieved January 4, 2008, from http://etext.library.adelaide.edu.au/k/kant/immanuel/k16p/. (Orig. publ. 1781/1787.)

—— (2004a). *Fundamental Principles of the Metaphysic of Morals*. Retrieved May 15, 2009, from www.gutenberg.org/etext/5682. (Orig. publ. 1785.)

—— (2004b). *The Critique of Judgment*. Retrieved January 15, 2009, from http://etext.library.adelaide.edu.au/k/kant/immanuel/k16j/. (Orig. publ. 1790.)

Katz, E. (1959). Mass Communication Research and the Study of Popular Culture: An Editorial Note on a Possible Future for this Journal. *Studies in Public Communication, 2*, 1–6.

Katz, J. E., and Aakhus, M. (Eds.). (2002). *Perpetual Contact: Mobile Communication, Private Talk, Public Performance*. Cambridge: Cambridge University Press.

Kay, A., and Goldberg, A. (1999). Personal Dynamic Media. In P. A. Mayer (Ed.), *Computer Media and Communication: A Reader*. Oxford: Oxford University Press. (Orig. publ. 1977.)

Kay, L. E. (2000). *Who Wrote the Book of Life? – A History of the Genetic Code*. Stanford, CA: Stanford University Press.

Kennedy, G. A. (1980). *Classical Rhetoric and Its Christian and Secular Tradition from Ancient to Modern Times*. Chapel Hill: University of North Carolina Press.

Kim, H., Kim, G. J., Park, H. W., and Rice, R. E. (2007). Configuration of Relationships in Diffferent Media. *Journal of Computer-Mediated Communicaiton, 12*(4).

Kiousis, S. (2002). Interactivity: A Concept Explication. *New Media & Society, 4*(3), 355–83.

Klapper, J. (1960). *The Effects of Mass Communication*. Glencoe, IL: The Free Press.

Klinger, B. (2006). *Beyond the Multiplex: Cinema, New Technologies, and the Home*. Berkeley: University of California Press.

Kripke, S. A. (1980). *Naming and Necessity*. Oxford: Blackwell.

Krippendorff, K. (2004). *Content Analysis: An Introduction to Its Methodology* (2nd ed.). Thousand Oaks, CA: Sage.

—— (2008a). Cybernetics. In W. Donsbach (Ed.), *International Encyclopedia of Communication* (Vol. 3, pp. 1152–59). Malden, MA: Blackwell.

—— (2008b). Information. In W. Donsbach (Ed.), *International Encyclopedia of Communication* (Vol. 5, pp. 2213–21). Malden, MA: Blackwell.

Kristeller, P. O. (1961). *Renaissance Thought: The Classic, Scholastic, and Humanist Strains*. New York: Harper.

Kristeva, J. (1984). *Revolution in Poetic Language*. New York: Columbia University Press. (Orig. publ. 1974.)

Kroeber, A. L., and Kluckhohn, C. (1952). *Culture: A Critical Review of Concepts and Definitions*. Cambridge, MA: Peabody Museum of American Archaeology and Ethnology.

Kuhn, T. S. (1970). *The Structure of Scientific Revolutions* (Revised ed.). Chicago, IL: University of Chicago Press.

Kuklick, B. (1977). *The Rise of American Philosophy, Cambridge, Massachusetts, 1860–1930*. New Haven, CT: Yale University Press.

Kvale, S. (1996). *InterViews: An Introduction to Qualitative Research Interviewing*. Thousand Oaks, CA: Sage.

Ladurie, E. L. R. (1972). *Times of Feast, Times of Famine: A History of Climate since the Year 1000*. London: Allen & Unwin. (Orig. publ. 1967.)

Lakoff, G., and Johnson, M. (1980). *Metaphors We Live By*. Chicago, IL: University of Chicago Press.

—— (1999). *Philosophy in the Flesh: The Embodied Mind and Its Challenge to Western Thought*. New York: Basic Books.

Lamb, H. H. (1995). *Climate, History, and the Modern World* (2nd ed.). London: Routledge.

Landow, G. P. (1997). *Hypertext 2.0: The Convergence of Contemporary Critical Theory and Technology* (2nd ed.). Baltimore, MD: Johns Hopkins University Press.

Lanza, J. (1994). *Elevator Music: A Surreal History of Muzak, Easy-Listening, and Other Mood-Song*. New York: Picador.

Lasswell, H. D. (1948). The Structure and Function of Communication in Society. In L. Bryson (Ed.), *The Communication of Ideas*. New York: Harper.

Latour, B. (1987). *Science in Action*. Milton Keynes, UK: Open University Press.

Lazarsfeld, P. F. (1941). Remarks on Administrative and Critical Communications Research. *Studies in Philosophy and Social Science, 9*, 2–16.

Lazarsfeld, P. F., Berelson, B., and Gaudet, H. (1944). *The People's Choice*. New York: Duell, Sloan, and Pearce.

Lerner, D. (1958). *The Passing of Traditional Society*. New York: Free Press.

Lessig, L. (2006). *Code version 2.0*. New York: Basic Books.

Lévi-Strauss, C. (1963). *Structural Anthropology*. New York: Penguin. (Orig. publ. 1958.)

—— (1991). *Totemism*. London: Merlin Press. (Orig. publ. 1962.)

Levy, M. (Ed.). (1993). Symposium: Virtual Reality: A Communication Perspective. *Journal of Communication, 43*(4).

Lewin, K. (1945). The Research Center for Group Dynamics at Massachusetts Institute of Technology. *Sociometry, 8*(2), 126–36.

Lewis, L. (Ed.). (1991). *The Adoring Audience*. London: Routledge.

Lincoln, Y. S., and Guba, E. G. (1985). *Naturalistic Inquiry*. London: Sage.

Ling, R. (2004). *The Mobile Connection: The Cell Phone's Impact on Society*. Amsterdam: Elsevier.

—— (2008). *New Tech, New Ties: How Mobile Communication is Reshaping Social Cohesion*. Cambridge, MA: MIT Press.

Ling, R., and Yttri, B. (2002). Hyper-coordination via Mobile Phones in Norway. In J. E. Katz and M. Aakhus (Eds.), *Perpetual Contact: Mobile Communication, Private Talk, Public Performance*. Cambridge: Cambridge University Press.

Liszka, J. J. (1998). Reading Peirce Postmodernly. *Semiotica, 121*(1/2), 113–32.

Lobkowicz, N. (1967). *Theory and Practice: History of a Concept from Aristotle to Marx*. Notre Dame, IN: University of Notre Dame Press.

Lomborg, B. (2001). *The Skeptical Environmentalist: Measuring the Real State of the World*. Cambridge: Cambridge University Press.

—— (2007). *Cool It: The Skeptical Environmentalist's Guide to Global Warming*. New York: Alfred A. Knopf.

Lovejoy, A. O. (1936). *The Great Chain of Being*. Cambridge, MA: Harvard University Press.

Lull, J. (1980). The Social Uses of Television. *Human Communication Research, 6*, 197–209.

Lund, A. B. (2001). The Genealogy of News: Researching Journalistic Food-Chains. *Nordicom Review, 22*(1), 37–42.

Lyotard, J.-F. (1984). *The Postmodern Condition*. Minneapolis: University of Minnesota Press. (Orig. publ. 1979.)

Lyytinen, K., and Yoo, Y. (2002). Issues and Challenges in Ubiquitous Computing. *Communications of the ACM, 45*(12), 63–65.

MacBride, S. (Ed.). (1980). *Many Voices, One World*. Paris: UNESCO.

Machill, M., Beiler, M., and Zenker, M. (2008). Search-engine Research: a European-American Overview and Systematization of an Interdisciplinary and International Research Field. *Media, Culture & Society, 30*(5), 591–608.

Machill, M., Neuberger, C., Schweiger, W., and Wirth, W. (2004). Navigating the Internet: A Study of German-Language Search Engines. *European Journal of Communication, 19*(3), 321–47.

Mann, C., and Stewart, F. (2000). *Internet Communication and Qualitative Research: A Handbook for Researching Online*. London: Sage.

McCombs, M. E., and Shaw, D. L. (1972). The Agenda-Setting Function of Mass Media. *Public Opinion Quarterly, 36*, 176–87.

McLuhan, M. (1962). *The Gutenberg Galaxy*. Toronto: University of Toronto Press.

—— (1964). *Understanding Media: The Extensions of Man*. New York: McGraw-Hill.

McMillan, S. J. (2002). Exploring Models of Interactivity from Multiple Research Traditions: Users, Documents, and Systems. In L. Lievrouw and S. Livingstone (Eds.), *Handbook of New Media: Social Shaping and Consequences of ICTs* (pp. 163–82). London: Sage.

McQuail, D. (1983). *Mass Communication Theory: An Introduction*. London: Sage.

—— (2005). *McQuail's Mass Communication Theory* (5th ed.). London: Sage.

McQuail, D., and Windahl, S. (1993). *Communication Models for the Study of Mass Communication*. London: Longman.

Mead, G. H. (1934). *Mind, Self, and Society*. Chicago, IL: University of Chicago Press.

Megarry, T. (1995). *Society in Prehistory: The Origins of Human Culture*. London: Macmillan.

Menand, L. (2001). *The Metaphysical Club*. New York: Farrar, Strauss, and Giroux.

Merleau-Ponty, M. (1962). *Phenomenology of Perception*. London: Routledge & Kegan Paul. (Orig. publ. 1945.)

Merton, R. K. (1968). *Social Theory and Social Structure* (Enlarged ed.). New York: The Free Press.

Messaris, P. (1994). *Visual 'Literacy': Image, Mind, and Reality*. Boulder, CO: Westview Press.

Meyrowitz, J. (1985). *No Sense of Place: The Impact of Electronic Media on Social Behavior*. New York: Oxford University Press.

—— (1989). The Generalized Elsewhere. *Critical Studies in Mass Communication*, *6*(3), 326–34.

—— (1994). Medium Theory. In D. Crowley and D. Mitchell (Eds.), *Communication Theory Today*. Cambridge: Polity Press.

—— (Ed.) (2008). McLuhan, Marshall. In W. Donsbach (Ed.), *International Encyclopedia of Communication* (Vol. 6, pp. 2801–3). Malden, MA: Blackwell.

Mill, J. S. (1973–74). *Collected Works of John Stuart Mill* (Vol. 7–8). Toronto: University of Toronto Press. (Orig. publ. 1843.)

Millard, A. (1995). *America on Record: A History of Recorded Sound*. Cambridge: Cambridge University Press.

Miller, C. R. (1984). Genre as Social Action. *Quarterly Journal of Speech*, *70*, 151–67.

—— (1994). Rhetorical Community: The Cultural Basis of Genre. In A. Freedman and P. Medway (Eds.), *Genre and the New Rhetoric*. London: Taylor & Francis.

Mills, C. W. (1959). *The Sociological Imagination*. London: Oxford University Press.

Morley, D. (1986). *Family Television*. London: Comedia.

Mortensen, F. (1977). The Bourgeois Public Sphere: A Danish Mass Communications Research Project. In M. Berg, P. Hemanus and J. Ekecrantz (Eds.), *Current Theories in Scandinavian Mass Communication*. Grenaa, Denmark: GMT.

Mukerji, C. (2006). Printing, Cartography, and Conceptions of Place in Renaissance Europe. *Media, Culture & Society*, *28*(5), 651–69.

Mumford, L. (1934). *Technics and Civilization*. London: Routledge.

Munakata, T. (Ed.) (2007). Beyond Silicon: New Computing Paradigms. *Communications of the ACM*, *50*(9), 30–72.

Murdock, G. (2002). Media, Culture, and Modern Times: Social Science Investigations. In K. B. Jensen (Ed.), *A Handbook of Media and*

Communication Research: Qualitative and Quantitative Methodologies. London: Routledge.

Murdock, G., and Golding, P. (1977). Capitalism, Communication, and Class Relations. In J. Curran, M. Gurevitch and J. Woollacott (Eds.), *Mass Communication and Society.* London: Edward Arnold.

Murphy, J. P. (1990). *Pragmatism: From Peirce to Davidson.* Boulder, CO: Westview Press.

Nagel, T. (1986). *The View from Nowhere.* Oxford: Oxford University Press.

Negroponte, N. (1995). *Being Digital.* London: Hodder & Stoughton.

Negt, O. (1973). Massenmedien: Herrschaftsmittel oder Instrumente der Befreiung? [Mass media: Means of domination or instruments of liberation?]. In D. Prokop (Ed.), *Kritische Kommunikationsforschung* [Critical communication research]. Munich, Germany: Carl Hanser Verlag.

Negt, O., and Kluge, A. (1993). *Public Sphere and Experience.* Minneapolis: University of Minnesota Press. (Orig. publ. 1972.)

Nellhaus, T. (1998). Signs, Social Ontology, and Critical Realism. *Journal for the Theory of Social Behaviour, 28*(1), 1–24.

Nelson, T. H. (1965). *Complex Information Processing: A File Structure for the Complex, the Changing, and the Indeterminate.* Paper presented at the 20th National ACM Conference, Cleveland, Ohio.

Nerone, J. C. (Ed.). (1995). *Last Rights: Revisiting Four Theories of the Press.* Urbana: University of Illinois Press.

Neuberger, H. (1970). Climate in Art. *Weather, 25*(2), 46–56.

Neuman, W. R., Just, M., and Crigler, A. N. (1992). *Common Knowledge: News and the Construction of Political Meaning.* Chicago, IL: University of Chicago Press.

Newcomb, H., and Hirsch, P. (1983). Television as a Cultural Forum: Implications for Research. *Quarterly Review of Film Studies, 8*(3), 45–55.

Norman, D. A. (1990). *The Design of Everyday Things.* New York: Doubleday.

Nott, J. J. (2002). *Music for the People: Popular Music and Dance in Interwar Britain.* Oxford: Oxford University Press.

Nyre, L. (2008). *Sound Media: From Live Journalism to Music Recording.* London: Routledge.

Ong, W. (1982). *Orality and Literacy.* London: Methuen.

Park, D. W., and Pooley, J. (Eds.). (2008). *The History of Media and Communication Research: Contested Memories.* New York: Peter Lang.

Parker, K. A. (2004). Josiah Royce. Retrieved January 25, 2008, from http://plato.stanford.edu/entries/royce/

Partridge, D. (1991). *A New Guide to Artificial Intelligence.* Norwood, NJ: Ablex.

Patton, M. Q. (1990). *Qualitative Evaluation and Research Methods* (2nd ed.). Newbury Park, CA: Sage.

Pavitt, C. (1999). The Third Way: Scientific Realism and Communication Theory. *Communication Theory, 9*(2), 162–88.

Pearson, R., and Uricchio, W. (Eds.). (1990). *The Many Lives of the Batman*. New York: Routledge.

Peirce, C. S. (1931–58). *Collected Papers*. Cambridge, MA: Harvard University Press.

—— (1955). *Philosophical Writings of Peirce*. New York: Dover.

—— (1958). *Selected Writings*. New York: Dover.

—— (1982). *Writings of Charles S. Peirce: A Chronological Edition* (Vol. 1). Bloomington: Indiana University Press.

—— (1986). *Writings of Charles S. Peirce: A Chronological Edition* (Vol. 3). Bloomington: Indiana University Press.

—— (1992–98). *The Essential Peirce*. (Vols 1–2). Bloomington: Indiana University Press.

Perry, D. K. (Ed.). (2001). *American Pragmatism and Communication Research*. Mahwah, NJ: Lawrence Erlbaum.

Peters, J. D. (1999). *Speaking into the Air: A History of the Idea of Communication*. Chicago, IL: University of Chicago Press.

—— (2005). *Courting the Abyss: Free Speech and the Liberal Tradition*. Chicago, IL: University of Chicago Press.

—— (2008). Communication, History of the Idea. In W. Donsbach (Ed.), *International Encyclopedia of Communication* (Vol. 2, pp. 689–93). Malden, MA: Blackwell.

Pettegree, A. (2005). *Reformation and the Culture of Persuasion*. Cambridge: Cambridge University Press.

Pike, K. L. (1967). *Language in Relation to a Unified Theory of the Structure of Human Behavior* (2nd ed.). The Hague: Mouton.

Pitt, J. (Ed.). (1988). *Theories of Explanation*. New York: Oxford University Press.

Polanyi, M. (1962). *Personal Knowledge*. Chicago: University of Chicago Press.

Popper, K. R. (1963). *Conjectures and Refutations: The Growth of Scientific Knowledge*. London: Routledge & Kegan Paul.

—— (1972a). *Objective Knowledge: An Evolutionary Approach*. London: Oxford University Press.

—— (1972b). *The Logic of Scientific Discovery*. London: Hutchinson. (Orig. publ. 1934.)

Porat, M. (1977). *The Information Economy: Definition and Measurement*. Washington, DC: Government Printing Office.

Radway, J. (1984). *Reading the Romance: Women, Patriarchy, and Popular Literature*. Chapel Hill: University of North Carolina Press.

Ramirez, A., Dimmick, J., Feaster, J., and Lin, S.-F. (2008). Revisiting Interpersonal Media Competition: The Gratification Niches of Instant Messaging, E-Mail, and the Telephone. *Communication Research*, *35*(4), 529–47.

Rekimoto, J. (2008). Organic Interaction Technologies: From Stone to Skin. *Communications of the ACM*, *51*(6), 38–44.

Rettberg, J. W. (2008). *Blogging*. Cambridge: Polity.

Ricoeur, P. (1981). *Hermeneutics and the Human Sciences: Essays on Language, Action and Interpretation*. Cambridge: Cambridge University Press.

Ritchie, D. (1999). *Probably, Probably Not: Rhetoric and Interpretation in Communication Research*. Paper presented at the International Communication Association Conference, San Francisco.

Rogers, E. M. (1999). Anatomy of Two Subdisciplines of Communication Study. *Human Communication Research*, *25*(4), 618–31.

—— (2003). *Diffusion of Innovations* (5th ed.). New York: Free Press.

Rorty, R. (Ed.) (1967). *The Linguistic Turn*. Chicago: University of Chicago Press.

Rorty, R. (1979). *Philosophy and the Mirror of Nature*. Princeton, NJ: Princeton University Press.

—— (1982). *Consequences of Pragmatism*. Minneapolis: University of Minnesota Press.

—— (1989). *Contingency, Irony, and Solidarity*. Cambridge: Cambridge University Press.

—— (1991a). *Essays on Heidegger and Others* (Vol. 2). Cambridge: Cambridge University Press.

—— (1991b). *Objectivity, Relativism, and Truth* (Vol. 1). Cambridge: Cambridge University Press.

—— (1998). *Truth and Progress* (Vol. 3). Cambridge: Cambridge University Press.

—— (2007). *Philosophy as Cultural Politics* (Vol. 4). Cambridge: Cambridge University Press.

Ross, D. (1923). *Aristotle*. London: Methuen.

Royce, J. (1969). The Possibility of Error. *The Basic Writings of Josiah Royce* (Vol. 1). Chicago: University of Chicago Press. (Orig. publ. 1885.)

Rudy, W. (1984). *The Universities of Europe 1100–1914: A History*. London: Associated University Presses.

Ruesch, J., and Bateson, G. (1987). *Communication: The Social Matrix of Psychiatry*. New York: Norton. (Orig. publ. 1951.)

Russill, C. (2005). The Road Not Taken: William James' Radical Empiricism and Communication. *Communication Review*, *8*, 277–305.

Ryan, M.-L. (1991). *Possible Worlds, Artificial Intelligence, and Narrative Theory*. Bloomington: Indiana University Press.

Ryle, G. (1949). *The Concept of Mind*. New York: Hutchinson's University Library.

Sacks, H., Schegloff, E. A., and Jefferson, G. (1974). A Simplest Systematics for the Organisation of Turn-Taking in Conversation. *Language*, *50*, 696–735.

Saussure, F. de (1959). *Course in General Linguistics*. London: Peter Owen. (Orig. publ. 1916.)

Sawyer, R. K. (2004). The Mechanisms of Emergence. *Philosophy of the Social Sciences*, *34*(2), 260–82.

Scannell, P. (2000). For-Anyone-as-Someone Structures. *Media, Culture & Society*, *22*(1), 5–24.

—— (2002). History, Media, and Communication. In K. B. Jensen (Ed.), *A Handbook of Media and Communication Research: Qualitative and Quantitative Methodologies*. London: Routledge.

Schafer, R. M. (1977). *The Tuning of the World*. New York: Alfred A. Knopf.

Schiller, H. I. (1969). *Mass Communications and American Empire*. New York: Kelley.

Schmidt, J. (2007). Blogging Practices: An Analytical Framework. *Journal of Computer-Mediated Communication, 12*(4).

Schramm, W. (1964). *Mass Media and National Development*. Stanford, CA: Stanford University Press.

Schrøder, K. C., Drotner, K., Kline, S., and Murray, C. (2003). *Researching Audiences: A Practical Guide to Methods in Media Audience Analysis*. London: Hodder Arnold.

Schudson, M. (1997). Why Conversation is Not the Soul of Democracy. *Critical Studies in Mass Communication, 14*(4), 297–309.

—— (2006). The Trouble with Experts – and Why Democracies Need Them. *Theory and Society, 35*, 491–506.

Schütz, A. (1962). On Multiple Realities. *Collected Papers: The Problem of Social Reality* (Vol. 1). The Hague: Martinus Nijhoff. (Orig. publ. 1945.)

Scribner, S., and Cole, M. (1981). *The Psychology of Literacy*. Cambridge, MA: Harvard University Press.

Searle, J. R. (1969). *Speech Acts*. London: Cambridge University Press.

Sebeok, T. A., and Umiker-Sebeok, J. (1983). "You Know My Method": A Juxtaposition of Charles S. Peirce and Sherlock Holmes. In U. Eco and T. A. Sebeok (Eds.), *The Sign of Three*. Bloomington: Indiana University Press.

Sennett, R. (1974). *The Fall of Public Man*. Cambridge: Cambridge University Press.

Shannon, C. E. (1948). A Mathematical Theory of Communication. *The Bell System Technical Journal, 27*, 379–423, 623–56.

Shannon, C. E., and Weaver, W. (1949). *The Mathematical Theory of Communication*. Urbana: University of Illinois Press.

Sheriff, J. (1987). *The Fate of Meaning*. Princeton, NJ: Princeton University Press.

Siebert, F., Peterson, T., and Schramm, W. (1956). *Four Theories of the Press*. Urbana: University of Illinois Press.

Silverstone, R. (1999). *Why Study the Media?* London: Sage.

Simonson, P. (2008). Pragmatism. In W. Donsbach (Ed.), *International Encyclopedia of Communication* (Vol 8, pp. 3858–60). Malden, MA: Blackwell.

Singer, M. (1984). *Man's Glassy Essence: Explorations in Semiotic Anthropology*. Bloomington: Indiana University Press.

Skagestad, P. (1981). *The Road of Inquiry: Charles Peirce's Pragmatic Realism*. New York: Columbia University Press.

Slater, D. (2002). Social Relationships and Identity Online and Offline. In L. Lievrouw and S. Livingstone (Eds.), *Handbook of New Media: Social Shaping and Consequences of ICTs* (pp. 533–46). London: Sage.

Snow, C. P. (1964). *The Two Cultures and a Second Look*. Cambridge: Cambridge University Press.

Sternberg, R. J. (2009). *Cognitive Psychology* (5th ed.). Belmont, CA: Wadsworth.

Stivers, T., and Sidnell, J. (2005). Introduction: Multimodal Interaction. *Semiotica, 156*(1/4), 1–20.

Surowiecki, J. (2004). *The Wisdom of Crowds*. New York: Doubleday.

Tejera, V. (1996). Has Habermas Understood Peirce? *Transactions of the Charles S. Peirce Society, 32*(1), 107–25.

Theall, D. F. (1971). *The Medium is the Rear View Mirror: Understanding McLuhan*. Montreal: McGill-Queen's University Press.

Thomas, W. I., and Thomas, D. S. (1928). *The Child in America: Behavior Problems and Programs*. New York: Alfred A. Knopf.

Thompson, E. P. (1991). *Customs in Common*. London: Merlin.

Thompson, J. B. (1984). *Studies in the Theory of Ideology*. Cambridge: Polity Press.

—— (1995). *The Media and Modernity*. Cambridge: Polity Press.

—— (2000). *Political Scandal: Power and Visibility in the Media Age*. Cambridge: Polity.

Thompson, K., and Bordwell, D. (2003). *Film History: An Introduction* (2nd ed.). Boston, MA: McGraw-Hill.

Toffler, A. (1981). *The Third Wave*. New York: Bantam.

Trenaman, J. S. M., and McQuail, D. (1961). *Television and the Political Image*. London: Methuen.

Turner, F. (2006). *From Counterculture to Cyberculture: Stewart Brand, the Whole Earth Network, and the Rise of Digital Utopianism*. Chicago: University of Chicago Press.

Turner, V. (1967). Betwixt and Between: The Liminal Period in Rites de Passage. *The Forest of Symbols*. Ithaca, NY: Cornell University Press.

Valenti, S. S., and Good, J. M. M. (Eds.). (1991). Social Affordances and Interaction I: Introduction. *Ecological Psychology, 3*(2), 77–98.

Vertegaal, R., and Poupyrev, I. (2008). Organic User Interfaces. *Communications of the ACM, 51*(6), 26–30.

Von Hippel, E. (2005). *Democratizing Innovation*. Cambridge, MA: MIT Press.

Wallerstein, I. (1974). *The Modern World-System* (Vol. 1). New York: Academic Press.

Warren, S. D., and Brandeis, L. D. (1890). The Right to Privacy. *Harvard Law Review, IV*(5). Retrieved July 15, 2009, from www.lawrence.edu/fast/BOARDMAW/Privacy_brand_warr2.html

Watzlawick, P., Beavin, J. H., and Jackson, D. D. (1967). *Pragmatics of Human Communication: A Study of Interactional Patterns, Pathologies, and Paradoxes*. New York: Norton.

Webb, E. J., Campbell, D. T., Schwartz, R. D., and Sechrest, L. (2000). *Unobtrusive Measures* (Revised ed.). Thousand Oaks, CA: Sage.

Webster, F., and Dimitriou, B. (Eds.). (2004). *Manuel Castells*. London: Sage.

Weiser, M. (1991). The Computer for the Twenty-First Century. *Scientific American, 265*(3), 94–104.

Weitzner, D. J., Abelson, H., Berners-Lee, T., Feigenbaum, J., Hendler, J., and Sussman, G. J. (2008). Information Accountability. *Communications of the ACM, 51*(6), 82–87.

Wells, K. J. (1996). Peirce's "Architecture of Theories" and *the* Problem of Pragmatism. *Metaphilosophy, 27*(3), 311–23.

West, C. (1989). *The American Evasion of Philosophy: A Genealogy of Pragmatism*. Madison: University of Wisconsin Press.

Westin, A. F. (1967). *Privacy and Freedom*. New York: Atheneum.

Wetherell, M., Taylor, S., and Yates, S. (Eds.). (2001). *Discourse Theory and Practice: A Reader*. London: Sage.

Wieland, W. (1962). *Die aristotelische Physik* [Aristotelian Physics]. Göttingen, Germany: Van den Hoeck & Ruprecht.

Wiener, N. (1961). *Cybernetics, Or Control and Communication in the Animal and the Machine* (2nd ed.). Cambridge, MA: MIT Press. (Orig. publ. 1948)

Wilden, A. (1980). *System and Structure: Essays in Communication and Exchange* (2nd ed.). London: Tavistock.

Williams, R. (1974). *Television: Technology and Cultural Form*. London: Fontana.

—— (1975). *Culture and Society 1780–1950*. Harmondsworth: Penguin. (Orig. publ. 1958.)

—— (1977). *Marxism and Literature*. London: Oxford University Press.

Wilson, N. L. (1958/59). Substances without Substrata. *Review of Metaphysics, 12*, 521–39.

Winch, P. (1963). *The Idea of a Social Science*. London: Routledge. (Orig. publ. 1958.)

Winnicott, D. W. (1971). *Playing and Reality*. London: Tavistock.

Winston, B. (1998). *Media, Technology, and Society – A History: From the Telegraph to the Internet*. London: Routledge.

Wittgenstein, L. (1953). *Philosophical Investigations*. London: Macmillan.

—— (1972). *Tractatus Logico-Philosophicus*. London: Routledge & Kegan Paul. (Orig. publ. 1921.)

Wober, J. M. (1981). Psychology in the Future of Broadcasting Research. *Bulletin of the British Psychological Society, 34*, 409–12.

Woo, J. (2006). The Right Not to Be Identified: Privacy and Anonymity in the Interactive Media Environment. *New Media & Society, 8*(6), 949–67.

Woolgar, S. (1988). *Science: The Very Idea*. London: Routledge.

Wurtzel, A. H., and Turner, C. (1977). Latent Functions of the Telephone: What Missing the Extension Means. In I. S. Pool (Ed.), *The Social Impact of the Telephone*. Cambridge, MA: MIT Press.

Yates, J., and Orlikowski, W. (1992). Genres of Organizational Communication: A Structurational Approach to Studying Communication and Media. *Academy of Management Review, 17*(2), 299–326.

Yin, R. K. (2003). *Case Study Research: Design and Methods* (3rd ed.). Thousand Oaks, CA: Sage.

Zimmer, M. (2008). The Externalities of Search 2.0: The Emerging Privacy Threats When the Drive for the Perfect Search Engine Meets Web 2.0. *First Monday, 13*(3).

Index

Related titles from Routledge

New Media: A Critical Introduction

2nd Edition

Martin Lister, Jon Dovey, Seth Giddings, Iain Grant and Kieran Kelly

New Media: A Critical Introduction is a comprehensive introduction to the culture, history, technologies and theories of new media. Written especially for students, the book considers the ways in which 'new media' really are new, assesses the claims that a media and technological revolution has taken place and formulates new ways for media studies to respond to new technologies.

The authors introduce a wide variety of topics including: how to define the characteristics of new media; social and political uses of new media and new communications; new media technologies, politics and globalization; everyday life and new media; theories of interactivity, simulation, the new media economy; cybernetics, cyberculture, the history of automata and artificial life.

Substantially updated from the first edition to cover recent theoretical developments, approaches and significant technological developments, this is the best and by far the most comprehensive textbook available on this exciting and expanding subject.

New case studies, further research and an interactive glossary can be found on the companion website at www.newmediaintro.com

ISBN13: 978–0–415–43160–6 (hbk)
ISBN13: 978–0–415–43161–3 (pbk)

Available at all good bookshops.

For ordering and further information please visit:
www.routledge.com

Related titles from Routledge

The New Media Handbook

Andrew Dewdney and Peter Ride

The New Media Handbook deals with the essential diversity of new media by combining critical commentary and descriptive and historical accounts with a series of edited interviews with new media practitioners, including young web developers, programmers, artists, writers and producers.

The New Media Handbook provides an understanding of the historical and theoretical development of new media, emphasising the complex continuities in the technological developments associated with particular cultural uses of media, rather than understanding new media as replacing or breaking what has gone before.

The New Media Handbook focuses upon the key concerns of practitioners and how they create their work and develop their projects – from artists to industry professionals, web designers to computer programmers. It includes a discussion of key concepts such as digital code, information, convergence, interactivity and interface and, finally, identifies key debates and locates the place of new media practice within contemporary culture.

The New Media Handbook includes:

- interviews with new media practitioners
- case studies, examples and illustrations
- a glossary of technical acronyms and key terms
- a bibliography and list of web resources.

ISBN13: 978–0–415–30711–6 (hbk)
ISBN13: 978–0–415–30712–3 (pbk)
ISBN13: 978–0–203–64578–9 (ebk)

Available at all good bookshops.

For ordering and further information please visit:
www.routledge.com